Compelling! Couldn't put it down! Must-reading for parents
as well as Christian leaders. God used this book to challenge
and change me in some areas of need. I will be using it
regularly as I counsel students.

JOE ALDRICH, PRESIDENT
MULTNOMAH SCHOOL OF THE BIBLE

This is a "must read" for those interested in effectively fighting
the "good fight of faith." The authors help us to understand
that Satan and his demons are not figments of human imagination.
They are real and whether we like it or not they can influence
us and our children, especially those of us who are ignorant
of their tactics. *Spiritual Protection for Your Children*
provides helpful information for dealing appropriately
with demon spirits.

RAY BEESON, AUTHOR
DIRECTOR OF OVERCOMERS MINISTRIES

Riveting! Pete and Sue Vander Hook will grab your attention
with the story of their three-year spiritual ordeal as Neil Anderson
gives you biblical, practical steps on how to establish spiritual
freedom in your home. Parents, grandparents, pastors,
missionaries and teachers have got to read
Spiritual Protection for Your Children!

JAY BELL, GLOBAL MINISTRY STAFF
GRACE BRETHREN INTERNATIONAL MISSIONS

Pete and Sue Vander Hook not only relate the fierce dimensions of battle sometimes experienced with the powers of darkness, but they also exalt the sufficiency of the believer's victory in Christ. Neil Anderson provides usable tools coupled with a balanced approach to spiritual protection. This book needs wide exposure in the Christian community.

MARK I. BUBECK, AUTHOR, PRESIDENT
INTERNATIONAL CENTER FOR BIBLICAL COUNSELING

Every Christian parent who is concerned about God's provision and protection for their children will benefit from this strategic book.

PAUL A. CEDAR, PRESIDENT
EVANGELICAL FREE CHURCH OF AMERICA

This book is must reading for every parent of small children. There is no greater insurance for your children's abundant future than freedom in Christ.

DAVID L. FINNELL
COLUMBIA INTERNATIONAL UNIVERSITY

Neil Anderson touches yet another nerve of vital need in the Body of Christ—sensitively defending against the adversary's calculated attacks on our children.

JACK W. HAYFORD, SENIOR PASTOR
THE CHURCH ON THE WAY

We are grateful to Neil Anderson for
Spiritual Protection for Your Children. It will spare many children,
parents and families years and perhaps a lifetime of grief.

DR. AND MRS. J. KENT HUTCHESON

This incredible story is must reading.
Once your start it, you don't want to lay it down.

EARL PICKARD, NATIONAL DIRECTOR
PRAYERWORKS

This book will dispel ignorance and equip every family with the
spiritual weapons that God has given us to prevent and overcome
whatever attack may come our way. No Christian home should be
without this dramatic and encouraging book!

C. PETER WAGNER
FULLER THEOLOGICAL SEMINARY

SPIRITUAL PROTECTION
FOR YOUR CHILDREN

HELPING YOUR CHILDREN
AND FAMILY FIND THEIR
IDENTITY, FREEDOM AND
SECURITY IN CHRIST

NEIL T. ANDERSON
AND PETE & SUE VANDER HOOK

Regal

A Division of Gospel Light
Ventura, California, U.S.A.

Published by Regal Books
A Division of Gospel Light
Ventura, California, U.S.A.
Printed in U.S.A.

Regal Books is a ministry of Gospel Light, an evangelical Christian publisher dedicated to serving the local church. We believe God's vision for Gospel Light is to provide church leaders with biblical, user-friendly materials that will help them evangelize, disciple and minister to children, youth and families.

It is our prayer that this Regal book will help you discover biblical truth for your own life and help you meet the needs of others. May God richly bless you.

For a free catalog of resources from Regal Books/Gospel Light please contact your Christian supplier or call 1-800-4-GOSPEL.

Unless otherwise indicated, all scripture quotations are taken from the *Holy Bible, New International Version®. NIV®.* Copyright © 1973, 1978, 1984 by International Bible Society. Used by permission of Zondervan Publishing House. All rights reserved.

Other versions used are:
NASB—Scripture taken from the *New American Standard Bible,* © 1960, 1962, 1963, 1968, 1971, 1972, 1973, 1975, 1977 by The Lockman Foundation. Used by permission. The Scripture references in Appendix A are taken from the *NASB.*
NKJV—Scripture taken from the *New King James Version.* Copyright © 1979, 1980, 1982 by Thomas Nelson, Inc. Publishers. Used by permission. All rights reserved.

Library of Congress Cataloging-in-Publication Data

Anderson, Neil T., 1942-
    Spiritual protection for your children / Neil T. Anderson and Pete and Sue Vander Hook.
    p.   cm.
    Includes bibliographical references (p.).
    ISBN 0-8307-1868-0 (hardcover)
    1. Spiritual warfare. 2. Family—Religious life. 3. Children—Religious life. 4. Devil. 5. Vander Hook, Pete. 6. Vander Hook, Sue. I. Vander Hook, Pete. II. Vander Hook, Sue. III. Title.
BV4509.5.A54 1996
235'.4—dc20
                                                                        96-30482
                                                                        CIP

1 2 3 4 5 6 7 8 9 10 11 12 13 14 15 16 17 18 19 / 03 02 01 00 99 98 97 96

Rights for publishing this book in other languages are contracted by Gospel Literature International (GLINT). GLINT also provides technical help for the adaptation, translation and publishing of Bible study resources and books in scores of languages worldwide. For further information, contact GLINT, P.O. Box 4060, Ontario, CA 91761-1003, U.S.A., or the publisher.

PETE

JARED

DAVID

SUE

JALENE

MYKAELA

FOR DAVID, JARED, JALENE AND MYKAELA
WHO KNOW THE TRUTH...
AND HAVE BEEN SET FREE.

Contents

PART II: LEADING YOUR CHILDREN TO FREEDOM IN CHRIST

APPENDICES

INTRODUCTION

You are about to read a remarkable story of one family's victory over the powers of darkness. What makes this testimony so unordinary is the ordinary nature of the Vander Hook family.

Pete is a mainline evangelical pastor in middle America. He and his wife, Sue, are morally righteous parents whose children have not only attended Christian school but also home school. As a family, they have courageously taken a stand for the sanctity of life.

Pete and Sue Vander Hook are biblically uncompromising Christians who found themselves in a spiritual battle for their family. Their struggle to help their children led to their own freedom in Christ and a ministry to others.

THE FAMILY—SATAN'S TARGET

I wish I could say the Vander Hooks' story is an exception, but it isn't. I have been privileged to help thousands of Christians find their freedom in Christ throughout the past several years. Most have been Christian leaders, their spouses or their children. Generally their problems originated during childhood.

Many parents believe a Christian home, an active church and a Christian school will insulate and protect their children from the world, the flesh and the devil. In reality, these families are often targets for the powers of darkness who seek to destroy their homes and their ministries. In preparation for writing *The Seduction of Our Children*, Steve Russo and I interviewed more than 1,700 professing Christian teenagers.

The following results are what we found in one evangelical Christian high school:[1]

- Forty-five percent said they have experienced a "presence" (seen or heard) in their rooms that scared them.
- Fifty-nine percent said they've harbored bad thoughts about God.
- Forty-three percent said they find it mentally hard to pray and read the Bible.
- Sixty-nine percent reported hearing "voices" in their heads, like there were subconscious voices talking to them.
- Twenty-two percent said they frequently entertain thoughts of suicide.
- Seventy-four percent think they are different than others (It works for others but not for them).

As bad as these percentages are, they rise considerably when teens have dabbled in the occult, followed counterfeit guidance or played certain fantasy games that no Christian should play. How do we explain that 7 out of 10 professing Christian young people are hearing voices? Are they paranoid schizophrenic, or psychotic? They could be, but we must also consider the truth taught in 1 Timothy 4:1: "The Spirit clearly says that in later times some will abandon the faith and follow deceiving spirits and things taught by demons."

Is that happening? It is happening throughout the world. During the past 10 years I have been privileged to individually help nearly a thousand adults who were struggling in their thought lives, having difficulty reading their Bibles or actually hearing voices in their heads. Their problems have consistently proven to be spiritual battles for their minds.

We have learned how to help them find their freedom in Christ in a single three- to four-hour setting. This discipleship/counseling process is explained in my book *Helping Others Find Freedom in Christ*. The following portion of the high-priestly prayer in John 17:13-20 explains the spiritual battle every Christian is waging:

> I am coming to you now, but I say these things while I am still in the world, so that they may have the full measure of my joy within them. I have given them your word and the world has hated them, for they are not of the world any more than I am of the world. My prayer is not that you take them out of the world but that you protect them from the evil one. They are not of the

world, even as I am not of it. Sanctify them by the truth; your word is truth. As you sent me into the world, I have sent them into the world. For them I sanctify myself, that they too may be truly sanctified. My prayer is not for them alone. I pray also for those who will believe in me through their message.

WE ARE NOT DEFENSELESS

Protection from the evil one was Jesus' concern for His disciples and those who would believe in Him. He was returning to the Father, but the disciples and the soon-to-be-established Church would remain on planet Earth where "the prince of this world" (John 14:30), "the ruler of the kingdom of the air" (Eph. 2:2), "your enemy the devil prowls around like a roaring lion looking for someone to devour" (1 Pet. 5:8).

Unlike concerned parents who may be tempted to isolate their children from the harsh realities of this world, Jesus did not ask that we be removed. That strategy would result in no growth for the children or the Church, thus no future ministry. Instead, His prayer was that we be protected from the evil one.

Scary thought, but Jesus has not left us or our children defenseless. First, "You have been given fullness in Christ, who is the head over every power and authority" (Col. 2:10). Christians are established in Christ and seated with Him in the heavenly realms (see Eph. 2:6). Our position in Christ provides all the authority we need over the evil one to carry out the delegated responsibility of fulfilling the Great Commission (see Matt. 28:18,19).

Second, "Having disarmed the powers and authorities, he made a public spectacle of them, triumphing over them by the cross" (Col. 2:15). "His intent was that now, through the church, the manifold wisdom of God should be made known to the rulers and authorities in the heavenly realms, according to his eternal purpose which he accomplished in Christ Jesus our Lord" (Eph. 3:10,11).

Paul was stating the eternal purpose of God—to make His wisdom known through the Church. To whom? To the rulers and authorities in the heavenly realm (i.e., the spiritual realm). "The Son of God appeared for this *purpose*, that He might destroy the works of the devil" (1 John 3:8, *NASB*, emphasis mine). If the battle is between the kingdom of darkness and the kingdom of light—

between the Christ and the anti-Christ—and God's eternal purpose is to make His wisdom known through the Church to the rulers and authorities in the heavenly realm, how are we doing?

Not very well I'm afraid. Some Christians don't even believe in a personal devil, an established doctrine of the historical Christian Church. Many believers live as though he doesn't exist, having little understanding about the spiritual world's ability to impinge on themselves or their families. A few would even insist no interaction occurs. Others, because of fear, make a conscious choice not to address the reality of the devil. In some educational circles it isn't academically credible. Many of us are like blindfolded warriors unable to identify our enemy, so we strike out at ourselves and each other.

As we confront this hostile world, the Lord has not left us defenseless. We have a sanctuary in Christ, and He has equipped us with the armor of God. We have all the resources we need in Christ to stand firm and to resist the devil. However, if we don't assume our responsibility those resources will go unused.

He has instructed us to put on the armor of God. What if we haven't? We have been told to "put on the Lord Jesus Christ, and make no provision for the flesh in regard to its lusts" (Rom. 13:14, *NASB*). What if we have made provision for the flesh? Clearly it is our responsibility to "resist the devil" (Jas. 4:7). What if we don't? God's provision for our freedom in Christ is limited only to the degree we fail to recognize our position in Christ and assume our responsibility.

The most common and naive response in the Western world is to ignore the battle, or to make the fatal assumption that Christians are somehow immune. Just the opposite is true. Ignorance is not bliss, it is defeat. If you are a Christian, you are the target. If you are a pastor, you and your family are the bull's-eye! Satan's strategy is to render Christians inoperative and to obliterate the truth that we are "dead to sin but alive to God in Christ Jesus" (Rom. 6:11).

How's the devil doing? The divorce rate and disintegration of the Christian family roughly parallels the secular world. The distinction between a Christian and a pagan is no longer obvious. The tragic fall of many visible Christian leaders indicates something is dreadfully wrong. Having an intellectual knowledge of Scripture is obviously not enough, because I'm sure those leaders had that. "Christianity doesn't work" is the mistaken message many are choosing to believe.

THREE LEVELS OF CHRISTIAN MATURITY

The apostle John shed some light on our dilemma when he categorized three levels of maturity in 1 John 2:12-14 (*NASB*). "Little children" of the faith are identified as those who know the Father, and have had their sins forgiven. In other words, they have overcome the penalty of sin. Satan loses the primary battle at this first level of maturity when we trust in Christ, but he doesn't curl up his tail and pull in his fangs. His strategy is to keep believers under the power of sin.

Twice John identifies a young person of the faith (the second level of maturity) by the person's ability to "overcome the evil one." How can people reach their full maturity in Christ if they have no idea how to overcome the evil one?

The unfortunate truth is that even many of our Christian leaders have not reached the second level of spiritual maturity as evidenced by their seemingly uncontrollable appetites and behaviors. The sin-confess-sin-confess-sin-confess-and-sin-again cycle does not deal with all of reality. It should be sin, repent and resist. Confession is only the first step in repentance. The third level of maturity is identified by those who have a deep knowledge of God.

If you are tempted to think you are spiritually immune to the attacks of the evil one, let me ask you three pertinent questions. First, have you experienced any temptation this week? Biblically, who is the tempter? It cannot be God. He tests our faith to strengthen it, but Satan's temptations are intended to destroy our faith.

Second, have you ever struggled with the voice of the accuser of the brethren? Before you answer, let me rephrase the question. Have you ever struggled with thoughts such as, "I'm stupid," or "I'm ugly," or "I can't," or "God doesn't love me," or "I'm different from others" or "I'm going down!" I know you have, because the Bible says he accuses the brethren day and night.

Third, have you ever been deceived? The person who is tempted to answer no may be the most deceived of all.

THE REAL BATTLE

Let me share what I believe is the real battle. If I tempt you; you know it. If I accuse you; you know it. But if I deceive you; you don't know it. If you knew it, you would no longer be deceived.

Now listen to the logic of Scripture: "If you hold to my teaching, you are really my disciples. Then you will know the truth, and the truth will set you free" (John 8:31,32). Jesus said, "I am the way and the truth and the life" (14:6). In the high-priestly prayer, Jesus prayed, "Sanctify them by the truth; your word is truth" (17:17). The first piece of God's armor we put on is the "belt of truth" (Eph. 6:14).

Why did God dramatically strike down Ananias and Sapphira in the Early Church? Pete asked, "How is it that Satan has so filled your heart that you have lied to the Holy Spirit and have kept for yourself some of the money you received for the land?" (Acts 5:3,4). The message is clear. If Satan can get us to believe a lie in any area of our lives—in our churches, our homes, our marriages or our personal identities—he can rob us of our victory in Christ. The Lord had to expose the battle for the mind as soon as Satan raised his ugly head in the Early Church.

This strategy is unveiled throughout the Old and New Testaments. Satan deceived Ananias and Sapphira to lie to the Holy Spirit. Satan had also *deceived* Eve, and she believed a *lie*. "Satan rose up against Israel and incited David to take a census of Israel" (1 Chron. 21:1). David bought the lie, and destruction came upon the nation. At the Last Supper, "The evening meal was being served, and the devil had already prompted Judas Iscariot, son of Simon, to betray Jesus" (John 13:2).

It wasn't David's idea to defy God's will, nor was it Judas's idea to betray Christ, but both probably thought it was. That is the deception. Good people and even people chosen by God can be deceived. The devil cannot make Christians do anything against their wills, but the father of lies will deceive us if we don't assume our responsibility to know the truth that sets us free. The primary battle is for our minds.

Why don't we know this? One reason is that we can't read each other's minds. People fear sharing demonic thoughts because they don't want to be wrongly labeled as mentally ill. They will usually share experiences of pain or abuse; however, rarely can they find a safe person with whom they are able to share their mental battles. Therefore, they keep them locked in their minds.

Are they mentally ill, or is there a battle going on for their minds? The lack of any balanced biblical contribution to mental health professionals has left them with only one conclusion. Any problem in the mind must either be psychological or neurological. A common medical explanation for those who hear voices, have panic attacks, suffer from severe depression or see things in their rooms is "You have a chemical imbalance." A prescription for medication will usually be given with the hope of curing the problem or eliminating the symptoms.

I believe our body chemistries can get out of balance and cause discomfort, and hormonal problems can throw our systems off. But I also believe other legitimate questions need to be asked. For example, "How can a chemical produce a personal thought?" and "How can our neurotransmitters involuntarily and randomly fire in ways that create thoughts we are opposed to thinking?"

Is there a natural explanation for that? I am willing to hear any legitimate answers and explanations because I really care for people. I want to see their problems resolved by the grace of God, but I don't think that will happen unless we consider the reality of the spiritual world.

When people say they are hearing voices, what are they actually hearing? The only way we can physically hear with our ears is to have a sound source that compresses air molecules. Sound waves move through the physical medium of air and strike our eardrums, sending a signal to our brains. That is how we physically hear. But the voices people hear or the thoughts they struggle with are not coming from that kind of source.

Similarly, when people say they see things (that others don't), what are they actually seeing? The only way we can naturally see anything is to have a light source reflecting off a material object back to our eyes, sending a signal to our brains. Satan and his demons are spiritual beings; they do not have material substance, so we cannot see spiritual beings with our natural eyes, or hear them with our natural ears. "For our struggle is not against flesh and blood, but against the rulers, against the authorities, against the powers of this dark world and against the spiritual forces of evil in the heavenly realms" (Eph. 6:12).

What do parents typically do when frightened children enter their bedrooms claiming they have seen or heard something in their rooms? They go into the child's room, look into the closet or under the bed and say, "There is nothing in your room, Honey, now go back to sleep!" If you as an adult saw something in your room, would you just forget about it and go back to sleep?

"But I looked in the room, and nothing was there," you respond. There never was anything in the room that could be observed by your natural senses. "Then it's not real," says the skeptic. Oh yes it is! What that child saw or heard was in his or her own mind, and it is very real.

I can't explain how people pay attention to deceiving spirits. I don't know how the devil does it, but I don't have to know how he does it to believe what Scripture clearly teaches. The spiritual battle for our minds does not operate according to the laws of nature. No physical barriers can confine or restrict the movements of Satan. The frightened face of a child testifies that the battle is real. Why not respond to the child as follows:

> Honey, I believe you saw or heard something. I did not hear or see anything, so that helps me understand that you may be under a spiritual attack, or you could be having bad memories from a movie you saw. Sometimes I can't tell the difference between what is real and a dream I just had.
>
> Before I pray for your protection, I want you to know that Jesus is much bigger and more powerful than any frightening thing you see or hear. The Bible says that greater is Jesus living in us than any monsters in the world. Because Jesus is always with us, we can tell whatever is frightening us to leave in Jesus' name. The Bible tells us to submit to God and resist the devil, and he will flee from us. Can you do that, Honey? Do you have any questions? Then let's pray together.

THE BRAIN VERSUS THE MIND

There is much we don't know about mental functioning, but we do know a fundamental difference exists between our brains and our minds. Our brains are organic matter. When we die physically, we will separate from our bodies, and our brains will return to dust. At that moment, we will be absent from our bodies and present with the Lord. But we won't be mindless, because the mind is a part of the soul.

Let me draw an analogy. Our ability to think is similar to how a computer functions. Both have two separate components: the hardware, which is the actual physical computer (brain); and the software (mind), which programs the hardware. If the software is removed from the hardware it still weighs the same. Likewise, if the spirit is removed from the body, it also remains the same weight. A computer is totally worthless without the software, but the software won't work either if the hardware shuts down.

Society assumes that if something is not functioning correctly between the ears, it must be a hardware problem. I do not believe the primary problem is the hardware; I think the primary problem is the software. If a person has organic brain syndrome, Down's syndrome or Alzheimer's disease, the brain won't function very well. Severe brain damage, however, is relatively rare, and little can be done about it. Romans 12:1,2 instructs us to submit our bodies to God (which includes our brains) and be transformed by the renewing of our minds.

Much of what is being passed off today as mental illness is nothing more than a battle for our minds. Proverbs 23:7 says, "For as he thinks within himself, so he is" (*NASB*). In other words, we don't do anything without first thinking it. All behavior is the product of what we choose to think or believe. We can't see what people think. We can only observe what they do. Therefore, when our children misbehave, we try to change their behavior when we should be trying to understand their thinking so we can change what they believe.

Because we cannot read another person's mind, we must learn to ask the right questions. In *The Seduction of Our Children*, I shared the story of five-year-old Danny who was sent to the office at the Christian school he attended for hurting several other children on the playground. He had been acting aggressively toward others and was restless in class. His teacher said, "I'm puzzled by his recent behavior. It isn't like Danny to act this way!" Danny's mother was a teacher at the school. When she asked her son about Jesus, he covered his ears and shouted, "I hate Jesus!" Then he grasped his mother and laughed in a hideous voice!

When we asked Danny if he ever heard voices talking to him in his head, he looked relieved. He volunteered that voices were shouting at him on the playground to hurt other kids. The thoughts were so loud that the only way to quiet them was to obey, even though he knew he would get into trouble. We told Danny he didn't have to listen to the voices anymore.

We led Danny through the children's version of the "Steps to Freedom" described later in this book, having him pray the prayers after us. When we finished we asked him how he felt. A big smile spread across his face, and with a sigh of relief he said, "Much better!" His teacher noticed a calmness the next day, as though he were a different child. The aggressive behavior in school ended completely.

A committed Christian couple adopted a young boy, receiving him into their home with open arms. Their innocent little baby turned into a monster before he was five. Their home was in turmoil when I was asked to talk to him.

After some friendly chatter, I asked him if it ever seemed like someone was talking to him in his head. "Yes," he said, "all the time." "What are they saying?" I asked.

"They're telling me I'm no good."

I asked him if he had ever asked Jesus into his life.

He said, "Yes, but I didn't mean it."

I told him that if he really did ask Jesus to come into his life, he could tell those voices to leave him. Realizing that, he sincerely gave his heart to Christ.

Another committed couple heard thumping on the wall of their son's room. He had taken a pair of scissors and stabbed the wall several times. They never caught him doing it nor did they find the scissors. Then the child began to cut up every piece of clothing in the house. Again they never actually caught their son doing it. Huge medical and counseling bills piled up as they desperately tried to find a solution.

Finally the parents were introduced to the Freedom in Christ material and began to believe this might be a spiritual problem. So they asked their son if he ever had thoughts telling him to do what he was doing. He said, "Yes, and if I don't do what they tell me to do, they said they will kill you (the father)!" The little boy thought he was saving his father's life. I have heard that scenario more than once.

THE BIGGER PICTURE

Let's look at the bigger picture. Before we came to Christ we had neither the presence of God in our lives, nor the knowledge of His ways. Consequently, we learned to live our lives independently from God.

When we committed our lives to the Lord and were born again, we became new creations in Christ. The good news is that salvation comes with a brand-new software package. The bad news is that there is no delete button. So the old software (flesh or old nature) is still loaded into the memory bank and the computer is vulnerable to viruses (the fiery darts of the evil one). We must consciously choose to renew (reprogram) our minds and check for viruses (demonic attacks).

Paul said, "For though we live in the world, we do not wage war as the world does. The weapons we fight with are not the weapons of the world. On the contrary, they have divine power to demolish strongholds. We demolish arguments and every pretension that sets itself up against the knowledge of God, and we take captive every thought to make it obedient to Christ" (2 Cor. 10:3-5). Every child of God must assume personal responsibility for choosing the truth and teaching his or her children to do likewise.

The computer terminology of "garbage in, garbage out" also applies to our minds. If we have watched a lot of horror films, those images have been filed into our memories. When we sleep, we have no conscious control of our minds. The "computer" between our ears can randomly access any file stored in our memories, providing the basis for many nightmares.

Most nightmares are probably not direct spiritual attacks on the mind, although horror films may indeed be demonically inspired. An October 1995 issue of *The Denver Post* reported that author Stephen King, speaking at a fund-raiser for the public library in his hometown of Bangor, Maine, said, "People pay a shrink $50 an hour to get rid of those sick thoughts. I write them down and people pay me."

Similarly, the theme of many "good" dreams centers around people we know, and precious experiences we have had. A dear lady asked me about hallucinations of weird Disney figures she had experienced while under heavy medication. I told her that because she had no conscious control of her mind under the influence of hallucinogenic medication and severe sickness, her mind was "free" to access whatever she had stored in her memory.

It was a credit to her that images of Mickey Mouse had filled her mind. Many people would have had far worse images available for recall. Spiritual attacks and poor data entry have caused many people to have "mental" problems.

Our Western mentality assumes there is a natural explanation for everything. After every medical possibility has been unsuccessfully explored, we say, "There is nothing left to do now but pray." I believe the order should be reversed. My Bible reads, "Seek first His kingdom and His righteousness" (Matt. 6:33). Why not go to God first?

I have a great respect for the medical profession; therefore I believe the Church should work hand in hand with committed doctors. Taking a pill to cure the body is acceptable, but taking a pill to cure the soul is deplorable. Every legitimate doctor will admit that the medical field does not have all the answers. Medical professionals conservatively estimate that 50 percent of their patients are physically sick for psychosomatic reasons.

Who has the answer? The secular world that has no knowledge of God? We shouldn't be intimidated as though the Church has no valid contribution. The Church is "the pillar and foundation of the truth" (1 Tim. 3:15), and the truth will set our people free.

Please don't assume I believe all our problems are spiritual, because I don't. But I do believe we must have a whole answer for a whole person. The Church must be careful not to attribute a "spiritual" solution to every problem. For the same reason the medical profession must not promote a "physical" answer for everything. We need each other because we are both physical and spiritual beings who live in both a physical and a spiritual world—both created by God.

I'm often asked how I know whether a person's problem is spiritual or psychological. That question forces us into a false dichotomy. Our minds, wills and emotions are always involved or pertinent to the situation; therefore, our problems are always psychological. Our humanity must be considered in every circumstance this side of eternity.

On the other hand, God is always present and relevant; therefore, our problems are always spiritual. He is right now "sustaining all things by his powerful word" (Heb. 1:3). It is never safe to take off the armor of God. The possibility of being tempted, accused or deceived is a constant reality.

The Bible teaches that the unseen world is more real than the seen world: "For what is seen is temporary, but what is unseen is eternal" (2 Cor. 4:18). Accepting that truth will eliminate our attempts to find solutions in one of two polarized ministries: (1) psychotherapeutic ministries that ignore spiritual reality or (2) deliverance ministries that ignore developmental issues and human responsibility. Neither extreme can adequately provide a comprehensive answer. We must consider all reality, and strive for a balanced message.

Basically the answer is "Submit yourselves, then, to God. Resist the devil, and he will flee from you" (Jas. 4:7). Trying to resist the devil without first submitting to God will result in a dog fight. That is often the error of confrontational-type deliverance ministries. On the other hand, we can submit to God without resisting the devil, and stay in bondage.

Tragically, many recovery ministries are not doing either. Submitting to God requires dealing with the sin in our lives. Sin is like garbage—it attracts flies. So get rid of the flies? No! Get rid of the garbage. If we get rid of the garbage, the flies will have no reason (right) to be there.

THE TRUTH ABOUT POWER

I didn't ask for my first encounter with the powers of darkness, it was thrust upon me. My feeble attempt was based on the most common perceived process of calling up the demon, getting its name and rank, then casting it out. I found the process ugly, exhausting and potentially harmful to the victim.

Often the process had to be repeated because the results were not permanent. In this procedure, the deliverer is the pastor, counselor or missionary. The information is procured from the demons. Why should we believe them? We are clearly told "there is no truth in him. When he lies, he speaks his native language, for he is a liar and the father of lies" (John 8:44).

I also found the process lacking transferability. The procedure is often based on giftedness, or an office of the Church. I believe a better, much more transferable procedure is available. I believe Jesus is the deliverer, and He has already come. We should get our information from the Holy Spirit because He is "the Spirit of truth," and "he will guide you into all truth" (John 16:13).

My thinking shifted when I realized it is truth that sets us free, and Jesus is the truth. His prayer in John 17 is that we be kept from the evil one by being sanctified in the Word of God, which is the truth. Therefore, I prefer to think of our battle as a truth encounter rather than a power encounter.

The Bible does not instruct us to seek power. We already have all the power we need due to our incredible position in Christ. Paul wrote, "I pray also that the eyes of your heart may be enlightened in order that you may know the hope to which he has called you, the riches of his glorious inheritance in the saints, and his incomparably great power for us who believe. That power is like the working of his mighty strength, which he exerted in Christ when he raised him from the dead" (Eph. 1:18-20).

The power for Christians lies in their ability to believe the truth; the power of the evil one is in his ability to deceive. When the lie is exposed, his power is broken. When Christians struggle, they often wrongly conclude that they lack power. They are tempted to pursue an experience that will give them more power, but it will be a false trip. Satanists pursue power because it has been stripped from them. Christians pursue the truth.

Pete and Sue Vander Hook did not ask for their encounter with the powers of darkness either. It came with their ministry. They discovered as I did that truth sets people free, and that each of us has to assume our own personal responsibility to resolve our personal and spiritual conflicts. I cannot fight your fight for you, or believe for you or confess for you. I can, however, help you as Paul outlined in the pastoral Epistle, 2 Timothy 2:24-26:

> The Lord's servant must not quarrel; instead, he must be kind to everyone, able to teach, not resentful. Those who oppose him he must gently instruct, in the hope that God will grant them repentance leading them to a knowledge of the truth, and that they will come to their senses and escape from the trap of the devil, who has taken them captive to do his will.

This is not a power model—it is a kind, compassionate and instructive model. It requires dependency upon the Lord, for only He can grant the repentance that eliminates the garbage. It identifies truth as the liberating agent, and implies that the battle is for the mind. It is totally transferable because it requires only a loving, mature bondservant of the Lord, who knows the truth.

I know the latter is true. We have had the privilege of training thousands of pastors, missionaries and laypeople throughout the world who are now setting other captives free in Christ. I deeply believe every parent can be equipped to protect and help his or her children.

SETTING THE CAPTIVES FREE

Does Christ want us free? Of course. "It is for freedom that Christ has set us free. Stand firm, then, and do not let yourselves be burdened again by a yoke of slavery" (Gal. 5:1). The context is freedom from the law. Legalism is a bondage. The answer for us and our families is not to just lay down the law. Should we be tempted to throw off all legal or moral constraints and go too far in the other direction, we must consider Galatians 5:13: "You, my brothers, were called to be free. But do not use your freedom to indulge the sinful nature."

The "Steps to Freedom" I have developed are simply a tool to help people resolve the critical issues between themselves and God, then to resist the devil. The "Steps" don't set you free. Christ sets you free when you choose to respond to Him in repentance and faith.

The process could not hurt anybody except possibly to create some false hope. The worst possible result from going through the "Steps to Freedom" would be complete readiness for communion the next Sunday. We are trying to help people resolve their personal and spiritual conflicts so the life of Christ will be manifested in them. Then they can do all things through Christ who strengthens them.

I don't believe in instant maturity. It will take the rest of our lives to renew our minds and conform to the image of God. If people are not free in Christ, they will go from book to book, counselor to counselor and church to church, unable to break free from their pasts and the bondage of sin.

Once they find their freedom in Christ, watch them grow! It doesn't take the rest of their lives to become free in Christ. In most cases, a single three- to four-hour session will help people resolve their issues and get radically right with God.

Our doctors prescribe tests to determine the cause of our illnesses. When the tests don't reveal the problem, we don't become angry with our doctors. Shouldn't Christians be able to turn to their churches, and children to their parents, to ascertain whether or not their problems are spiritual? We should not be angry with the secular world for refusing to consider the reality of the spiritual world. It is not their responsibility—it is the Church's responsibility to resolve spiritual conflicts.

Paul said, "I am afraid that just as Eve was deceived by the serpent's cunning, your minds may somehow be led astray from your sincere and pure devotion to Christ" (2 Cor. 11:3). I share the same concern for every child of God. My desire is to see every Christian live his or her life free in Christ. It is our spiritual birthright. And I desire to see every marriage, family and ministry alive in Christ and free to be all God has called them to be.

I love Pete and Sue's story because it demonstrates how people, marriages, families and churches can be free in Christ. Then and only then can the Body of Christ join in unity to fulfill the Great Commission.

As you read Pete and Sue's story (told from Sue's perspective), understand that your situation may be quite different. The rise of New Age teaching in our public schools, the increasing violent and anti-Christian attitude of society (especially in public television) as well as the less-than-innocent games many children are playing have made it necessary to recognize the spiritual battle children of Christian families may be experiencing. We definitely do not believe all our problems are spiritual, but we must be able to recognize the ones that are so we can provide a balanced biblical answer for them.

In telling their story, Pete and Sue do not share the ideal way of resolving a spiritual attack. They did not perfectly do what is right. None of us do! They moved from ignorance to biblical enlightenment and from defeat to victory in Christ—so can you!

They share their story for one purpose: to help other parents who find themselves in a spiritual battle and don't know how to resolve it. You may be tempted to think that sharing their story and exposing the reality of the spiritual world will cause some to have imaginary fears and start looking for demons that aren't even there.

That would be tragic, because we believe just the opposite. Ignorance is not bliss—it is defeat. Truth sets us free. We must know who we are in Christ, as Pete and Sue discovered. We must know the position, authority and protection every child of God has in Christ. We need to know that Satan is a defeated foe. We should never let the devil set the agenda. Jesus is Lord, and we must fix our eyes upon Him, the author and finisher of our faith. This is the basic and balanced message Pete and Sue discovered as they read *Victory over the Darkness* and *The Bondage Breaker*.

At the end of their story, I will provide some specific instructions for parents and pastors. I just want you to know there is an answer for you and your family. Jesus is the answer, and His truth will set you and your family free. He is the bondage breaker.

Note
1. Neil T. Anderson and Steve Russo, *The Seduction of Our Children* (Eugene, Oreg.: Harvest House, 1991), p. 33.

PART I

SETTING YOUR FAMILY FREE

1

A MIGHTY FORTRESS

A MIGHTY FORTRESS
IS OUR GOD, A BULWARK...

My mouth continued to form the words, but my emotions clogged any sounds that might follow. I wanted to boldly sing those words of strength and truth. As I stood in church that early spring Sunday morning in 1995, I was oblivious to the hundreds of others who stood with me raising their voices to our Creator and Savior.

I was remarkably impervious to anyone's attempt to analyze my grief—or was it my joy—or perhaps my past association with the truths of Martin Luther's great hymn. It probably appeared as though I were still singing as I mouthed the words...

A bulwark never failing.
Our helper, He amid the flood
Of mortal ills prevailing.
For still our ancient foe
Doth seek to work us woe—
His craft and pow'r are great,
And, armed with cruel hate,
On earth is not his equal.

I longed to sing those words that expose our ancient foe who formerly sought with all his craft and power to bring a flood of havoc on our family and our church. I clearly identified with Martin

Luther's description of Satan's nature. He is armed with cruel hate, and he has no regard for the human lives fashioned by his greatest nemesis, God the Creator. I knew all too well that Satan has no earthly equal, and that in our flesh we are defenseless under his offensive.

As my husband, Pete, stretched his arm around me grabbing my trembling shoulders with his strong hand, I heard him sniffling back his own tears. We were moved by the culmination of a victorious weekend of repentance and renewal for the elders of our church after completing the Setting Your Church Free conference by Neil Anderson and Charles Mylander. The thought of 12 men—the spiritual leaders of our church—about to share the intimate details of their own repentance stirred our emotions.

But more than that, the song reminded us of the painful yet triumphant memories of our past. We both felt an overwhelming sense of God's great continuing power and ability to be a "Mighty Fortress."

The reality of God's role in our lives as a protective citadel, a bastion, a bulwark and a defender extended beyond the scope of that day and that weekend. It was rooted in another year, another city and another situation.

THE BASEMENT PIANO

The words to that mighty song ignited memories that rushed through my mind, creating a huge panoramic scene that now seems almost remote. It carried me back to many emotionally painful days and nights during a three-year period of our family's life. I remembered the many sleepless nights and hours spent agonizing about our children, who had become the target of Satan's attack. I was reminded of the big old brown piano in the basement where we lived in Madison, Wisconsin.

Six men had struggled to move that piano into our house. They had to remove the front door and take the piano apart so it would fit through the doorway. But we were determined to have music in our house. It finally found its place in the basement, standing tall and firm on its very old legs.

But the resounding tones from that piano one particularly cold January night in 1993 were beautiful, not because of any intrinsic loveliness of the resonance, but because of the healing effect from the hymn played on it: "A Mighty Fortress Is Our God."

Did we in our own strength confide,
Our striving would be losing,
Were not the right man on our side,
The man of God's own choosing.
Dost ask who that may be?
Christ Jesus, it is He–
Lord Sabaoth His name,
From age to age the same,
And He must win the battle.

As I played and sang every word to every verse of that hymn, I related to the spiritual warfare Martin Luther had experienced as he stood for godly truth and spiritual accuracy. I cried from the string of our present circumstances. But I refused to let my tears deter me from singing every word—probably in defiance of Satan and all the powers of darkness seeking to destroy our family.

"Be self-controlled and alert. Your enemy the devil prowls around like a roaring lion looking for someone to devour" (1 Pet. 5:8). Through the power of Jesus Christ who defeated Satan on the cross (see Heb. 2:14), I sang my song of victory, belting out every verse in triumph:

And tho this world, with devils filled,
Should threaten to undo us,
We will not fear, for God hath willed
His truth to triumph thru us.
The prince of darkness grim,
We tremble not for him–
His rage we can endure, for lo, his doom is sure:
One little word shall fell him.

That word above all earthly pow'rs,
No thanks to them, abideth;
The Spirit and the gifts are ours
Thru Him who with us sideth.
Let goods and kindred go,
This mortal life also–
The body they may kill; God's truth abideth still.
His kingdom is forever. A-men.

THE HOUSE

The house in Madison where we lived with that old piano was a "decorator's nightmare" when we bought it. The dark-colored walls throughout most of the rooms, black sheers, black swag lamps with amber light covers, black kitchen cabinets and orange and black kitchen floor all contended with each other to make it a dark experience. The basement didn't disappoint the rest of the house with its walls of dark mustard yellow and matching curtains. The carpet was badly in need of cleaning. Three recessed amber lights tried their best to illumine the area, succeeding only in casting a shadowy yellow light throughout the dirty cobwebbed corners of the L-shaped room.

LITTLE DID WE KNOW THAT ALTERING THE OUTWARD APPEARANCE OF OUR HOME WOULD NOT CHANGE WHAT ACTUALLY HAPPENED WITHIN ITS WALLS.

But the price was attractive, and our funds were limited. In our enthusiasm, we looked beyond the offensive decorating and optimistically saw the benefits of a few gallons of paint, some new window coverings and a lot of muscles, Lysol and rags.

After closing escrow on our new home in 1985, we eagerly began cleaning every corner and painting every dark wall. We replaced the dark light fixtures and some window coverings with anything that would exude light. But as the rejuvenation projects became more expensive, we had to slow down, doing one project at a time. We held garage sales to pay for more changes.

With our eagerness and hard work came difficulties for our family. Little did we know that altering the outward appearance of our home would not change what actually happened within its walls. Our sons—four and two—began having nightmares for the first time in their lives. Remembering some of our own childhood dreams, Pete and I attributed them to inevitable occurrences for children. Initially, we just prayed with our sons and comforted them until they went back to sleep.

Two years later (in 1987), we were blessed with another child— a daughter. In need of more space, we redecorated the third bedroom. We rented an electric sander to repair one badly damaged wall, then gladly removed the dark paneling from another wall, discovering a once black wall underneath. We enthusiastically covered the nefarious sight with bright, cheery blue wallpaper trimmed with airplanes and space shuttles. The other walls we adorned in pure white while we dressed the windows with blue miniblinds. Soon the room was ready, and our two boys eagerly moved into their brand-new room.

Covering up the old and giving it the appearance of new life did not change our circumstances. The nightmares not only continued in their new room, they intensified. Our oldest son, Dave, would often shout fearfully in the middle of the night. By the time we entered his room, he was wide awake and well aware of the all-too-realistic, terrifying details of his dream. We would pray with him, reassuring him of the power and protection of God: "You are my hiding place; you will protect me from trouble and surround me with songs of deliverance" (Ps. 32:7). Eventually he would go back to sleep.

But our second son, Jared, now four, never woke up during his nightmares and never remembered any part of his dreams the next day. It was impossible to awaken him from his deep sleep to tell us what was terrorizing him. He just sat up and cried hysterically, sometimes screaming in terror. We didn't know what made him so afraid.

On two separate nights his fright was so intense he couldn't stop crying out in fear, screaming whenever he looked into our faces. His open, sleeping eyes looked through us and not at us. Only the singing of "Jesus Loves Me" and the repetition of John 3:16 would calm him. After almost an hour and a half of singing and quoting the verse, he finally went to sleep. The words to that familiar children's song became a weapon we used often in the spiritual battles to come for our family.

Our bedtime prayers with our three children became progressively stronger, and included Scriptures to provide courage and

strength. But it was our family's involvement in the pro-life movement that turned our struggle into a crisis—a crisis that would only
be resolved by the awesome power of God in our lives.

2

THE ENEMY OF LIFE

THE LIFE CHAIN

Our involvement in defending life for the pre-born began in 1991 when abortion was very popular, very accepted and very politically correct—even in the Church. Sermons about life in the womb were not only politically improper, but often incited outspoken debate and controversy.

My husband, Pete, who pastored a church in Madison, disregarded public pressures and began supporting the scriptural basis for life from conception. He did not hesitate to preach on Psalm 139 as it applied to the viability of life in the womb. He endured some polemic discussions after the service about the poignant verses: "My frame was not hidden from you when I was made in the secret place. When I was woven together in the depths of the earth, your eyes saw my unformed body. All the days ordained for me were written in your book before one of them came to be" (Ps. 139:15,16).

That spring, we, along with 700 others, attended the annual banquet for our local crisis pregnancy center (Pregnancy Information Center). The humorous, motivating style of the guest speaker, Cal Thomas, encouraged Pete to be even bolder and to become more involved in pro-life activities. I was inspired to volunteer my time at the crisis pregnancy center.

A few months later, I was serving on its board of directors. Pete was speaking at walk-a-thons and rescue rallies, encouraging people to get involved in the first rescue and the first Life Chain in our city. Many from our own congregation joined in pro-life activities, standing side by side with others in the city for the cause of life.

At the first Life Chain, our human chain resembled a cross from an aerial view. But for those of us who stood as a speck in that formation, the cross of Jesus Christ was clearly our motivation, our reason for wanting every baby to live and know its Creator.

On that windy October Sunday afternoon, our entire family did its part to complete the message of the figurative cross in our liberal Wisconsin city. We boldly but silently held signs that in brave letters emblazoned our cause: ABORTION KILLS CHILDREN and JESUS HEALS AND FORGIVES.

People who opposed our message shouted obscenities from their cars and gestured to us in disdain, but we did not retaliate. For an hour we stood proclaiming our opposition to abortion and our promotion of God's forgiving and healing power. Only a few observers gave us a "thumbs-up" to show their agreement.

But in spite of the weak support and strong opposition, when the Life Chain disassembled, our children (ages 10, 7 and 4) wanted to drive through the city holding up their signs in the windows of our van. Exhilarated from the afternoon, Dave enthusiastically asked to keep the sign that read ABORTION KILLS CHILDREN so he could tape it in his window, a place obvious to all passersby. He wanted every driver or jogger to think twice about having an abortion and adding another unknown name to the list of millions already killed.

THE MARCH

Soon after the rescue and Life Chain in 1991, a pro-life group in Madison organized a countermarch around the Capitol building in opposition to a pro-abortion march and rally. The march was to culminate on the Capitol steps with a fervent speech by one of the state's liberal, gay, pro-choice politicians. Pete heard about the march shortly before it was to begin and called home to see if we all wanted to go. Our children were anxious to save some babies, so off we went planning to arrive at least 30 minutes prior to the scheduled pro-choice march.

The turnout was disappointing. Only 10 other people accompanied us, so more than enough signs were available. We each took the sign of our choice. Dave wanted to carry two. Even our four-year-old daughter, Jalene, chose a little sign to carry as we walked. Thus started our walk around the "square," the four streets encasing the beautiful white majestic Capitol building. There was only one rule for the march—we were not to speak.

As we walked around and around the Capitol, we didn't understand what all the opposition talk was about because no one bothered us at all. Some people glanced at us, some stared, some just ignored us—we thought this march was a "piece of cake." Suddenly we heard one of our fellow picketers say, "Here they come," and the mood of our group quickly changed.

As we stood at the corner by the Capitol where State Street stretches down through the distinctive shops and restaurants to connect the square to the University of Wisconsin campus, we could only hear the faint sound of a group of people. But soon we saw a wave of people in the far distance by the campus entrance. The increasing volume of their voices chanted phrases again and again that were as yet indistinguishable.

As they got closer, I felt as though a tidal wave of evil were surging toward us, rising in strength and speed as it advanced. They became closer and closer, louder and louder, until we could hear distinctly their angry shouts and demands for the government to leave them alone and not allow coat hangers back in the alleys. Some waved coat hangers angrily in the air in symbolic protest. Soon hundreds of people were marching past us, most of them dressed entirely in black and adorned with an abundance of gold and silver jewelry, much of it molded and shaped into occult symbols.

As those leading the march saw our small band of picketers carrying pro-life signs, their unison demands that the government stay out of their wombs changed to a chant directed at us. With visible anger, their voices rising to screams and their fingers and signs pointing at us in disdain, they shouted:

> Racists, bigots, anti-gay,
> Born-again Christians, go away!
> ## Racists, bigots, anti-gay,
> ## Born-again Christians, go away!
> # Racists, bigots, anti-gay,
> # Born-again Christians, go away!

Again and again they intoned their disgust at our presence. We stood in silence, perplexed that our opponents did not attack our pro-life stance or our signs heralding piercing statements and pictures. Instead they called us racists, bigots and anti-gay, assailing our Christianity—something our signs did not reveal.

Our emotions were running high as we saw this tidal wave engulf the sidewalks and stairs leading to the Capitol. Tears flowed

---

I KNEW SATAN WAS DISTORTING THE TRUTH AND THAT HE HAD ORCHESTRATED AND REVELED IN THE EASINESS AND EXCESS OF ABORTION, BUT I HAD NEVER SEEN SUCH A DELUGE OF HIS DECEPTIVE POWERS.

---

as we realized the utter darkness these people were in. Even Dave asked us, "Why are they so mad?" And Jared joined in, "Yeah, Daddy, why are they mad?" Pete answered them honestly and succinctly, "Because they can't stand the truth."

The lies they believed and their blindness to the truth was the most poignant display I had ever witnessed of Satan's attempt to destroy life. I knew Satan was distorting the truth and that he had orchestrated and reveled in the easiness and excess of abortion, but I had never seen such a deluge of his deceptive powers.

The pregnant woman standing beside me with her toddler was overcome with emotion as she watched the debacle of darkness press us. She seemed to cry for joy that her toddler was alive and that her unborn baby would live. But she also wept in sorrow for the babies who would never take their first breath or see the light of the morning sun, just so women could have a choice.

Soon the crowd's attention, as well as our own, was turned to the top of the Capitol stairs where the politician's treble voice had been given power and resonance only by the strength of a large amplification system. As the dark crowd heeded their political leader, our small group quietly turned in their signs and left.

As we traveled home, we renewed our desire to promote life for every baby and every person God created. But we were definitely sobered, gravely realizing that Satan truly is the ruler of the power of the air, the deceiver of the whole world, the father of lies, the accuser, our enemy (see Eph. 2:2; 6:11). "He was a murderer from the beginning, not holding to the truth, for there is no truth in him. When he lies, he speaks his native language, for he is a liar and the father of lies" (John 8:44). We had observed by graphic example on those Capitol stairs the agenda of God's chief antagonist—to thwart God's plan for all humanity and deceive people with lies, hatred and death.

But we did not walk away defeated by the power of our opposition. We rode home triumphantly rejoicing that we were on God's side, not helpless victims without hope in the face of evil. We rejoiced that through the death and resurrection of God in the flesh, the power of Satan was broken so that "by his death he [Jesus] might destroy him who holds the power of death—that is, the devil" (Heb. 2:14). We left with great faith that God would ultimately win this battle against abortion, and we determined to continue our fight for life. The most zealous, enthusiastic supporter in our family for the cause of life was Dave.

3

THE AGENDA OF DEATH

THE ATTACK

As our enthusiasm for life mounted, so did our involvement with pro-life activities. By the December 3rd board meeting for the crisis pregnancy center, I had agreed to fill the vacancy as editor for its newsletter. Not only was I eager to write, but I was also zealous for the cause of life and eager to circulate God's truth.

Instead of a December newsletter, several volunteers worked on a Christmas card. It featured the babies who had come into the world that year because the center had in some way helped its mothers choose life. We were pressed for time, but the card was completed, labels were applied and they were mailed. The cards arrived on Christmas Eve, heralding a simple yet poignant message next to the pictures of each of the newborns allowed to live that year. It simply stated, "I'm alive!" We would later realize its full impact on many people.

By December 19th, having no idea that God's archenemy was agitated by our pro-life activities and our church ministry, we were taken by surprise when the "father of lies" convinced Dave (age 10) that life was not worth living. He suddenly believed he should either shoot himself in the head or be given to someone else for adoption to spare us from living with him.

Does it sound ridiculous that a boy who had been so fervently promoting life from his bedroom window and marching around the Capitol in opposition to abortion would now espouse a death plan? It was absurd! The great deceiver and liar had been lulling Dave's mind during the night in the secret recesses of his dreams into believing death was the answer to some nebulous problem in his life.

I faced this unexpected turn of events alone with Dave for the first two hours as I awaited Pete's return from a meeting at church. It was Thursday at 9:00 P.M. and I was reading at the kitchen table. I had put all three children to bed about an hour before. I noticed Dave walking down the stairs slowly and sleepily. He approached me with glassy eyes and a stone-cold face, handing me a piece of paper on which he had drawn a picture. Unemotionally he said, "Here," and sat down on a chair.

He loved to draw, so I presumed he had just forgotten to show me a special picture. I eagerly opened the folded paper, but immediately received the greatest shock of my 10 years of parenting. It was a drawing of a young boy with a gun pointed at his head. Below the picture was scribbled, "It's either this or adoption."

My smiling face suddenly metamorphosed into an open mouth aghast with shock and furrowed brows filled with unbelief and fear. Thoughts whirred inside my head as I desperately tried to evaluate what could have prompted my son to feel such despair. I weakly asked, "What does this mean?"

He replied, "Just what it says." I could think of no family or relational problems that might have provoked such hopelessness and despondency. He had gone to bed not wanting a hug and a kiss that night, but I wasn't concerned. I told myself he *was* getting older.

Because we had adopted him when he was just one month old, I immediately interpreted the drawing to mean that he thought adoption was as bad as death itself. I began to ask him why he felt so badly about adoption, but he stopped me from continuing along that line of thinking. He assured me he didn't mean his own adoption was bad. I continued my questioning. Once again, he confirmed his security about his adoption. He finally looked at me with eyes that showed some love and assurance.

He explained that for the good of the family, he should die or we should rid ourselves of him. I tried desperately to convince him of our love for him and of his own worth, but his significance was almost gone. No matter what I said during the next two hours, he refused to believe me or come out of his sudden depression.

I realized these thoughts and feelings were far beyond the scope of Dave's own thoughts, or his young age or his secure Christian circumstances. I asked him what had prompted him to think these thoughts or draw the picture. At first he was uncommunicative. I wondered if it had been a big mistake not to find out why he didn't want a hug and kiss at bedtime; but how would such a small thing create such a repulsive decision?

CHERISHED MEMORIES

Between my own despairing thoughts, I reflected back on a precious day when Dave was three years old. I had knelt beside his bed to pray with him before he went to sleep. I remembered how he mat-

---

I REALIZED THAT A SPIRITUAL BATTLE HAD BEEN RAGING IN OUR CHRISTIAN HOME DURING THE SILENCE OF THE NIGHT AND IN THE FEAR OF OUR CHILD'S MIND.

---

ter-of-factly said, "Mom, I want Jesus in my heart." I remembered how he had prayed that simple prayer of belief in Jesus to save him from his sins and come into his heart. Then reflections of his love for Jesus throughout the years came to me.

I recalled a time when he was seven. He reaffirmed his salvation that day because he didn't remember his young three-year-old experience. Oh, how my heart flooded with joy when I remembered that Sunday evening in 1988. He had donned a little white robe and walked into the baptismal at church to be baptized by his father. I was waiting for him behind the tank with a towel as he came dripping up the stairs. He was sobbing, not from fear or embarrassment, but from joy—the joy of knowing Christ. His elation was so great, I knew God had done something spectacular in his life. As Dave later explained, he was really "pumped with the Spirit."

Those memories on the dark night we were now experiencing gave me confidence that Dave's thoughts of death were not his own. I was, however, totally unequipped to deal with the frightening prospect of suicide.

UNWELCOME VOICES

Dave finally began to talk and communicate openly, as he had always done, even though he was still cold and unresponsive. He related how, after he had been unable to go to sleep that night, a voice had told him exactly what to draw and write on that piece of paper. The voice had also told him to find his survival knife, which was fortunately not easily found in his messy room.

As we continued to talk, he told me of terrifying recurring nightmares that had plagued him for years, and voices he had heard as far back as he could remember. He later told me how for years his nights had been filled with horrifying dreams that often awakened him and silenced him in fear. He shared how he had desperately tried to pray during those times of terror, but had been unable to pray or utter the name of Jesus.

As I listened to and observed my son, I realized that a spiritual battle had been raging in our Christian home during the silence of the night and in the fear of our child's mind. Understandably, Dave had been afraid to tell us about the voices in his head. After all, it sounded like good grounds for the psychiatric ward. And why should he snivel about a dream? Wouldn't that be childish or insignificant? But we constantly thank God he didn't obey the voices, and that he cried out for help with a picture he was compelled to draw against his own beliefs.

YOU CREATED MY INMOST BEING

Undoubtedly we were now on the front lines of spiritual warfare, in a tug-of-war for our son. I realized nothing small had ignited this incident. As we would later discover, it involved an agenda of death developed by the principalities and powers of darkness themselves. I kept Dave close by my side, talking and praying with him until Pete, the spiritual head of our home, returned from his meeting.

Pete finally arrived shortly after 11:00 P.M. I feebly relayed the incidents of the night to him. My husband was as shocked as I had been by the sudden change that had taken place in his son whom he loved so much. He started to pray. His prayers cried out to God for help, claiming the promises that He would never leave us or forsake us (see Josh. 1:5; Heb. 13:5). Pete claimed the promise that God would take away our fears even when we walk through the valley of the shadow of death (see Ps. 23:4).

As Pete and I talked with Dave, attempting to break through to the core of his sudden despondency, Dave grew even colder, drifting off into blank stares, refusing to listen. Sometime after midnight, when all reason and discussion had failed, Pete opened his Bible to the Scripture that was able to mightily silence Satan's agenda of death that night—Psalm 139:13-16:

> For you created my inmost being;
> you knit me together in my mother's womb.
> I praise you because I am fearfully and wonderfully made;
> your works are wonderful, I know that full well.
> My frame was not hidden from you
> when I was made in the secret place.
> When I was woven together in the depths of the earth,
> your eyes saw my unformed body.
> All the days ordained for me were written in your book
> before one of them came to be.

Pete handed his worn, marked-up Bible to Dave, and asked him to read those four verses. Dave unwillingly held his father's Bible and began to read in a disgusted tone. He quietly and rebelliously started to read the printed words: "For you created my inmost being; you knit me together in my mother's womb." Unable to read any further, he bowed his head and began to sob. He reached out with wide open arms to embrace both his father and mother, something he had refused to do for the past few hours.

The truth of God's Word, the simple proclamation of God as the Creator of all life, had broken Satan's death agenda for our son. We had Dave back with a renewed zeal for life. He began his fight against the one who was trying to destroy him.

In the quiet hours well past midnight, Dave earnestly searched for every knife and possible weapon in our house. Determined to rid his room of other products of the lies he had believed, he found other pictures he had drawn that were prompted by thoughts of violence or death. We found an old cookie sheet, went outside to the backyard in the chill of that December night, and Dave set fire to every drawing that had been prompted by the father of lies.

Dave slept on the floor beside our bed that night, enduring the constant torture of voices and demons he alone could hear and see. He covered his ears, attempting to block out the noise of a myriad of voices shouting at him to deny God and embrace death. Because he had always been painfully honest, abounding in realism, I had no reason to doubt the existence of evil in our room.

Pete and I also felt the darkness and the oppression. Dave would sleep for 30 to 45 minutes before he was again awakened in terror. All three of us prayed each time he awoke. We realized as the night progressed just how inexperienced we were in spiritual warfare. Each prayer brought peace, but quoting Scripture verses brought victory, until another attack would come.

As the battle raged through the early hours of the morning, I wondered why. What was the reason for this vicious invasion of our home? Why was our child the target of this ugly assault? Was our house more than a "decorator's nightmare"? Was it our pro-life activities? Had a curse been placed upon us during the sinister march at the Capitol? Was it our ministry? Was it Pete's pointed sermons? Was it our belief in Jesus as the Son of God?

For whatever reason, Satan had decided to attack our child. Perhaps he was really attacking *us* by hurting one of our children whom we loved more than any other earthly thing. I don't believe we will ever know the real reason for Satan's attack. After all, he's the great liar and deceiver.

We *do* know that God did not leave those who believe in Him and serve Him as helpless victims without hope in the face of an evil world. We had total confidence that through the death and resurrection of God in the flesh (Jesus Christ), the power of Satan had already been broken and that "greater is He [Jesus] who is in you [us] than he [Satan] who is in the world (1 John 4:4, *NASB*). We only had to tap our source of power, God Himself, and defeat the one who had already been defeated! But how would we do that? What was the answer to our battle? As we would later look back and realize, our victory did not come easily.

4

WHO AM I?

CHRISTMAS FESTIVITIES

When our horrifying night finally ended, the sun brought a welcome light to our home. We eagerly arose, hoping our appointment with hell had concluded forever. But our meeting with evil was not over. We were fortunately unaware (lest we might have lost hope) that our strife with the principalities of darkness would last almost three years.

Life did go on, in spite of the unwelcome invasion of evil into our home and family. We ate breakfast as usual and sent our two sons off to school, praying and trusting God to protect them. We asked the Lord to give Dave strength to concentrate after his nearly sleepless night.

I busily gathered up some kitchen utensils to use for preparing the Christmas banquet at church. It was just five days before Christmas. Pete and I packed up Jalene with her bag of dolls to keep her busy, while I joined a good friend to cook roast beef and decorate for our church's biggest dinner of the year.

My hands prepared for celebration, but my body rebelled from lack of sleep. My heart ached for my suffering son. If his enemy had been flesh and blood, I would have called the police or attempted to fight his foes myself. But his contenders were the unseen powers of darkness, so all I could do was pray to God in whom I had total confidence. The humanity of my heart, however, was still breaking.

While we ate and celebrated with our church family that evening, the children had their own party in another room. Memories of our problems from the previous night seemed to fade when our children presented us with beautiful crude bells designed from upside down plastic cups accented with pipe-stem clappers and an assortment of stars and stickers. I silently thanked the Lord for the joy and light that still outweighs the darkest of nights.

ANOTHER NIGHT OF TERROR

Afraid that no one at the banquet would understand and not wanting to ruin a beautiful evening of celebration, I did not mention our previous night.

AT THE TIME, I COULDN'T EXPLAIN THAT STRIPPED OF ALL TALENTS, ABILITIES, GIFTS AND PHYSICAL CAPABILITIES, DAVE WAS STILL TOTALLY SIGNIFICANT, ENTIRELY SECURE AND COMPLETELY ACCEPTED JUST BECAUSE HE WAS A CHILD OF GOD!

We returned home and privately prayed with each child before bed. We tried to make bedtime as normal as possible, attempting to forget the events of the night before and alleviate fear. Although Jared and Jalene didn't know exactly what had transpired, they understood things were not right in our family. They knew something was bothering Dave, and that their mom and dad were extremely troubled and tired. So they joined in the fervency of our prayers, somehow understanding the urgency of the hour.

After putting all the kids to bed, Pete and I prayed together for protection, for strength, for wisdom to know what to do, for God's power in our home and for our children. We enthusiastically welcomed the sleep we had been robbed of the night before.

Within 45 minutes of our much needed slumber, we were awakened by Dave's trembling, fearful presence in our room. Our prayers began again and our ordeal with evil continued into another night. Again our son "camped out" in his sleeping bag on the floor beside our bed. Again the three of us prayed through another night of terror.

During those sleepless nights and times between attacks, my son and I just talked about things in general. He had always asked a lot of questions with an insatiable desire to learn. Suddenly he needed to be affirmed, to know he had self-worth. I enthusiastically validated all of his good qualities and abilities, but he wasn't satisfied.

At the time, I couldn't explain that stripped of all talents, abilities, gifts and physical capabilities, he was still totally significant, entirely secure and completely accepted just because he was a child of God! So I affirmed him then as best as I knew how. I knew I had failed to convince him that he was worthy.

THE WONDERFUL POWER OF GOD

In spite of my failure to communicate truth, and in spite of the terror and darkness of those first few nights, every skirmish was countered with the wonderful power of God. Every fear was overcome with the peace of God. We only had to repeat those well-worn verses we had learned as children, and the forces of evil left us alone. Psalm 23 was popular each night. Pete would say a phrase and Dave and I would repeat it. It was comforting to know as we walked through our valley of the shadow of death, we did not have to fear because God was there.

For whatever reason, God in His infinite wisdom did not choose to put an immediate end to our walk through the valley. The battle was far from being over and our quest for freedom had just begun.

CLEANING HOUSE

Two days after Dave's first attack, our children zealously searched the house for things that had brought fear into their lives. We had carefully tried to purchase toys that were not evil, so we were surprised at some of the things our children gathered. They threw away action figures, video games that were innocent until the last level when they tried to defeat a diabolic monster, and numerous other unsuspecting toys.

But we were just beginning to realize Satan's cunning deception and ability to use anything to affect the minds of children. By the time we finished "cleaning house," we had filled two bags with devices the enemy had used to bring fear upon our children (see *The Seduction of Our Children* by Neil Anderson and Steve Russo for a list of occult artifacts and symbols).

Meanwhile, we resolved to "be strong in the Lord and in his mighty power. Put on the full armor of God so that you can take your stand against the devil's schemes....Therefore put on the full armor of God, so that when the day of evil comes, you may be able to stand your ground, and after you have done everything, to stand" (Eph. 6:10,11,13).

I AM

During the next few nights of nightmares and terror, we learned much about the power of prayer and Scripture. Battles were won, faith replaced doubt and things *were* getting better. But we also knew we needed more help.

It was Monday, four days after Dave had been violated by evil and the first day of Christmas break from school. It was also Pete's day off after a busy Sunday of preaching and teaching. Pete visited a Christian bookstore where he searched through the "Spiritual Warfare" section for a book that would answer our questions and solve our problems. He avoided books that recommended face-to-face combat with demons or exorcisms. He also avoided authors with whom he disagreed doctrinally and those who didn't base their advice on Scripture.

He had emphasized throughout his 15 years as a pastor that if the Bible doesn't back up what you believe, don't believe it. So I wasn't surprised when he brought home a book replete with Scripture. And I wasn't surprised that the author was the chairman of the Practical Theology Department at Talbot School of Theology. I'll admit I was disappointed when he didn't bring home a book entitled *How to Get Rid of the Demons in Your House* or *Three Easy Prayers to Defeat Satan*. But I fully trusted my husband's judgment in spiritual matters.

Pete spent most of the afternoon reading his new book, *Victory over the Darkness* by Dr. Neil T. Anderson. The title was compelling because we had definitely been invaded by darkness and needed victory over it. I had hoped the chapter titles might include those easy steps to eliminate evil or some mighty supernatural prayer to forever free our family from demonic attacks. It didn't. But I still believed something in the book would help us.

After Jared and Jalene went to bed, Pete called Dave over to his big recliner where he was still reading the book. As Dave stood behind the chair, Pete held the open book above his shoulder and asked him to read a list entitled "Who Am I?" Dave willingly read the first few lines of the list, which ended at the bottom of the page.

I am the salt of the earth (Matt. 5:13).

I am the light of the world (Matt. 5:14).

I am a child of God (John 1:12).

I am part of the true vine, a channel of Christ's life (John 15:1,5).

I am Christ's friend (John 15:15).

I am chosen and appointed by Christ to bear His fruit (John 15:16).

He started to walk away, but Pete turned the page and said, "There's more." Hesitant to read another page and a half, Dave slowly returned to the chair to read the remainder of the "I Am" list. Between sighs of reluctance, he read on.

I am a slave of righteousness (Rom. 6:18).

I am enslaved to God (Rom. 6:22).

I am a son of God; God is spiritually my Father (Rom. 8:14,15; Gal. 3:26; 4:6).

I am a joint heir with Christ, sharing His inheritance with Him (Rom. 8:17).

I am a temple—a dwelling place—of God. His Spirit and His life dwells in me (1 Cor. 3:16; 6:19).

I am united to the Lord and am one spirit with Him (1 Cor. 6:17).

I am a member of Christ's Body (1 Cor. 12:27; Eph. 5:30).

I am a new creation (2 Cor. 5:17).

Then our son's voice lost its tone of unwillingness and seemed to gain confidence.

I am reconciled to God and am a minister of reconciliation (2 Cor. 5:18,19).

I am a son of God and one in Christ (Gal. 3:26,28).

I am an heir of God since I am a son of God (Gal. 4:6,7).

I am a saint (1 Cor. 1:2; Eph. 1:1; Phil. 1:1; Col. 1:2).

I am God's workmanship—His handiwork—born anew in Christ to do His work (Eph. 2:10).

I am a fellow citizen with the rest of God's family (Eph. 2:19).

I am a prisoner of Christ (Eph. 3:1; 4:1).

I am righteous and holy (Eph. 4:24).

I am a citizen of heaven, seated in heaven right now (Phil. 3:20; Eph. 2:6).

I am hidden with Christ in God (Col. 3:3).

I am an expression of the life of Christ because He is my life (Col. 3:4).

His voice was beginning to get louder and his articulation was reflecting confidence.

I am chosen of God, holy and dearly loved (Col. 3:12; 1 Thess. 1:4).

I am a son of light and not of darkness (1 Thess. 5:5).

I wanted to shout "AMEN!" from the kitchen when I heard that one! How wonderful it was to know we were all children of the light and didn't belong in the darkness of the night.

I am a holy partaker of a heavenly calling (Heb. 3:1).

I am a partaker of Christ; I share in His life (Heb. 3:14).

I am one of God's living stones, being built up in Christ as a spiritual house (1 Pet. 2:5).

I am a member of a chosen race, a royal priesthood, a holy nation, a people for God's own possession (1 Pet. 2:9,10).

I am an alien and stranger to this world in which I temporarily live (1 Pet. 2:11).

I am an enemy of the devil (1 Pet. 5:8).

I am a child of God and I will resemble Christ when He returns (1 John 3:1,2).

I am born of God, and the evil one—the devil—cannot touch me (1 John 5:18).

His voice was now sure and firm, obviously encouraged by the truth that he was protected from the evil one. From the kitchen I wanted to yell "PRAISE GOD." Instead, tears welled up in my eyes as I recalled 1 John 5:18: "We know that anyone born of God does not continue to sin; the one who was born of God keeps him safe, and the evil one cannot harm him." Then Dave emphatically stated the last "I Am":

I am not the great "I am" (Exod. 3:14; John 8:24,28,58), but by the grace of God, I am what I am (1 Cor. 15:10).

In just a few minutes, my son's questions about his significance were answered. My former feeble attempts to affirm him had paled in the power of God's Word and the truth of his identity in Christ. The Bible had supplied the answers he needed.

He now knew he was a child of God and he had become a new creation in Christ. His total significance depended upon who he was in Christ! Knowing his position as God's child had given him acceptance and security. He walked away from that chair with a big smile on his face, his shoulders held high. We put Dave to bed with a new respect for himself and the power of God's Word.

In spite of our fatigue, Pete and I stayed up late, indulging in the Scriptural truths pouring forth from the Bible and *Victory over the Darkness*. We gratefully embraced the reality of who *we* were in Christ. Pete was clearly excited. He stopped often to tell me exactly what he had discovered (I often don't have to read good books—he tells me all about them!).

We had been searching for help for Dave, but God also wanted to teach us things that would liberate our Christian lives, strengthen our family and change my husband's preaching. When Pete finished reading chapter 4, "Something Old, Something New," he was a changed person.

Realizing he was not the rope in a tug-of-war between two natures, he stopped wondering whether his old nature or his new nature were winning the battle. He realized that his old nature had been crucified when he trusted in Christ as his Savior. He rejoiced in being a new creation—not part light and part darkness, nor part saint and part sinner, but a completely new creature in Christ. Neil Anderson had challenged him to accept his new identity in Christ with these words using the *New American Standard Bible*:

> Since God "delivered us from the domain of darkness, and transferred us to the kingdom of His beloved Son" (Col. 1:13), can we still be in both kingdoms? When God declares that we are "not in the flesh but in the Spirit" (Rom. 8:9), can we be in the flesh and in the Spirit simultaneously? When God says that "you were formerly darkness, but now you are light in the Lord" (Eph. 5:8), can you possibly be both light and darkness? When God states that "if any man is in Christ, he is a new creature; the old things passed away; behold, new things have come" (2 Cor. 5:17), can we be partly new creature and partly old creature?[1]

Pete began to live in the light and in the Spirit instead of struggling in his own strength to defeat the old nature within him. He no longer had to live in defeat. He started living the victorious life of a new man, letting the old things pass away.

Did he start living a sinless life? No—a wife should know! But a newness developed. He now understood that his present sins were a result of his flesh that had been trained to sin, not a result of the old nature winning out over the new nature. He realized that being in Christ was not a helpless struggle between two natures over which we have no control, but when we sin we choose to walk according to the flesh and act as we were trained to do before our old nature was crucified (see Rom. 8:12,13).

As a child of God—a saint—you are no longer under the authority of your old man. He is dead, buried, gone forever. Getting rid of the old self was God's responsibility, but rendering the flesh and its deeds inoperative is our responsibility.[2] We have God's promise: "But I say, walk by the Spirit, and you will not carry out the desire of the flesh" (Gal. 5:16, *NASB*).

That night as Pete and I prayed together we thanked God for being new creations in Him. We thanked Him that we are children of God. We thanked Him that we are sons of light and not of darkness, that we are born of God and that the evil one cannot touch us. The focus of our prayers changed from a feeble cry for help to a declaration of our position in Christ. What a difference that began to make.

Dave slept peacefully in his own bed that entire night. He woke up on Christmas Eve morning refreshed and optimistic. We were amazed that we had been able to sleep all night, thankful for the power of God in our lives.

Notes

1. Neil T. Anderson, *Victory over the Darkness* (Ventura, Calif.: Regal Books, 1990), p. 71.
2. Ibid., pp. 79-81.

5

PRESSING ON

CHRISTMAS EVE

Christmas Eve morning was joyfully spent making cut-out cookies in every creative shape that could be iced and strewn with sprinkles. The kids took possession of the flour canister, which served as an arsenal for their flour war. After photographing their flour-white faces, I cleaned up the mess and finished decorating the cookies by myself.

Late that morning, we welcomed the mailman, wondering what last-minute cards and gifts might arrive. We were not disappointed when two huge boxes arrived, plastered with Priority Mail stickers. As the mailman carried those cardboard cartons into our living room, our children shrieked with delight. Their exuberance brought a grin to the mailman's face, which seemed to say it had been worthwhile working on Christmas Eve.

I was eagerly sifting through the mail when I noticed a plain envelope from the crisis pregnancy center. Opening that envelope first, my heart danced with emotion. I was relieved the card had arrived before Christmas, thankful I had participated in its creation and stirred by its poignant message.

The inside flap celebrated pictures of babies delivered—not aborted—that year because of the crisis pregnancy center's ministry. Next to each cherublike face were the simple yet powerful words...*I'm alive...I'm alive...I'm alive*. I shed tears of joy as I taped the card in a special place on our Christmas-card wall.

Later that day we baked our traditional birthday cake for Jesus, which usually splits down the middle before we can ice it. But we always decorate it anyway, filling in the cracks with extra icing and carefully topping it with edible letters proclaiming: Happy Birthday, Jesus! The final touch was putting on the four numbers identifying the year—1991.

We enjoyed a quick supper that evening followed by the ceremonial lighting of the candles on the cake. The annual picture with

> IN FEAR AND TERROR, DAVE UNDERSTOOD THAT BEING A CHRISTIAN DID NOT MEAN HE COULD PERSONALLY CHALLENGE EVIL FORCES STRONGER THAN HIMSELF.

the cake was taken, followed by the joyous singing of "Happy Birthday" to Jesus, our unseen guest of honor.

After opening a few out-of-town gifts, we all jumped in our van and sped to Toys "R" Us to exchange the duplicates. What fun it was to skid into the parking lot, race into the store and quickly pick out some new toys before the store's 7:00 P.M. closing.

When we finally settled the kids into bed, they certainly seemed to have "visions of sugar plums dancing in their heads." Assured that the kids were definitely asleep, Pete and I wrapped last-minute presents and made our annual trek to the tree, trying not to crinkle the paper as we passed our children's rooms. It was officially Christmas Day when we finally crawled into bed. We were thankful for such a great Christmas Eve and anticipating the most important day of our year.

COME AND GET ME

Our joy and celebrations were brought to an abrupt halt about 2:00 A.M. Satanic powers attempted to ruin our celebration of Jesus' birth by again attacking Dave's peaceful sleep. Pete and I woke up with a start when we heard our son shout, "Mom!" in a voice louder than I thought possible from such a young boy. We immediately sprang out of bed and ran into his room. As I flipped on the light, we saw Dave leaping from his top bunk, bypassing the steps and landing on the floor. A look of terror filled his eyes that no parent ever wants to see on his or her child's face.

When he was finally able to talk, Dave described being held down in bed by a large, ugly, black demon. It had descended from his ceiling and landed on top of him, relentlessly refusing to release him until he shouted in his loudest voice.

Months later, Dave confessed that his confidence in who he was in Christ had been so empowering that night that he had defied Satan and his evil workers to "Come and get me!" The powers of darkness had definitely taken the challenge. In fear and terror, Dave understood that being a Christian did not mean he could personally challenge evil forces stronger than himself. He had the armor to stand against their schemes (see Eph. 6:11), but a face-to-face dare was not part of the Christian life.

Again I asked myself—and God—WHY? Why was this happening to us? Why did it keep coming back? Why didn't one small word or one powerful prayer stop all this from happening? Why were the attacks on our children instead of us? I felt six days of spiritual warfare was enough for any child of God, and I prayed and prayed for it to end.

I thought about Job's long ordeal with Satan and how the battle was for his family. I thought about the many trials Paul endured because he was in a front line ministry. I also thought about Jesus' battle with Satan, a time of relentless temptation in the desert when Jesus was very hungry and extremely tired. But no one in our family was a Job, or a Paul, or a Jesus. I honestly didn't believe the ordeal of an ordinary, modern-day Christian family would be as long or its trials as plentiful as of those famous biblical stalwart leaders, prophets and martyrs. Each day I believed we would soon be delivered and life would return to normal.

THE GOD OF ALL COMFORT

Christmas Day came and went, but we were too exhausted to enjoy it. We went through the motions of opening presents and pretending to be joyful. We even attended the Christmas Day service at our church where Pete preached in spite of his fatigue. Our turkey meal lacked some of its traditional side dishes because I was just too tired to make them. After a quick dinner, Pete and I slept most of the afternoon while the kids played with their new toys.

As the days went by, our struggles continued. I began the new year with a concerted effort to produce a meaningful newsletter for the crisis pregnancy center. My efforts were impeded by computer problems when I worked on the newsletter and chaos among the children when I tried to write. The director of the crisis pregnancy center and I developed a close friendship—we could talk for hours about anything and she was a source of genuine comfort as I struggled to produce the newsletter.

Liz shared how demonic spirits had harassed her at least twice. Undoubtedly they were upset with her faith in Jesus Christ and subsequent change of profession—from an abortion clinic nurse to the director of a crisis pregnancy center. She was now *saving* babies' lives instead of piecing their body parts back together on the counter to make sure everything had been removed from the woman's uterus.

Liz's sensitivity and empathy for our situation was one of the greatest consolations God provided during that time. She told me how others had also struggled with the powers of darkness when they had attempted to produce the newsletter. But we would pray, share ideas, laugh together and encourage one another with God's Word. We were committed to saving lives, so we pressed on with the work that needed to be done.

The work Liz did at the crisis pregnancy center was not without opposition either. When hateful graffiti was spray painted on the center's exterior wall, the board and volunteers all prayed. As a result, God raised up someone to sandblast the angry words off the bricks. When angry picketers threatened to circle near the door of the center, we prayed again. Most of them didn't show up. The others dispersed soon after Liz kindly offered them donuts and coffee. When the news media arrived to interview Liz, we prayed for Liz to speak the truth in love and for the reporter to accept the truth. Our prayers were answered when Liz befriended the reporter, who then wrote a positive article about the center. And our prayers were answered when newsletters were printed and the truth went out.

Our strife with the rulers of darkness continued at the center and in our home, but so did our search for a solution. Pete, still deeply engrossed in the biblical truths in *Victory over the Darkness*, began preparing sermons about our identity in Christ. He enthusiastically phoned Freedom in Christ Ministries, founded by Dr. Neil Anderson, to ask permission to copy charts and portions of the book for his congregation. They granted him permission without hesitation.

A CRITICAL MISTAKE

Circumstances greatly improved as our nightly devotions became times to put on our spiritual armor for the night ahead...until we made a major mistake. Pete and I left our children in someone else's care while we went to a church in New Mexico for some meetings that had been planned well in advance. Why we didn't have the wisdom to cancel our plans during our children's time of greatest vulnerability to the evil one is still beyond our understanding. But we left, believing things were okay and that our trip was too important to cancel.

Satan's demons had a heyday in our home while we were gone. It began the moment Pete and I drove away. Little did we know that great fear had gripped Jared as we left. Little did we know that Satan's messengers had convinced him we would one day abandon him forever. Little did we know that Jared had run down the street behind our car, believing he would never see us again.

Both of our sons were terrorized with fear. The voices and nightly demonic harassment continued throughout the four days we were gone. As a result, we were on the phone with our children every night, praying with them and repeating the "I Am" list and Scripture verses.

By the time we arrived home, we faced a battle worse than the one we had left. The spiritual authorities in our children's lives had been removed from our house when Pete and I drove away to the airport. The powers of darkness almost had free reign over our kids. What a hard way to learn that we as parents have spiritual authority over our children!

UNFATHOMABLE FEAR

When we returned, Dave and Jared both started "camping out" on our bedroom floor every night. The nightmares and terror had eluded Jalene, but Dave's fear returned and Jared's nightmares became much more frequent and intense. Soon after Jared fell asleep, he was tormented by fear in his dreams. We still couldn't wake him out of his deep sleep. We would pray over him, turn him over and he would become quiet for a while.

Because the boys weren't sleeping in their room—the room where all the demonic activity had taken place—I quietly shut the door to it one afternoon, hoping I would never have to open it again. In my fear, I presumed I could somehow lock the evil into that room. The door stayed closed at night for about a week. No one would go in unless it was light outside.

A week later Pete was scheduled to go to a Sonlife seminar at Moody Bible Institute in Chicago, but I was afraid to stay home alone with the kids. I begged Pete not to go because I wasn't sure I could handle the attacks by myself. I needed the strength of working as a team in Christ. I feared what would happen without the head of our household being there to take his authority over our children. I began to hate the night and hate our house. I didn't want to be alone there when the sun set and darkness moved in—the darkness of the night and the darkness of evil.

Attending the seminar was imperative for Pete, so we came up with a solution—we *all* packed our bags and piled into the van to go to Chicago with him. What a wonderful idea that was! I was glad to get out of the house, and a vacation seemed like a good idea—something we all could use.

In spite of my expectations, however, it became one of our worst times together as a family. We all fought with each other most of the time. While Pete attended Sonlife classes, I found myself constantly uptight with the kids; they were rebellious toward me and angry with each other. No one slept much at night as the nightmares and fear continued. But it *was* better than being home alone in a house we were all beginning to fear and dislike.

SEEKING HELP

Two weeks later, Pete was being filmed as part of a promotional video for the crisis pregnancy center. He was also meeting with a fellow pastor for prayer and help in our situation. So we invited that pastor, as well as a member of the crisis pregnancy center board and a dear Christian friend of ours, to our home to talk and pray for our family. What a wonderful evening! We shared, cried and read

Scripture together. Then these wonderful people anointed each member of our family with oil and prayed over each of us as we knelt before God. We recalled the verses in James: "Is any one of you in trouble? He should pray...The prayer of a righteous man is powerful and effective" (Jas. 5:13,16).

It was an affirming time as each of our friends spurred us on and encouraged us to keep fighting (see Heb. 10:24,25). What wonderful encouragement it was to be motivated by one of our friends to read and remember Philippians 4:6-8:

> Do not be anxious about anything, but in everything, by prayer and petition, with thanksgiving, present your requests to God. And the peace of God, which transcends all understanding, will guard your hearts and your minds in Christ Jesus. Finally, brothers, whatever is true, whatever is noble, whatever is right, whatever is pure, whatever is lovely, whatever is admirable—if anything is excellent or praiseworthy—think about such things.

Before they left, we all went from room to room, dedicating the rooms to God and His truth. We barred Satan and his workers from residing there or affecting anyone who entered. Spiritual opposition occurred mostly in our sons' bedroom—the room that had been closed for several days now. As we prayed in that room, Dave and I could hear distinct noises under the bunk bed.

Our friends suggested Dave remove the anti-abortion sign from his window, but he adamantly refused to succumb to anything that might please our adversary. He would not retreat for a pseudovictory. So the sign stayed up, defying our enemy and trumpeting life from Dave's window.

NO DEALS

Our guests left, some assured that our home was cleansed, but our family could still sense the oppression and darkness. We pressed on, relying on verse after verse, promise upon promise in God's Word. Passages such as 1 Peter 1:6,7 were edifying:

> In this you greatly rejoice, though now for a little while you may have had to suffer grief in all kinds of trials. These have

come so that your faith—of greater worth than gold, which perishes even though refined by fire—may be proved genuine and may result in praise, glory and honor when Jesus Christ is revealed.

Although we were not yet at the point of rejoicing in our suffering, we knew that if our battle *was* the result of our pro-life activities or our church ministry, we would refuse to surrender to the enemy just to achieve "peace" in our home. We could have easily removed the sign from Dave's window, stopped writing the crisis pregnancy center's newsletter, resigned from its board of directors and moved to a different house. Pete could have stopped preaching against abortion and started watering down his sermons to appease the popular liberal agenda.

How easy it would have been to make a deal with Satan and say, "I won't bother you if you won't bother me." But what a high price we would have paid for bargaining with the devil, the father of lies and master of deceit who never would have kept his part of the bargain. Backing away from any of our ministries would have been negotiating with Satan himself. We were compelled to press on, believing that God had entrusted us with His truth and with the armor to proclaim that truth.

God is the faithful general in all our wars, and He never puts us on the front lines without first equipping us with the right armor and weapons for the battle. We can make the choice to put on the available armor to fight the battle or shrink back and bargain with Satan. God, our faithful general, will always go to war before us— He will never leave us or forsake us. He will never allow us to be in a battle that He will not empower us to handle.

Our general has already won the war—we only have to fight those obnoxious demons who think they still have a chance to win!

6

STEPS TO FREEDOM

God honored our refusal to retreat from our seemingly impossible battle. Our unwillingness to cower before our ugly enemy led to an in-depth study of the Scriptures and the spiritual tools God has made available. We were reading Scripture, praying and reciting the "I Am" list nightly during our family devotions. God gave us specific verses that not only proclaimed the truth, but also encouraged us and provided the weapons we needed for our warfare.

Verses from the book of James were especially encouraging:

> Consider it pure joy, my brothers, whenever you face trials of many kinds, because you know that the testing of your faith develops perseverance. Perseverance must finish its work so that you may be mature and complete, not lacking anything (1:2-4).
>
> Blessed is the man who perseveres under trial, because when he has stood the test, he will receive the crown of life that God has promised to those who love him (v. 12).

Pete continued to preach sermons from *Victory over the Darkness* and *The Bondage Breaker*. As a result, we began to realize the power of our identity in Christ. Pete soon became zealous about Neil Anderson's "Steps to Freedom in Christ," a biblical process of repentance and renunciation to break Satan's strongholds. It facilitates personal freedom as we choose truth by verbally confessing, forgiving, renouncing and forsaking those things that have kept us in bondage.

NOTHING TO LOSE

Pete's own liberation through the "Steps to Freedom" (see appendix A) proved to be so beneficial that he proclaimed their effectiveness "from the rooftops." He encouraged his family, his church and all

---

DAVE SAID HIS LIFE RESEMBLED A BUILDING SEVERELY SHAKEN DURING AN EARTHQUAKE. THE BUILDING HAD BEEN DAMAGED; BUT AS A RESULT, HE REBUILT IT STRONGER SO FUTURE QUAKES WOULD NOT BRING IT DOWN.

---

who would listen to go through them. "After all," he persuaded, "you have nothing to lose. If you don't believe you have any strongholds in your life, you can only get very right with God!"

Soon our dear Dave was asking for a day to stay home from school to fast, pray and go through the Steps. I was surprised at his request and his determination to include fasting in his spiritual journey. He must have heard that God acknowledges the seriousness of our prayers when we fast, and he was definitely serious.

JOURNEY TO FREEDOM

A few days later Dave and I replaced our breakfasts with fasting and prayer and began the journey toward his personal and spiritual freedom. Praying was a struggle for him. Halfway through his second sentence, he was interrupted by a noise that sounded like a babbling crowd of people. We both prayed, renouncing the voices and claiming the power of God—not just in the room, but also in our lives. The voices immediately stopped.

Dave continued the prayer with steadfast determination to win this battle; but before he was finished, more interference occurred. As he read, Dave would unknowingly mix up words or add a negative, changing the meaning entirely. Instead of saying, "I do take a stand against all the workings of Satan that would hinder me in this time of prayer," he would say, "I don't take a stand against all the workings of Satan that would hinder me in this time of prayer." That little negative contraction was difficult to hear, but what a difference it made in the meaning!

Satan's other cunning strategy was to cause Dave to only negate half of the sentence, so half of it was true and the other half was not. Isn't that what Satan did in the Garden of Eden? He deceived Eve because his lie had just enough truth in it to make her believe it. How often we ignore small nuances of untruth because we feel most of what is said is true.

I stopped Dave several times that day to let him know he had changed the sentence. Unaware of what he had done, he would back up and carefully read it again, distinctly saying each word correctly. So I acted as a guard for the truth that day, looking for ways in which we could be deceived.

We learned to maintain control by calmly taking our place in Christ and not letting the devil set the agenda. We found that the Steps to Freedom are a comprehensive means of submitting to God by resolving personal and spiritual conflicts—then we can resist the devil (see Jas. 4:7).

The strength of the Scriptures again proved to be sharp and powerful, penetrating to the dividing of soul and spirit (see Heb. 4:12). That day my 10-year-old son was set free from the footholds in his life. Although I would never desire to relive the battle that brought Dave to this point of need, I also would never want to exchange those few precious hours with him—hours when he humbled himself before his Lord with a contrite and broken spirit. Clearly he had one driving desire: to become right with Jesus.

Dave proclaimed the truth with the fortitude of someone three times his age, but with the gentleness and innocence of a child. As he began the first Step, I was thankful he had only been willfully involved in three non-Christian experiences: Once he had played with a magic eight ball at a friend's house, another time he had read his fortune in the horoscope section of the newspaper and once inside a fortune cookie. He did renounce those things, no matter how small they may have seemed.

But Dave still had to renounce those non-Christian experiences he had unwillingly been involved in, things that had caused much fear in his mind. He had to renounce the demonic voices he had occasionally complied with and the uninvited demon that had visited him in his room. Burdens were immediately lifted after that first Step, and footholds that had been affecting Dave's life were now gone.

The second Step, a declaration of truth, proved to be a good impetus for progressing toward harder Steps. As we approached the third Step on forgiveness, Dave agonized about the prospect of forgiving people he felt really deserved his hatred or revenge. Forgiving did not come without internal resistance as he chose to let go of the hurts and offenses that had embittered him even at his young age. He made a list of people he had to forgive, from the first-grade bully who had always pushed him and berated him on the way home from school to the neighbor kid who always pushed him around and the kid he had never liked at school.

Dave successfully struggled through the process of forgiving these people for their hurts against him, but I could tell Dave's list was incomplete. With a bit of trepidation and much reliance upon God, I said, "Dave, if you need to forgive me or Dad for anything at all, I want you to feel free to do that. I will be very comfortable and accepting of what you say." He assured me he had nothing to forgive us for, but I knew something was unresolved.

So I asked him how he felt about his adoption, and if he was bitter or angry about it. He maturely expressed his feelings: He was completely secure with being adopted, knowing he was where God wanted him to be. But he still couldn't understand how his birth mother could give him up. We openly discussed that difficult subject.

He needed to know how a woman could plan an adoption for her child, not because she doesn't want him, but because of her incredible love for him and her desire to have God's absolute best for him. I was able to explain that his birth mother was unable to provide a stable, healthy home in her difficult circumstances and had sought to do the very best for him—out of love. He understood, and a seed love for her took root. But he also agreed that he needed to forgive her.

How painful it was for him to admit that and to decide to forgive her and to put an end to the mixture of love and resentment, attachment and rejection he had harbored. When he finished the forgiveness prayer, we embraced each other tightly as our tears flowed. It was almost as if Dave's birth mother were there, too, sharing in our hug and in the unrestricted love we both had for her. What a special person she was to both of us, and what freedom Dave now enjoyed.

The most liberating verses Dave read that day were Ephesians 4:31,32:

> Get rid of all bitterness, rage and anger, brawling and slander, along with every form of malice. Be kind and compassionate to one another, forgiving each other, just as in Christ God forgave you.

He was also transformed by 1 Peter 5:6-11.

> Humble yourselves, therefore, under God's mighty hand, that he may lift you up in due time. Cast all your anxiety on him because he cares for you. Be self-controlled and alert. Your enemy the devil prowls around like a roaring lion looking for someone to devour. Resist him, standing firm in the faith, because you know that your brothers throughout the world are undergoing the same kind of sufferings. And the God of all grace, who called you to his eternal glory in Christ, after you have suffered a little while, will himself restore you and make you strong, firm and steadfast. To him be the power for ever and ever. Amen.

Step by Step, our son was set free that day and released from the footholds that had caused him to live in fear and miss God's best for his life. He renounced pride, repented of his sins and renounced any generational sins that might have been passed down to him. Because we didn't know the details of his heritage, he had to include everything that might have been a sin in his ancestral background. His awareness of Exodus 20:5 compelled him to do this:

> For I, the Lord your God, am a jealous God, punishing the children for the sin of the fathers to the third and fourth generation of those who hate me.

Later, the reality of Jeremiah 32:18 would confirm the necessity for all of us to liberate ourselves from the past.

You show love to thousands but bring the punishment for the fathers' sins into the laps of their children after them.

The Steps to Freedom were life changing for Dave. He was now secure in his position in Christ, equipped to finish his battle and confident he was on the winning side. He was definitely free from that day on. On only one occasion did a single voice return to assault him. Dave was praying and the voice said, "Shut up!" But my undaunted son immediately renounced that voice in the name of Jesus. It left, never to return again. Praise God!

Three years later when Dave was 13 years old, I asked him to reflect on his ordeal and the freedom he found in Christ. He said his life resembled a building severely shaken during an earthquake. The building had been damaged; but as a result, he rebuilt it stronger so future quakes would not bring it down.

During the months to come, our family learned the importance of constantly maintaining our "buildings." We realized we could never allow them to get run down or in disrepair, and never permit them to be vulnerable to another earthquake. When I asked Dave what he believed would be the long-term benefit of his victory, he anticipated that someday he would teach his children the truth and show them how to have freedom in Christ. It's exciting to think that another generation will be given the chance to know the truth and be set free!

Through Christ, our son won his battle. In his victory he found Scripture that helped him not only understand the warfare, but also celebrate the triumph of overcoming his accuser by the blood of the Lamb. He was encouraged and excited to know that Satan's time on earth was short and that a day would come when he would not be able to bother us. He had found a passage in Revelation that explained why Satan was becoming so active:

Now have come the salvation and the power and the kingdom of our God, and the authority of his Christ. For the accuser of our brothers, who accuses them before our God day and night, has been hurled down. They overcame him by the blood of the Lamb and by the word of their testimony;

they did not love their lives so much as to shrink from death. Therefore rejoice, you heavens and you who dwell in them! But woe to the earth and the sea, because the devil has gone down to you! He is filled with fury, because he knows that his time is short (12:10-12).

We typed those verses into the computer right away and printed several copies in large print to tape on various walls in our house. Passing those verses daily would cause us to say, "Praise God! Satan's time is short!"

Praise God that while Satan *is* here, we can overcome him by the blood of Jesus Christ, the sacrificial Lamb!

7

UNEXPECTED VICTORY

Joy and elation followed Dave's completion of the Steps to Freedom, but our closing prayer was interrupted by a phone call reporting the sudden death of Pete's father. In our shock and sorrow, Dave and I shed tears of grief that we would never see Grandpa on earth again.

We picked up Jared early from school and Jalene from a friend's house, then headed to church where Pete was just concluding a funeral he had officiated—the third one for Pete that month. We told him his father had been found that morning at the church where he worked, leaning back in his parked truck after suffering a massive heart attack.

The strain from our past three months of spiritual warfare and the many funerals Pete had performed for our church members that year had left him emotionally depleted. Pete spent most of the night fondly reminiscing about his father and writing a poem in his memory.

We all left for New Jersey early the next morning, exhausted from sorrow and affliction, but thankful for Dave's new freedom in Christ. Those who attended Grandpa's funeral affirmed the effectiveness of his Christian life and his acceptance of all people. We gloried in his knowledge of Christ as his Savior and that he was rejoicing in heaven with Him. We gloried that although his death was unexpected, it was a victory for him—a joyful homecoming.

We returned to Wisconsin after a week's stay in New Jersey, reluctantly entering our dark and oppressive house. Not being people who depend on our feelings to verify reality, we believed there was some validity to the darkness and gloom we all felt there. Because Jared was still having many nightmares, which had not been as frequent while we were in New Jersey, we wanted to eliminate at least one of the contributing factors—our house. We didn't want to run away from our troubles, but we were weary. So we asked God to provide another house if it was His will.

We launched a diligent search for the ideal house, but the doors kept closing. We finally trusted that God knew what He was doing by leaving us where we were. Admittedly, we felt we were trying to run away from our situation and our adversary. We also knew we couldn't try to gain a false victory for Jared and avoid the inevitable confrontation with his enemies.

Pete and I insisted on moving the "Abortion Kills Children" sign to the living room and traded bedrooms with our two sons, challenging the powers of darkness to aggravate us, the authorities in the home, rather than our children. And aggravate they did! After a few nights in the boys' room, we had no doubt someone had previously committed some never-to-be-discovered diabolic acts in that room. But again through prayer and Scripture, God gained the victory, and the powers of darkness were forced to leave. (In hindsight, however, we realize they undoubtedly just moved to another room in our house—the side of the master bedroom where Jared now slept.)

When circumstances settled down a bit for us, I felt God tugging at my heart to go through the Steps to Freedom. I had seen them transform my husband and liberate my son, so why wasn't I attending to my own relationship with God? Was it the false excuse that I had no time alone? Probably. Was it pride? Probably. Was it my need to help everyone else except myself? Probably. So I put aside my pride and my rescuing attitude and reserved a few hours to go through the Steps.

While the boys were in school and Jalene was in preschool, I sat alone with God at the dining room table, willing and ready for Him to work in my own life.

SEVEN STEPS TO LIBERTY

I was confident the Steps would help my relationship with God. I wasn't, however, prepared for the life-changing effect they would have in liberating me from the strongholds that had kept me in bondage for years. I confirmed my commitment to God to only go through these Steps if I could be totally honest before Him.

This pledge of honesty took me back to my salvation experience.

One Sunday evening when I was seven years old, my pastor announced an upcoming baptismal service in the church. He said those interested should contact him. When I arrived home that night, I told my mother I wanted to be baptized. My mother then explained what baptism meant: It was a testimony of one's faith in Jesus Christ, and I first needed to ask Jesus into my heart. She explained that if I believed Christ died for my sins, and if I repented of them and asked Jesus into my heart, I would be saved. Then I could be baptized. I prayed the prayer of salvation that night as my mother and I knelt beside the couch.

I knew I was saved that evening, but I had to admit that my decision had some selfish motives—I wanted to be a part of the baptismal service. So now, having made a total commitment to honesty with God, I confessed that my decision to trust in Him had been tainted with a selfish, childish ulterior motive. In one sense I realized that no one comes to Christ on the basis of pure motives. If we did, then salvation would be by pure motives rather than by grace through faith in what God did for us in Christ (see Eph. 2:8,9). God reaches out to us, mixed motives and all, in His grace. On the other hand, I wanted to deepen my commitment to Christ; I didn't want my relationship with Him to be marred by anything. So in the quietness of that morning, I said:

Oh Jesus, when I first asked You to come into my heart, my motives were not pure. I selfishly wanted to take part in a baptismal service at church. But right now I want You to know that I am trusting in You as my Savior because I believe wholeheartedly that You are the only way to heaven and that trusting in You is the only way to restore my relationship with God. I also want You as my Savior just because I love You from the depths of my heart. I want You to know that if there had never been a baptismal service, I would now trust in You just because You love me so much that You sent Your Son to die for my sins on the Cross, and just because I love You so much. There is no other motivation. If my salvation experience when I was seven was impure in Your sight for any reason, I now recommit myself to You in total honesty and purity.

I felt a newness in my relationship with God at that moment. I knew God had honored my childhood prayer, even though it had been tainted by impure motives, and that I was saved eternally from my sins at that time. But how fresh and unblemished our relation-ship was now. How new and guilt free was my salvation experience (see Ps. 32:1).

Now I knew I was ready to plunge into the first Step (Counterfeit Versus Real) in which I would renounce any previous or current involvements with occult practices or false religions. I didn't antici-pate any difficulty with this Step, because I was raised in a Christian home and had attended a good church all my life.

But even with my religious background, I *had* played with a Ouija board at several friends' homes, successfully seeing it give answers to private matters no one in the room would know. I had attributed its power to the electricity in our fingertips. I also had a magic eight ball I used as a toy when I was a child, and I had attempted to lift a table by supernatural powers at a friend's home in grade school. I had read my horoscope, tried the fortune machines and hoped the more desirable messages in those Chinese fortune cookies would come true.

As I grew up, I stopped participating in those things, believing that if I had no further involvement with them, their effect on my life would vanish. Rather than sins that had to be confessed or strongholds that had to be broken, I viewed them as innocuous childhood escapades. The truth is that each of those shadowy ven-tures, whether I had participated knowingly or innocently, had given Satan a foothold in my life. They had allowed Satan to get a toe, or perhaps a foot, in the doorway of my life.

But by the power of God, those strongholds were broken that day, not by a display of supernatural powers or a dramatic exorcism of my soul, but by a simple confession of the truth and a renuncia-tion:

Lord, I confess that I have participated in the Ouija board. I ask your forgiveness, and I renounce the Ouija board.

One by one each stronghold was broken and deception was replaced with the truth—the truth from the Word of God—which brought blessing upon blessing.

The second Step (Deception Versus Truth) was basically a prayer and a doctrinal affirmation, a declaration of biblical truth. But declaring those truths became much more meaningful and power-ful sitting before God, allowing Him to search my heart and expose every foothold and every sin—past and present. I willfully desired any deceptive schemes of Satan to be revealed in my life.

As I began the prayer, I experienced a new transparency with myself and God. I not only had a new relationship with God, but I was tearing down all the walls that had hidden my innermost being. I read the prayer from the Steps, which would begin to knock down more walls in my life.

Dear heavenly Father,

I know that You desire truth in the inner self and that facing this truth is the way of liberation (John 8:32). I acknowledge that I have been deceived by the "father of lies" (John 8:44) and that I have deceived myself (1 John 1:8). I pray in the name of the Lord Jesus Christ that You, heavenly Father, will rebuke all deceiving spirits by virtue of the shed blood and resurrection of the Lord Jesus Christ.

By faith I have received You into my life and I am now seated with Christ in the heavenlies (Eph. 2:6). I acknowledge that I have the responsibility and authority to resist the devil, and when I do, he will flee from me. I now ask the Holy Spirit to guide me into all truth (John 16:13). I ask You to "Search me, O God, and know my heart; try me and know my anxious thoughts; and see if there be any hurtful way in me, and lead me in the everlasting way" (Ps. 139:23,24, NASB). In Jesus' name, I pray. Amen.

The doctrinal affirmation that followed was authoritative and commanding—it was one declaration after another of biblical truths, almost biblically verbatim. After stating who God is, what He did for me, who I am, how I can stand in my faith, what He has commanded me to do and why I can have victory and freedom, I was overwhelmed with God's greatness and His goodness. What a wonderful Savior I have!

I FORGIVE

The third Step (Bitterness Versus Forgiveness) was not quite as easy for me. During Dave's struggle through this Step on forgiveness, I had silently and hastily forgiven someone I knew I had to forgive. But on this day, it went much deeper. The words in 2 Corinthians 2:10,11 poignantly stuck in my mind:

If you forgive anyone, I also forgive him. And what I have forgiven—if there was anything to forgive—I have forgiven in the sight of Christ for your sake, in order that Satan might not outwit us. For we are not unaware of his schemes.

> # FREEDOM WAS NOW MY CHOICE. I COULD WAIT ALL MY LIFE FOR AN APOLOGY, ALL THE TIME BOUND TO THAT PERSON IN BITTERNESS, OR I COULD CHOOSE TO FORGIVE AND BREAK THE CHAINS THAT BOUND ME.

Had Satan actually outwitted me all those years I had been bitter toward that person? But that person never repented of what he did to me! No sooner had I said those words to myself than I saw the unforgettable words emblazoned on the page of the Steps:

You don't forgive someone for their sake; you do it for your sake, so you can be free. Your need to forgive isn't an issue between you and the offender; it's between you and God.

Was it possible that in my unforgiveness I had been hurting myself more than I had been hurting my offender? How could I get past what he had done to me? Then more words stood out on the page.

Forgiveness is agreeing to live with the consequences of another person's sin. Forgiveness is costly. You pay the price for the evil you forgive. You're going to live with those consequences whether you want to or not; your only choice is whether you will do so in the bitterness of unforgiveness or the freedom of forgiveness.

Freedom was now my choice. I could wait all my life for an apology, all the time bound to that person in bitterness, or I could choose to forgive and break the chains that bound me. With great pain in the emotional core of my heart, I chose to acknowledge all the hurts and the hate. I forgave that person and some others on my list for each offense and every hurt. I left their offenses at the Cross and gave them to God in obedience to Romans 12:19:

> Do not take revenge, my friends, but leave room for God's wrath, for it is written: "It is mine to avenge; I will repay," says the Lord.

Words cannot express the emancipation of my heart that day. A flood of tears ran through the river of my soul and purified my yesterdays and my todays. The chains of bondage were broken and I could look at other people without seeing my offender in the faces of everyone I met. I could love other people without the mistrust and skepticism that had tainted previous relationships.

MORE STEPS

I needed an emotional break after that Step, but I knew I had to press on before Pete brought Jalene home from preschool. The fourth Step (Rebellion Versus Submission) helped me comprehend how seriously God deals with rebellion. I wondered: *Had my questioning nature and my challenging spirit been rebellion? Had my independent personality actually been a defiant character?* Knowing "rebellion is like the sin of divination, and arrogance like the evil of idolatry" (1 Sam. 15:23), I had to confess my rebellion toward many people who had been in authority over me throughout my life. I agreed to "submit to one another out of reverence for Christ" (Eph. 5:21).

I proceeded with Step five (Pride Versus Humility), confessing the pride that so often had accompanied my rebellion and motivated a false confidence. Choosing to "put no confidence in the flesh" (Phil. 3:3) and to "be strong in the Lord and in his mighty power" (Eph. 6:10) calmed my spirit and provided the freedom to discard my false masks of egotism and rest in the will of God.

Regarding others as more important than myself was a puzzle piece that connected perfectly to the forgiveness of and submission to others:

> Do nothing out of selfish ambition or vain conceit, but in humility consider others better than yourselves (Phil. 2:3).

More than two hours had passed, and I was tired yet excited about finishing the Steps. My heart's desire was to experience total freedom, complete cleansing and a radically right relationship with my Savior. I enthusiastically plunged into Step six (Bondage Versus Freedom), anxious to see what other burdens could be lifted and what other unnecessary baggage could be discarded.

I asked God to search my heart and reveal to my mind every sin in my life that had transgressed His moral law and grieved the Holy Spirit. One by one God showed me sins I needed to confess—not only present sins, but sins from my childhood, teens, early adulthood and beyond.

Because I had been saved at an early age, I had been effectively deceived into believing I was pretty good and had lived a good Christian life. I had confessed the big sins, but many other sins had just slid by because I was so involved in church and felt pretty good. I believed refraining from doing them was tantamount to confession. As a result, I carried extra baggage all those years that prevented me from living life to the fullest and experiencing the joy of a righteous and holy life. God's promises proved to be true:

> If we confess our sins, He is faithful and righteous to forgive us our sins and to cleanse us from all unrighteousness (1 John 1:9, NASB).
>
> I came that they might have life, and might have [it] abundantly (John 10:10, NASB).

For the first time I felt totally clean before my Lord. I understood that "just as he who called you is holy, so be holy in all you do; for it is written: 'Be holy, because I am holy'" (1 Pet. 1:15,16). I understood what it really means to "offer your bodies as living sacrifices, holy and pleasing to God—this is your spiritual act of worship" (Rom. 12:1).

By the final Step (Acquiescence Versus Renunciation), I was

emotionally depleted yet saturated with the blessings and grace of God. I had gone as far back as I could remember into my past, and further, as God had searched my heart. Although I didn't think anything could possibly be left to confess and renounce, I wanted to complete all the Steps. It proved to be important for me, and later for my family, not to skip this Step in which I renounced the sins of my ancestors and any curses that may have been placed on our family (see Exod. 20:5; Jer. 32:18).

My Native American (Indian) heritage extended back three generations on my mother's side. My great grandmother was an Indian (I'm not sure what tribe) taken off the reservation by a white man. When my great aunt was asked to share the family history she knew so well, she refused, explaining that our past was much too shameful to tell.

Because the possibility of an ungodly history in our family heritage was so great and because a curse upon a succeeding generation was feasible, my children and I definitely needed to renounce any generational sins or curses. There was also murder, depression, anger and bitterness in my ancestry that needed to be renounced. I also believed that our pro-life activities may have caused us to be targeted by satanist groups, so I applied all the authority and protection I needed in Christ to renounce the sins of my ancestors and any curses and assignments that may have been imposed on me or my family.

I was filled with great freedom by the time I finished that last Step. An indescribable burden was lifted. I will probably never know what ancestral sins or curses were affecting our family, but I do know that freedom was found in that last Step. Pete had also experienced great release in the last Step because both alcoholism and suicide existed in his heritage.

After completing all seven Steps in great physical and emotional fatigue, I was renewed spiritually and mentally as I had never been before. I was cleansed to "not conform any longer to the pattern of this world, but be transformed by the renewing of your mind" (Rom. 12:2).

I gave God my sins and my past. I gave him my burdens and my children. But it was more difficult than I had anticipated to give Him our children. Pete and I had suffered through 10 years of infertility before God gave us a baby through adoption—our cherished Dave. Then, almost miraculously, I became pregnant and we were blessed with a precious baby boy—our dear Jared. Finally after a disappointing miscarriage, we were again blessed with another pregnancy and a baby daughter—our lovely Jalene. With each child we thanked God for performing a miracle. With each child I identified with Hannah in the Bible: "I prayed for this child, and the Lord has granted me what I asked of him" (1 Sam. 1:27). With each child we praised God and thanked Him, forever grateful that our barrenness had been triply blessed, lavished with God's goodness and His grace. But now I had to follow Hannah's example and unreservedly give them back to God: "So now I give him to the Lord. For his whole life he shall be given over to the Lord" (1 Sam. 1:28).

I also had to accept the fact that neither Pete nor I could remove the strongholds in our children's lives. They could only be removed by the power of God and by the truth of His Word. They could only be removed when each child personally confessed, renounced and submitted to God. I gave myself and my children to God that day, relinquishing them to the One who had given them to Pete and me.

I rested in the promise that through Christ we are overcomers. I rested in the promise that our faith in Christ is the victory that has overcome the world:

> Everyone born of God overcomes the world. This is the victory that has overcome the world, even our faith. Who is it that overcomes the world? Only he who believes that Jesus is the Son of God (1 John 5:4,5).

8

REACHING OTHERS

With three people in our family now free in Christ, we rejoiced. We knew, however, that the battle was not over. After failing to find another house to buy, we agreed we were where God wanted us to be so we determined to persevere in our house.

Jared (age 8) was still experiencing terrible nightmares in the recesses of his subconscious. And Jalene was also beginning to have intermittent nightmares, but she would remember the details of her dreams and renounce them right away.

As Jared witnessed our excitement over the Steps to Freedom, he also wanted to go through them. Because he had trusted Christ as his Savior when he was three years old and reaffirmed his faith when he turned seven, we felt confident the Steps would be effective for establishing his freedom in Christ.

One evening I sat down with him privately and took him through the Steps (see chapter 19 for the Steps for ages 5-8). Soon after he began I was assured of his understanding and sincerity. He renounced, repented and proclaimed everything with great willingness and candor before his Lord. He was honest about every detail of his life, humbly coming before God, willing to do anything necessary to eliminate both his fear and his nightmares.

But in spite of his honesty as we went through each Step, Jared struggled with his inability to remember certain things from his past. He couldn't remember anything about the horrible nightmares he had experienced for years, nor could he recall what had precipitated them. He knew he had an inordinate fear that Pete and I would leave him forever, but he couldn't remember why. He knew something very frightening had happened to him long ago, but he couldn't remember what it was. His memory was completely blocked.

We pressed on in spite of his memory block. When Jared finished the Steps, he clearly understood who he was in Christ and was definitely as free in Christ as possible. Things hidden in the deep recesses of his memory still bound him. As a result, our family's journey toward total freedom persisted for more than two years. But he faithfully prayed daily for God to search him and know his heart, and we trusted God to reveal those things, in His time.

In her own five-year-old way, Jalene also went through the Steps to Freedom. One of my greatest joys had already been to hear her invite Jesus into her heart the year before. The memory of her simple prayer that she loved Jesus and wanted Him to come into her heart was precious. She loved Jesus from the first time she had heard about Him, so trusting in Jesus as her Savior was a natural response.

Because Jalene was so young, I simplified the Steps as we went along. It was exciting to hear her proclaim her position in Christ and become free from every fear and sin. She manifested childlike faith and simple humility as she prayed her way through the Steps. I'm sure some parts were beyond her comprehension (such as saying no to the sins of your ancestors), but because she loved God and trusted me to provide her with the truth, she earnestly stated the simple renunciations. Her lack of understanding, however, did not preclude the power of the truth being spoken. When the truth is proclaimed, God's foes are paralyzed and rendered ineffective.

Jalene also learned some battle tactics that day to use when she was tormented by fear or nightmares. She learned to quickly and simply say, "I'm a child of God and the evil one cannot touch me" (see 1 John 5:18).

"I HAVE COME THAT THEY MIGHT HAVE LIFE"

Our children were not the only ones to find their freedom in Christ that year. The Lord sent us a steady flow of people who wanted to go through the Steps to Freedom. It was exciting to finally have a scriptural counseling tool to emancipate people from their hidden bondages and bring them into the freedom of an abundant life in Christ (see John 10:10).

In our 16 years of ministry we had not known how to lead Christians to an abundant life in Christ—a totally right relationship with God—free from their pasts, their sins and their bitterness.

Never before had *we* experienced such freedom in Christ, and now we were also seeing others set free (see *Helping Others Find Freedom in Christ* by Neil Anderson).

While Pete was still preaching his way through the truths encompassed in *Victory over the Darkness* and *The Bondage Breaker*, he also began a Sunday School series for parents using the video series on *The Seduction of Our Children*. God was working in the hearts of many people who requested to go through the Steps to Freedom in Christ. As they bowed before God in honesty and repentance, not only did they find their own personal lives in right relationship with God, but their marriages were also strengthened and they tuned in to their children's spiritual needs.

That year, Pete and I took several husbands and wives through the Steps simultaneously, Pete with the husband in one room and I with the wife in another. When they came together afterward, they met with a new acceptance for each other that only comes from spiritual freedom. Some of their children also wanted to go through the Steps. They had been prompted by the change in their parents.

It was a joy to take kids through the Steps, knowing they wouldn't have to live with the bondages that so often begin in childhood and manifest as fears, phobias and mental instability during adulthood. Satan doesn't have to be permitted to plant footholds of fear or violence or inordinate thoughts of worthlessness, death or sex. He doesn't have to be allowed to emotionally disable children for a life of silent terror, unexplainable anxieties or schizophrenic-like symptoms.

"Jesus said, 'Let the little children come to me, and do not hinder them, for the kingdom of heaven belongs to such as these'" (Matt. 19:14). We saw children learn that in Christ they are accepted (see Eph. 1:4,5). We saw children acknowledge their security in Christ (see Rom. 8:35,37). Stripped of all earthly talents and importance, children began to understand their significance in Christ (see Eph. 2:4,5).

Children *can* know that they are seated with Jesus Christ in the heavenlies, far above all principalities and powers of darkness, armed with Christ's incomparable power to fight the enemy (see Eph. 1:19-21; 2:6).

QUEST FOR TRUTH

Pete's sermons in conjunction with *The Seduction of Our Children* class at our church piqued the interest of a woman named Carol to go through the Steps to Freedom in Christ. She had trusted in Christ as her Savior, but her past still unmistakably had an effect on her Christian life.

Carol trembled when she began to tell me her story. As she continued, she was unable to hold still—she just shook all over. As Carol later explained, "It was frightening; there was some real fear there wrapped up in my past." We both prayed, renouncing Satan's attempts to prevent her from becoming free in Christ, and she immediately stopped shaking and was able to proceed.

The first Step revealed that Carol had tried almost every religion, cult and occultish practice on the Non-Christian Spiritual Experience Inventory in the Steps. She eagerly began to renounce each one of them. As she made her way through her long list of non-Christian involvements, which included false religions, drug use, occult practices, demonic visitations and a guru who used to appear and disappear in the blink of an eye, the ceiling began to rumble and clatter. Carol stopped, renounced the demonic interference, and the noises and clattering ceased immediately. She then completed the Steps. Carol left free in Christ, unencumbered by her past involvements and her past hopelessness.

When Carol arrived home, she realized her children's music and their tape or CD covers were causing her a lot of satanic opposition. Her children didn't believe her, but they did get rid of the music. As she expressed her freedom in Christ, the two younger children (ages 12 and 9) became eager to go through the Steps themselves. Carol had the privilege of taking them through the Steps, and they were set free from fear and nightmares.

It Hit Her Like a Sledgehammer

Sharon, another dear friend of ours who has been a single parent since her adult daughter was a baby, asked us for a copy of the Steps to Freedom in Christ. She decided to go through them herself. (Although it is better for a facilitator to take a person through the Steps, it certainly is acceptable to go through them alone.) Sharon began to read and apply the portions of the Steps she thought she needed. Little by little, piece by piece, she was going through them. Weeks passed before she finally finished three Steps. The third Step on forgiveness was so painful—yet liberating for her—that she thought she had done all she needed to do.

Some time later she decided to finish Steps four through seven. When she completed the last Step, rejecting and disowning all the sins of her ancestors, she said it hit her "like a sledgehammer." The release of the bondage from those last four Steps and the release from the sins of her ancestors were overwhelming. She realized how important it was to remove the footholds from her life—the same footholds Satan had had on her parents and on her parents' parents. The chains were broken and she was free!

She also realized how important it was to go through all the Steps at one sitting. She had experienced partial freedom as she applied portions of the Steps each week, but Satan was still working because total freedom had not yet been achieved. Impacted by that realization, she set aside a block of time to go through all seven Steps at once. Then she invested time alone with her Lord, not withholding anything or postponing any part of her path to freedom.

Sharon has been through the Steps several times, not because she didn't have freedom the first time, but because Satan has fought to regain a position in her life. He is always trying to regain a foothold of sin or a bondage of bitterness back in our lives. The Bible calls it temptation and explains it in the following terms:

> So, if you think you are standing firm, be careful that you don't fall! No temptation has seized you except what is common to man. And God is faithful; he will not let you be tempted beyond what you can bear. But when you are tempted, he will also provide a way out so that you can stand up under it (1 Cor. 10:12,13).

When our minds are being deceived into bondage again, we *can* maintain our freedom by taking control of every thought in obedience to Christ before it takes control of us (see 2 Cor. 10:5). Maintaining freedom means recognizing and rejecting the patterns of our flesh and relying on the truth found in the Word of God so that we do not have to sin (see Rom. 12:2).

Three years after Sharon's first attempt to go through the Steps, she is still free in Christ and has grown in her faith and willingness to minister for Christ on the front lines. She is involved in a new ministry to the gay community in Madison, a ministry of forgiveness and restoration through Jesus Christ (see *A Way of Escape* by Neil Anderson).

Sharon has experienced severe demonic opposition because of her commitment to this ministry, but every attack has been overcome through the power of Jesus. Just as Satan's agenda is abortion and we were his target for our pro-life ministry, so Satan's agenda is sexual bondage in homosexuality. But in the name of Jesus, every foe is defeated and every bondage broken. What power there is in the name of Jesus (see Phil. 2:9-11)!

THE BONDAGE BREAKER

That year, as we endured our own spiritual battles, God sent us 40 people who wanted to go through the Steps. Most of them found

---

THERE IS NO FREEDOM WITHOUT FIRST KNOWING CHRIST AS SAVIOR.

---

complete freedom in Christ by their willingness to be open, honest and repentant before God and to proclaim the truth.

One person didn't find freedom because she was on medication for depression. Her senses were dulled and her emotions were numbed so the truth became unclear. She actually laughed through the forgiveness Step, making us wonder if the drugs were preventing her from experiencing her true emotions. Another person wanted freedom from the demons that had harassed him for more than 20 years, but he was unwilling to first give his life to Jesus Christ (see Acts 4:10,12).

There is no freedom without first knowing Christ as Savior and believing Jesus' own words: "I am the way and the truth and the life. No one comes to the Father except through me" (John 14:6). As much as we wanted this man to be free from his tormentors, his refusal to accept Jesus as his Savior rendered all who sought to help him powerless.

But for those who trusted in Christ and allowed Him to search and know their hearts, powerful bondages were broken. God performed miracles in many lives right before our eyes. An alcoholic not only came to know Jesus as Savior, but was also freed from addiction and achieved a right relationship with his wife who was ready to leave him.

One person who had been a victim of abominable satanic ritual abuse as a child was gloriously set free from the bondages of those atrocities. She was able to renounce her wedding to Satan and announce that she was the bride of Christ (see Eph. 1:13,14).

Some young engaged couples also wanted to go through the Steps to get their marriages off to the right start. It was a pleasure to see these couples become clean before their Lord and each other before they entered into marriage. The baggage of bondage they carried in the past was gone; prior uses of their bodies as instruments of unrighteousness were renounced and they presented their bodies to Christ as living sacrifices, holy and pleasing to God (see Rom. 12:1). Then they reserved any sexual use of their bodies only for marriage, renouncing the lie that their bodies are not clean or in any way unacceptable as a result of their past sexual experiences. What a beautiful way to enter the marriage union! (See *A Way of Escape* by Neil Anderson.)

AWAY FROM IT ALL

That summer, we were blessed with the best vacation our family has ever had. For three weeks we explored the Pacific Northwest, avoiding any interstate highways along the way. We camped in a tent or just slept in our van, lavishing in the richness of His beautiful creation and design.

As we traveled more than 7,000 miles throughout rural America, I read *The Bondage Breaker* by Neil Anderson, realizing with each mile how much the people in every town and city we passed needed to know Christ and have the chains of their bondages broken. But as I ached for those people and as I bolstered my strength to fight my own family's battles, I was caught off guard when one of the case scenarios in the book unveiled a blocked memory and a forgotten foothold in my life.

When we stopped at the next gas station, I hurried into the bathroom to pray. It was not the most desirable place to bow before the Savior of the world, but I knew God wasn't concerned with the surroundings—He cared about the condition of my heart. So I renounced a long-forgotten memory.

For the first time in my life I had formed a habit of saying, "Search me, O God, and know my heart; test me and know my anxious thoughts. See if there is any offensive way in me, and lead me in the way everlasting" (Ps. 139:23,24). I realized that "the truth will set you free" (John 8:32), and that time does *not* heal all wounds. Freedom felt so good that I said to God, "Search me some more...expose every foothold."

The trip was a wonderful time of emotional renewal for our family after six months of spiritual warfare. It was spontaneous and full of surprises and blessings, blemished only at night when we were awakened by Jared (age eight). Still in a deep sleep, he would sit up in his sleeping bag, babbling words we couldn't understand, often yelling and screaming. At times he would scurry around the tent, apparently looking desperately for something or perhaps running to avoid something. Our attempts to calm him down were futile, so we just prayed over him and tried to get him to say the name of Jesus.

SUSTAINING GRACE

When we returned home, I continued my involvement with the crisis pregnancy center, and Pete and I both continued to take other people through the Steps. Precious believers in Jesus Christ came into Pete's office to be freed from anxiety attacks, recurring dreams, influences of the New Age, nagging thoughts of suicide, satanic rituals, violent video games, sexual spirits, self-hypnosis, false religions, etc. A phenomenal number of people were forgiven from the core of their hearts.

By the end of that year, we reviewed our struggles and our battles, our victories and our triumphs, and we thanked God for sustaining us (see 1 Cor. 1:8,9).

That memorable year, which included months of personal spiritual warfare for our family, the death of Pete's dear father, the deaths of 11 people in our church family, the relocation to nursing homes for many of the precious saints in our church, numerous lengthy sessions through the Steps and the moral fall of one of our respected church leaders, rendered us physically and emotionally depleted. Only through the sustaining grace of God did we survive that year (see Pss. 18:35-37; 94:18,19; Rom. 5:1-5).

When the next Christmas season joyfully came and went, void of any spiritual warfare or attacks during the holiday season, we not only remembered the events of the year before, but celebrated that perhaps our darkest hour was over and would not reoccur. We soon realized our battle was not over and that God would demonstrate His sustaining, amazing grace to us in even greater ways.

9

THE SECOND ASSAULT

HAPPY NEW YEAR?

After an enjoyable Christmas hallmarked by sugar cookies, flour-covered faces and another birthday cake for Jesus, we looked forward to a good New Year. New Year's Day was relaxing and reminiscent as we spent it with friends. We enjoyed warm friendship, homemade soup and the laughter of children.

THE ACCIDENT

The day after New Year's was typical of wintry Wisconsin days when hot chocolate is a must and cabin fever is a great possibility. By evening our family decided a drive would alleviate our boredom, so we piled into our van and headed downtown. The roads were not slippery where we lived, but by the time we reached the downtown exit, we were on a sheet of ice. Pete had no control of our van and was unable to stop at a red light. He carefully swerved to the right, trying to make it sound like a fun adventure as he shouted, "Here we go, guys! Wheeeee!"

The uncooperative ice underneath our van refused to allow the tires to grab. Pete cried out, "Lord, please turn this van," but we just kept on sliding. He braced himself and warned, "Hang on! We're going to hit that tree!" Dave conveniently put a cardboard box over his head so he wouldn't see what was inevitably going to happen, while Jared and Jalene intently watched the tree.

Although we weren't going very fast, the impact was forceful enough to put our seatbelts to their optimum test, bring us to an immediate halt and cause $2,500 worth of damage to the front of our van. After we recovered from the sudden jolt, we looked back to see if the kids were okay. Dave had removed the cardboard box from his head in time to see us collide with the tree, and Jalene was on the floor, a victim of not wearing her seatbelt—but unhurt.

Everyone was able to force a smile after the impact—everyone except Jared who was screaming in terror. No one was hurt physically, but we spent quite some time allaying Jared's fears and near hysteria. Pete got the van running, and we slowly drove home in our injured, limping vehicle. We tried to laugh and joke about the box on Dave's head and about our dilemma in general, giving thanks that no one was physically hurt, but aware that some emotions had been injured.

The next day was an uneventful Sunday as we all squeezed into our rusty old Honda to go to church, out to eat with friends afterward and then to a nursing home to read Scripture and give communion to a dear lady near death. Church was canceled that evening because of icy road conditions, so we all cuddled up to watch a football game and enjoy the wintry night. The kids went to bed praying the ice would endure until morning so Christmas break would be extended one more day.

GABRIEL

In the middle of that seemingly peaceful night, Pete and I were awakened by noises from the boys' room—noises that sounded desperate. By now we were accustomed to sleeping lightly, so we dashed from our small bedroom (formerly the boys' room) into the master bedroom where we discovered Jared (now nine) trying to cry out through muffled sounds. We both frantically asked, "What's wrong? What's wrong?" He couldn't answer—he just held his neck and choked on every attempt to communicate.

I immediately concluded he was sick, so I said, "If you're going to throw up, get to the bathroom—QUICK!" He reacted immediately, almost sliding down the bunkbed stairs and darting into the bathroom.

When Pete and I arrived at the bathroom door, we saw Jared still grabbing his throat, still trying to talk. I attempted to hold his forehead as I always did when the kids were vomiting, but he pushed me away, swiftly running out of the bathroom. Pete intercepted him in the hallway. Stopping him was difficult for Pete—even with his six-foot-tall, 220-pound body. But Pete did manage to hold him.

When Jared finally started talking, he asked, "Why are you here? What are you doing here?" We logically explained that we wanted to see what was wrong. Then he started asking with a fearful, glassy stare, "Who are you?" At that point, we knew he was not awake and that we had a problem.

Attempting to calmly and rationally answer his questions, we said, "We're your parents. This is Mom and Dad."

His eyes looked vacant as he replied, "You're not here...because I'm dead!" He repeatedly insisted he was dead...and then that we were dead...and that we were trying to kill him...or that we also should die. The theme of death was oppressive, to say the least. Pete and I just looked at each other with mouths agape, overwhelmed by yet another spiritual attack.

Pete and I held onto our son in the hall that night, unsure of what might happen if we let go of him. We didn't know how we were going to awaken him from such a horrible attack upon his mind. But we knew that now was the time to meet these ugly experiences head-on.

Jared was unquestionably listening to deadly lies. We looked our otherwise gentle son in the face that night and emphatically stated the untainted truth: "You are alive! You are alive! We are alive! You are not dead! We would never hurt you! We love you!" He climbed up on a chair in the hallway shaking his head in disagreement and arguing that he was surely dead. We continued to confront him with the truth: "You *are* alive! You are not dead! Jesus loves you! Jesus is alive in you!"

With sudden belief in his eyes at the mention of Jesus, he woke up. The name of Jesus ceased the fear. He transformed from a victim of a horrible nightmare into a warrior, ready to defeat his foe. He suddenly knew we were not his enemies, but that an ugly demonic enemy who had been annoying him since he was two years old had now surfaced and revealed his disgusting plan—death.

Pete and I were replete with questions for Jared, who was now fully awake: "What was the dream that started all this? What did you see? Did you hear any voices? What did they say? What made you think you were dead? Who or what told you we all were dead?"

He didn't answer all our questions because he didn't know the answers, but he did know he had been told he was dead, that we should die and then that we were dead. When he heard us say that he was alive, the voice told him he *had* to die. But the name of Jesus broke the hold of his horrible nightmare. Finally Pete asked him, "What is the name of this demon?"

Jared matter-of-factly answered, "His name is Gabriel."

How typical of God's archenemy to use deceit and half-truths, to distort Scripture just enough to make it seem right, especially to a child. If this demon's name had been Slimeball or Spitwad, Jared would have recognized him as evil from the very start, but the name "Gabriel" not only evokes thoughts of the birth of Christ (see Luke 1:26,30,31), but also elicits feelings of grandeur and majesty in the heavenlies as we envision Gabriel and Michael with their hosts of angels surrounding them in the sky.

Jared renounced Gabriel in the name of Jesus, and Gabriel left at the mention of His name. Within minutes, however, he was back again, challenging Jared to the fight of his life. Jared was fighting his foe, jumping down almost all seven steps descending into the living room, then heading for the large picture window behind the couch. Pete was right behind him, trying to reach him before he punched the window. As Jared leaped onto the back of the couch with his fist aimed at the window, Pete grabbed him and pulled him back with all his strength.

I tried to hug my precious son, but he struggled and pushed with great strength. As I held on to his wiggling, twisting body, I realized I was going to lose this struggle. I also knew he was deeply asleep again, vulnerable to satanic attack.

"Pete! Help me!" I pleaded. Pete clutched all three of us together.

Jared looked at us and yelled, "Let go of me! You're going to kill me!"

We held on to him, repeating again and again, "We love you. Jesus loves you. We would never hurt you. We love you. Jesus loves you. We would never hurt you."

Jesus' powerful name finally woke him up again and he could hear the truth. But all he could say was, "Help me! Please help me! Oh God, please help me!"

His body finally relaxed, and I was overcome with anguish for our son. But I knew God was greater than Satan, and that through faith, Jared had Christ in his life. I also knew that Satan's activities were limited to what God would allow (see Job 1:12) and that God promises His children that "the evil one cannot harm him" (1 John 5:18).

Looking back, Pete and I realize we should have just calmly taken our place in Christ and by His authority commanded Satan and all demon powers to stop bothering Jared. We also realize the reason the Steps to Freedom and our prayers were ineffective for Jared was that deep-rooted fears were imbedded in his blocked memory—fears that allowed Satan to maintain powerful footholds in his life.

We could only assure Jared that God *would* help him and that we would help him in every way possible. I said, "Jared, hold on to me as tight as you can and don't let go. I am going to hold you real tight so you can't run away." As we held each other tightly, Pete prayed

ONE THING WE CHRISTIANS MUST REMEMBER IS THAT IN OUR OWN FLESH, WE ARE TOTALLY HELPLESS TO BATTLE THE POWERS OF DARKNESS.

fervently, proclaiming truths from God's Word while calling upon the name of Jesus for power and authority over Jared. And with Pete's help, Jared prayed mightily that this battle would end.

During the few minutes of peace that followed, we spoke calmly with Jared who had returned to his normal, mild, awake self. We sat on the couch and talked for a while, repeating well-known Scripture verses and praying with intensity. The peace of God contrasted greatly with the chaos of evil we had just experienced. The power of God was obvious whenever we called on the name of Jesus or recited Scripture. When God's truth was proclaimed, the demons would flee. But the persistence of this demon seemed tireless.

Seated on the couch, Jared calmly pointed toward the dining room table and said, "There he is."

"Who?" we asked.

He answered, "Gabriel—Gabriel is right there by the table." We couldn't see Gabriel, but we had no reason to disbelieve that what our son saw was very real. Attempting to show Jared he was on God's winning team and that Satan's demons could not harm him, we lightheartedly told him to go punch that ugly old demon's lights out. So Jared ran to the dining room table, pushed it forcefully against the wall and began punching and buffeting his adversary with his fists as hard as he could.

Had we made a mistake? Definitely! One thing we Christians must remember is that in our own flesh, we are totally helpless to battle the powers of darkness. It is *only* through Jesus Christ that we have any authority over the demonic realm, and we can never enter into battle unless we go through Jesus. Our physical strength and our mortal courage mean nothing in the face of the prince of the power of the air and his demons. Only through Jesus Christ do we have any power, and then our power is in the proclamation of His truth, not in a dogfight.

Jared's attempts to physically contend with his assailant were clearly futile and resulted only in another chaotic episode with Gabriel. Pete caught up with Jared on his bunk bed where Pete grabbed him and held him close, praying and calling upon the name of Jesus. Out of breath, Jared began calling out to God for help.

My heart was broken at that moment. I had always been able to protect my kids and provide a safe, Christian home. But now there was nothing I could do but appeal to God, the only one who could help us.

We prepared a bed for Jared beside our bed and declared once again that Jared was a child of God and Satan could not touch him. After praying, reading the Bible and repeating the "I Am" list together, we felt some victory and peace as we tried to get some sleep. Pete and I knew we had to sleep lightly, but I never did go back to sleep. Every 30 to 45 minutes Jared would again go through another terrifying episode, and we would all pray his way through it. Jared used Scripture repeatedly to disarm the enemy and cause fear to subside.

We saw the great power of God that night and gained a new respect for the Bible. By morning, we had acquired an unusually high esteem for the helmet of salvation and the sword of the spirit, which is the Word of God.

Pete and I welcomed the light of morning, scurrying in the fog of our sleeplessness to get Dave and Jalene ready for school. They were disappointed the ice had melted and school wasn't canceled. We kept Jared home that day, partly because he was so exhausted, but primarily because he wanted to go through the Steps to Freedom in Christ again and be freed from the footholds remaining in his life. He believed God would liberate him from his darkest night.

Fortunately, we didn't know then that because of the deeply imbedded footholds of his early years, it would be almost two and a half years before he was completely free.

10

BATTLE WEAPONS

FAMILY TIME

Jared was not only willing to go through the Steps that cold Monday morning, but also ready to do whatever the Bible said to be set free. He renounced Gabriel and any footholds from the nightmare he had. He renounced the sins of his ancestors and all generational curses. When he finished the seven Steps, he was relieved by renouncing the horrible events of the night before. But his attempts to remember footholds produced from repressed memories and years of terrifying dreams would make it necessary to repeat them again. He began to pray daily that God would expose what was keeping him in bondage.

That night before bed, Pete planned a family time saturated in the Scriptures and warfare prayers. Each family member read part of a psalm followed by one "I Am" (see appendix A) while everyone else repeated after them. Even Jalene, who was just learning to read in kindergarten, slowly and deliberately read a verse of a psalm, and reveled in the administration and leadership of her one special "I Am" found in the back of the Steps to Freedom.

Pete had also scanned his copy of *The Adversary* by Mark I. Bubeck, gathering warfare prayers to use before entering into battle that night and for the nights to come. We were unaccustomed to reading prayers, but because we were on the front lines of spiritual warfare, we found it helpful to use written prayers. They provided biblical accuracy and relevancy in our time of fatigue and fear. Even when we read them, however, we occasionally mixed up the words and added negatives that changed the meaning. To assure accuracy, therefore, everyone watched the text intently while one person read. When our intense time of warfare prayers ended, we prayed our own personal prayers. Our family times increased to more than 45 minutes as we armed ourselves with our battle weapons.

BATTLE "SWORDS"

Jared again slept in our room, tossing and turning, shouting and chattering. He would often bolt upright in bed, ready to run out of the room in his sleep to either follow his enemy or fight with him—it was difficult to tell. But we were prepared to grab him at all times. Sometimes we slept so lightly we wondered if we had slept at all.

When Jared began one of his battles, I would quickly hold him close so he couldn't run out of the room. I would instruct him to hug me and not let go, and Pete would grab one of the many "swords" (Bibles) we had strategically placed throughout the room. We had placed a Bible by Jared's pillow, 2 Bibles on our bed and about 12 Bibles on the dresser. We had put on our spiritual armor before going to bed, and we were not willing to be caught without our weapon—the Word of God.

As I held Jared tightly, Pete would read a phrase from the Bible, and Jared would repeat it. Even though Jared was still asleep when the battles began, he was responsive to our directives. Unfortunately, that compliance also worked for the powers of darkness as he succumbed to their suggestions and lies. So we fought for the truth to prevail in his mind; and when it did, he would wake up with determination to win his spiritual battle. We eventually realized that during sleep we have no conscious control of our minds. If we have unresolved issues in our lives, sleep can give Satan easy access.

When Jared was fully awake he would immediately ask for a Bible, unconcerned about what portion he read because all of it revealed truth. The truth was always triumphant, dispelling the lies and forcing the adversary to leave.

Tuesday morning Pete and I unwillingly arose, dissatisfied with the two hours of intermittent sleep we had accumulated in 30-minute intervals throughout the night. Jared was finally sleeping well.

Pete dressed and was ready to leave for an early morning men's prayer time in his office, when fear gripped me. I pleaded with him to stay home in case Jared was attacked again. I wasn't sure I could handle it alone, because we had seen a marked difference in the battle when Pete took his authority as the leader of our home. Pete did stay home and we both waited in anticipation for another invasion of our spiritual lives. No more attacks occurred that morning, and we learned that usually the sunlight brought an appreciated respite of peace.

DANGER AT SCHOOL

Dave and Jalene had again slept peacefully, divinely protected from the dark chaos of the night. We kept Jared home again that day, but we took Dave and Jalene to school, though we were running about 30 minutes late.

While Pete stayed home with Jared, I drove the other two kids to school, stopping at the big new school building first to sign them in at the office. Dave stayed there because his fifth grade class was in that building. Then I drove Jalene to another building about 200 yards away where her kindergarten class met. After parking our van, we both got out to walk into the building. Because we were so late, no cars were coming or going.

As Jalene started to run just ahead of me, a car appeared from nowhere, speeding through the parking lot and headed directly toward Jalene. Everything happened so fast—all I could do was quickly pray, "God, save her!" As I let out a quivering scream, Jalene hesitated slightly and the driver of the car swerved just enough to miss her by no more than a few inches.

After two nearly sleepless nights of contending with hideous attacks at home, death had seemingly followed us to school and dangled its peril in Jalene's face. Jalene was unnerved by the incident, but I almost collapsed on the pavement. I thought to myself, *Are we going to be like Job and lose all of our children before this is over?*

THE SWORD OF THE SPIRIT

When I returned home, I told Pete and Jared what had happened, and we immediately prayed for protection and safety for our family. After Pete left for church, Jared did his school work while I sat at the computer typing Scripture verses we later printed in very large letters to read in the middle of the night.

Jared and I taped the verses to the walls of the hallway and all the upstairs bedrooms—especially on the walls and closet doors where Jared had been sleeping by our bed. Now we could quickly grab a sheet of paper off the wall and have God's Word at our fingertips. The verses provided encouragement to get us through another hour, another day, another week of our battle. Some of the verses that adorned our walls were Job 23:10-12; Psalm 27:1,3; 91:5;

WE DON'T HAVE TO MATURE TO A CERTAIN LEVEL IN OUR CHRISTIAN LIVES BEFORE GOD MAKES US SOLDIERS AND EQUIPS US WITH ARMOR AND WEAPONS.

Proverbs 1:33; 3:24,25,26; Isaiah 41:13; 43:2; John 3:16; 14:27; Romans 3:23; 6:23; Romans 8:15,37,38,39; Ephesians 6:10-18; Philippians 1:21; 2 Timothy 1:7; 1 John 4:1-6; Revelation 12:12.

ARMED FOR BATTLE

That night during family devotions we prepared for battle by spiritually and verbally putting on the armor of God, piece by piece (see Eph. 6:10-13).

We don't have to mature to a certain level in our Christian lives before God makes us soldiers and equips us with armor and weapons. He has told us to only *put on* what He has already provided and we will be able to stand against Satan.

So every night we *put on* our armor—we put on the belt of truth by making declarations of truth from the Bible, stating who God is and who we are in Him by declaring the "I Am" list. We put on the breastplate of righteousness by confessing our sins to each other and then repenting of those sins before God. We prepared our feet with readiness for the gospel of peace by agreeing not to waver in our willingness to help others find truth and find freedom in Christ. Nightly we raised our shield of faith, affirming our belief and confidence in God our Creator and Jesus our Savior and Lord (see Heb. 11:1). By faith we believed that God's shield of faith would extinguish the arrows of our adversaries. Then, of course, we took our helmet of salvation—praise God, we all were saved—and we took our sword of the Spirit, which is the Word of God, and sharpened it for battle by reading it, memorizing it and taping it on the walls of our house. Finally we prayed:

> *Heavenly Father, we acknowledge that You are Lord of heaven and earth. In Your sovereign power and love, You have given us all things richly to enjoy. Thank You for this place to live. We claim this home for our family as a place of spiritual safety and protection from all the attacks of the enemy. As children of God seated with Christ in the heavenly realm, we command every evil spirit, claiming ground in the structures and furnishings of this place based on the activities of previous occupants, to leave and never to return. We renounce all curses and spells utilized against this place. We ask You, heavenly Father, to post guardian angels around this home to guard it from attempts of the enemy to enter and disturb Your purposes for us. We thank You, Lord, for doing this, and pray in the name of the Lord Jesus Christ. Amen.* (Prayer for Cleansing Home from Steps to Freedom in Christ, see appendix A.)

THE MINISTRY OF ANGELS

That night we also went outside together and stopped at each corner of our yard to hold hands in a circle and pray for God to post His angels on the corners of our property. We said an extra prayer by our neighbor's window—a window exposing occultish symbols and sounds of non-Christian music. Then we prayed for hosts of God's angels to surround us and fill our home. We understood that "Satan himself masquerades as an angel of light" (2 Cor. 11:14), so we carefully proclaimed God's truth, forcing any false angels to leave. As we endured the battle of the following nights, we knew we were not fighting alone—God had promised "Never will I leave you; never will I forsake you" (Heb. 13:5). We knew His mighty angels were in combat with us because "The angel of the Lord encamps around those who fear him, and he delivers them" (Ps. 34:7; see also Ps. 91:11,12).

THE POWER OF THE WORD

Our battle did not end there, but we knew we were not alone. Jared was attacked in his sleep night after night, but God enabled him to wake up and maintain control by reading Scripture aloud and refusing to entertain the lies bombarding his mind.

When Jared would sit up in bed, yelling or babbling in unknown words and overcome by terror, we would first have him say the name of Jesus, or phrases such as, "I am a child of God" or "In the name of Jesus, I renounce you." We could tell when the battle for Jared's mind was raging at full force because it became difficult for him to say the name of Jesus. But we continued to press him. When he finally was able to say "Jesus," he woke up and moved from a defensive to an offensive position in his fight against the adversary. Reading the Bible verses we had taped to the walls enabled him to become the victor.

We became eyewitnesses to the power of God's Word to dispel Satan's schemes. We remembered that Jesus had used the Scriptures as His weapon when he battled Satan in the desert. Thus we plunged into the Bible to find more ammunition for warfare. Pete and I discovered more powerful yet comforting passages of Scripture. There were psalms of victory (Psalm 30), psalms of petition (Psalm 31), psalms of quiet comfort (Psalm 23) and psalms to encourage patience (Psalm 40).

But our favorite psalm was Psalm 91, which became a powerful resource for us every night. First, He promised that He is our fortress, our bulwark and our citadel, sheltering us with His protection under His wings. What a wonderful place to be—under God's wings. Then He promised to save us from Satan's attack—a comforting guarantee at a time when we weren't sure our ordeal would ever end. His promise that we would not fear the terror of night came at a time when we were almost too afraid to sleep. And His promise that His angels would lift us up in their hands came at a time when we were almost too tired to lift ourselves out of bed each morning.

Verse 14 of Psalm 91 really gave us the freedom to love our Lord and lift His name during a time when it was easy to despair and wonder when He would finally intervene. God was saying to us in this verse that He would rescue us because we love Him! "'Because he loves me,' says the Lord, 'I will rescue him'" (Ps. 91:14). And He would protect us simply because we acknowledged His name, simply because we kept repeating the name of Jesus at 2:00 in the morning! "'I will protect him, for he acknowledges my name.'"

God promised to answer our cries for help (see Ps. 91:15). We could simply love Him, praise His name and say "Help!" and He would deliver us—and *honor* us! How amazing that He would care enough to rescue us, but how unthinkable to receive *honor* from the One to whom all honor is due. God said, "Those who honor me I will honor" (1 Sam. 2:30).

THE SPIRIT HELPS US IN OUR WEAKNESS

The next seven days and nights slowly ticked by as Jared, Pete and I continued to endure almost sleepless nights. We continued to keep Jared home from school for a few of those days so we could spend time with him in an attempt to discover what the footholds were in the deep recesses of his mind.

One morning after Dave and Jalene had gone to school, Pete and I shared a spiritually intimate time alone with Jared. Instead of just praying together with Jared, Pete had Jared kneel at the foot of our bed. Then Pete and I placed our hands on our dear nine-year-old son as he knelt down, and we asked God to fill all of us with His Holy Spirit so we could effectively pray. Then we asked God to open up the memories of Jared's past to reveal what hold Satan had on his life. We asked Him to open up the subconscious areas of Jared's mind where the memories of his dreams had dwelt for several years. And we asked God to completely deliver Jared from his darkest hour. Then, in great fervency and humility, Jared prayed that God would reveal the source of his fears to his mind so he could be free.

Our prayers that morning were powerful, not from our own abilities to articulate beautiful orations to God, but because we weren't praying in ourselves, rather by the power of the Holy Spirit who was crying out, "*Abba*, Father" on our behalf. We felt a boldness to approach God with confidence as never before (see Heb. 4:16).

Pete and I knew the Holy Spirit was interceding for us in ways we could not express in our weak, tired flesh. Our words and our petitions on behalf of Jared were not our own that morning (see Rom. 8:26,27). Even though we didn't know it right away, God did begin then to slowly reveal to Jared's mind the strongholds of Satan.

YOU MUST COME THROUGH ME

As wonderful as that prayer time was with Jared, we didn't always do everything right. Sometimes our flesh got impatient and insisted on intervening for Jared instead of patiently waiting on the Lord. Occasionally we accepted wrong counsel from other well-meaning people who were trying to help us. Our impatience and our failure to align the counsel of others with Scripture resulted in trouble one night during an intense struggle.

That day, Pete had been told by someone that because parents have spiritual authority over their children, they can tell evil spirits they have to come through the parent to get to the child. Thus the parent is much more able to fight the battle than is the child.

So that night, in the middle of another nightly attack, Pete, in his anguish over what Jared was experiencing, proclaimed that Satan and his workers had no right to Jared or any of our other children and that all evil spirits had to come through him to get to any of our children. And that's exactly what the demons did! They attacked Pete with horrible thoughts, with headaches and with such excruciating back pain that he could hardly walk. What a mistake it was to think we had any authority over Satan or his demons in our mere humanity! We had left out the only One who has authority over Satan, and that is Jesus Christ. We have authority over the powers of darkness because we are *in* Christ, but not because we are merely parents.

Several days passed while Pete endured agonizing back pain, until we realized what a mistake we had made. One evening the whole family gathered around Pete as he slumped over the kitchen counter in pain. We all placed our hands on the most painful part of his back and prayed. First Pete and I confessed our mistake in commanding the demons to go through Pete. Then we proclaimed the truth that because we are children of God in Christ, bought by the blood of Jesus, all powers of darkness had to first go through Jesus Christ before they could come near us (see Col. 2:9,10). Even as we prayed, the children and I felt a surge of immense heat from Pete's back. When we all said "Amen," Pete stood upright with ease, free of any pain.

We would never invite emotional, mental or physical attacks upon our family again, but the magnitude of God's power we witnessed through our spiritual combat is something we wouldn't exchange for anything. The great darkness of evil revealed the awesome light of God in much greater intensity.

11

CHILDREN OF MINISTRY

ON THE FRONT LINES

On January 15, 1993, 12 days after Jared had his first skirmish with the kingdom of darkness, the family piled into our rusty little Honda and we drove to Rockford, Illinois, to attend a spiritual warfare seminar. We had determined not to repeat the mistake we made the year before when we left our children with someone else in the midst of spiritual warfare.

The seminar was taught by Dr. Timothy Warner, who had just left Trinity Evangelical Divinity School in Deerfield, Illinois, to become the vice president of International Ministries for Freedom in Christ Ministries. Pete had announced this seminar in church, hoping many would attend, but only one other couple chose to go. After the first session, the wife became ill, so they packed their bags and went home early. She was fine as soon as they arrived home.

But Pete and I eagerly attended every session, poring over the materials and listening to every word Dr. Warner said. Our aim was to gain more biblical ammunition to win our battle. Having served with his wife Eleanor as missionaries in a tribal village in West Africa, Dr. Warner taught with great insight. He exposed the primary spiritual reasons for the unprecedented overt demonic activity in the United States today: growth of the New Age movement, interest in Eastern religions, rock music with occultic messages, certain games and toys, certain movies, videos, TV programs and publications, interest in the paranormal/supernatural and the rise in satanism. Pete and I began to understand why our children were experiencing struggles and personal conflicts foreign to us when we were growing up.

Dr. Warner used material printed in the back of the seminar workbook, contributed by Tom White of Frontline Ministries, that applied directly to our situation:

Under the sovereignty of God, Satan and his forces may legally influence and oppress a life on the basis of unconfessed, uncleansed sin—personal or ancestral. Release from affliction is achieved through the removal of sin ground, exposure of suspected enemy schemes/spirits and resistance

CHILDREN ARE ALSO IN THE MINISTRY, SERVING ON THE FRONT LINES OF A RAGING SPIRITUAL BATTLE.

in the authority of the name and blood of Jesus Christ. Generally, if oppression occurs in young children it is primarily rooted in the previous uncleansed sin of ancestors that has opened doors of advantage in the blood line to the influence of enemy spirits.

A possible application to this reason for demonic affliction was "ungodly ancestral heritage from parents who are believers but through ignorance and lack of diligence fail to dedicate and pray for release of children from genealogical influences." Now we knew why such a powerful release of oppression had occurred the night we renounced the sins and curses of our ancestors. Pete and I continued to renounce any ancestral influences on ourselves or our children for months to come because that stronghold was so oppressive.

Another possible reason powerfully illuminated our situation:

Children of actively involved Christian servants are subject to intensive enemy attack devised to diminish the effectiveness of the parent's ministry. Specific, diligent prayer for protection and wise parenting must be employed as defense against this type of oppression.

So our pro-life activities *did* have an effect on our children, and our ministry in the church *did* affect our home life. We began to ask ourselves: *Is it any wonder pastors' kids often have problems bigger than others? Is it any wonder missionaries' kids often experience struggles that oppose the biblical teaching provided in their homes? Is it any wonder Satan defeats those in ministry, along with their children? Is it any wonder people in ministry avoid frontline issues to protect themselves and their families from satanic anger and retaliation?*

We not only began to pray for the protection and wise parenting of our own children, but we also began praying for the children of the director of the crisis pregnancy center. We began praying for the children of a pastor friend of ours in Florida. We prayed for the children of our missionary friends who were serving an unreached tribe. The list of children whose parents are in ministry and who need our prayers could go on and on because the children are also in the ministry, serving on the front lines of a raging spiritual battle. "But thanks be to God! He gives us the victory through our Lord Jesus Christ" (1 Cor. 15:57).

Should we stay out of ministries on the front lines of the spiritual battle just so we can live in tranquility? Absolutely not! But we must be spiritually alert and aware of Satan's schemes because of our greater vulnerability. God has not only called us, He has also gone before us in our battle, already having won the victory (see Heb. 2:14,15; Rom. 8:28-31).

12

BREAKING STRONGHOLDS

ENCOURAGED BY OTHERS

While Dr. Warner's conference was going on, so was our own nightly spiritual warfare in the hotel room. We spoke with Dr. Warner and his wife about our intense battle, and they encouraged us to keep doing what we were doing.

When we returned home, Jared's former attacks continued. So we began to ask God to search Jared and know his heart (see Ps. 139:23,24). We were totally dependent upon God to reveal those things in his life he couldn't remember. We were also perusing the Scriptures for answers and talking with trusted Christian friends to receive godly counsel. Many people were compassionate and understanding—especially the dear people in our church. Because Saturday night was a favorite time for the diabolic skirmishes (probably in an attempt to ruin Pete's effectiveness on Sunday morning), we were often physically exhausted and emotionally depleted at church. Many people would ask us week after week how things were going.

When the congregation reached across the aisles each Sunday for corporate prayer, people often prayed for us. And when Pete choked on his tears during a sermon, the people showed compassion, often crying with us. Church board meetings became a time for Pete to share our struggles and pray with the leaders. During the women's Bible study when I would share my prayer request (freedom from demonic harassment), the women didn't look at me in judgment as if I were going crazy or not a strong enough Christian to handle my own problems. They believed me and they prayed (see Eph. 5:19-21).

Few people, however, actually understood in the spiritual sense what was happening to us; and no one had any real answers to our dilemma, but their compassion and empathy sustained us (see Col. 3:12).

Jalene's kindergarten teacher, a wonderful compassionate Christian woman who had gone through her own spiritual warfare, was one who did understand our circumstances. She was a tremendous help to me when I daily brought Jalene to her classroom. Every morning, this teacher stood in the classroom doorway to greet a long line of five- and six-year-olds who anxiously awaited her hug and tender hello. This remarkable teacher, who was responsible for about 40 kindergarten students, took time to pray with me almost every day.

It was so comforting to know she had been praying for us at 2:00 A.M. when she couldn't sleep. Perhaps God had kept her awake just so she could intercede for us. It was also comforting to know I could call her in the middle of the night and pray with her. The effectiveness of her prayers was noticeable, not only because her prayers were in accord with Scripture as she prayed, but because she prayed from personal experience and from past victories.

She also prayed with Jared one day after school. It was encouraging to have an intercessor praying for us when we were so weary. She discerned I felt like giving up one day, so she called me into her room after morning kindergarten was out, sat me down by her desk and she showed me some Bible verses I will never forget. They kept me going when I thought I couldn't handle any more.

So do not throw away your confidence; it will be richly rewarded. You need to persevere so that when you have done the will of God, you will receive what he has promised. For in just a very little while, "He who is coming will come and will not delay. But my righteous one will live by faith. And if he shrinks back, I will not be pleased with him." But we are not of those who shrink back and are destroyed, but of those who believe and are saved (Heb. 10:35-39).

During our darkest time when so few people understood what was really happening to our family, I thanked the Lord for providing a godly teacher to encourage us and spur us on in love.

Pete was also receiving encouragement from some of the people he talked with throughout his day. He and a pastor on the other side of Madison often talked and discussed solutions. And every week when Pete went to the Christian radio station to record his weekly program, he unloaded his burdens on the station manager. God uses encouraging people to help us endure—people who "spur one another on toward love and good deeds" (Heb. 10:24).

THE CRACK OF FEAR

Just when we thought we were the only ones in the world who had ever fought against the powers of darkness for our children, God sent someone who could identify with our situation. It was our phone call to a pastor we had never met before that helped us discover the reason for Jared's demonic episode.

This pastor told us how he had driven home with his daughter during a terrible thunderstorm with lightning, thunder and torrential rains. They pulled up in front of their closed garage door, and he ran out to open it. Finding it locked, he ran to the back of the house to go in the access door. While he was behind the house, lightning struck and thunder roared almost simultaneously, terrorizing his daughter who was alone in the car. When he returned to the car, his daughter was crying and screaming hysterically. That night her ordeal began. The trauma of the storm had caused a crack of fear in her life, opening the door to a demonic attack.

Pete and I began to think of the trauma in Jared's life. We immediately recognized the door of fear had opened for him when our van slid off the icy road and hit the tree. At the time, we didn't understand his hysterical screaming or his extreme reaction to such a moderate accident. How could such a small crash cause such great fear? That accident had been the "icing on the cake" to the fears he had experienced for years in the silence of his dreams and forgotten memories. Satan was using his primary tactic—FEAR—to victimize our son and hold him in bondage.

In our attempt to help Jared break the hold of fear in his life, we returned to the site of the accident. Just as the rider needs to get back on a horse right after the person has fallen off, so we believed Jared should revisit the scene of the accident to prevent fear from growing.

We traveled the same route we took the night of the accident, but this time the roads weren't icy. We pulled our Honda around to the spot closest to the tree, walked across the snow and stood by the tree we thought we had hit. After arguing lightheartedly about two trees and moving from one tree to the other several times, Pete and I insisted the tree we were standing by was the right tree.

We all jokingly debated about the trees—everyone except Jared who stood silently frozen in fear. Pete and I still believed we were right, so we stayed by "our tree" and each one of us prayed to renounce any stronghold of fear caused by the accident. We also made it clear that the tree was not inhabited by demons. But we did emphasize that Jared's fear had begun there; and in that same place where fear had been birthed, it could be overcome through prayer and renunciation.

SATAN'S PLOY HAS ALWAYS BEEN

TO CONFUSE THE MIND.

Two days passed, and Jared's nights were no better. Finally, at the kids' insistence that we had prayed by the wrong tree, we all piled into our Honda again and went to the scene of the accident. This time we prayed by the "kids' tree" and again renounced the fear of the accident. When we finished, one of them reached down in the snow and picked up a piece of metal at the base of the tree. Then someone found another piece nearby. We recognized it as part of the front grill of our van. The kids had been right—we were finally praying beside the right tree! Although it was not imperative to pray by the right tree to break the foothold, Jared felt better about it. He slept better that night, not because we found the right tree, but because he began to believe there was no reason to fear the tree or the scene of the accident. The foothold of fear was definitely beginning to break.

BATTLE FOR THE MIND

Fear still gripped Jared's mind, fear that went back years. We had all memorized 2 Timothy 1:7: "For God has not given us the spirit of fear, but of power and of love and of a sound mind" (*NKJV*). It bolstered our courage to know we don't have to live in fear (see 1 John 4:18).

Satan's ploy has always been to confuse the mind—he convinced Eve God didn't really say what she thought He said. Satan battered Job's mind with sorrow, death and pain. Satan knew Jesus would not fear him, so he tried to entice Him with a desire for earthly power and authority. Satan will find our weakness and work on our minds in that area. Satan was battling for Jared's mind with the weapon of fear because he knew he was dealing with a gentle, trusting child who could be easily shocked into silence.

SEARCHING THE PAST

While we waited on God to open up Jared's memory, we searched what we did know about his life and renounced everything we could think of. We started with an incident that occurred while he was still in the womb. Pete and I attended Lamaze birthing classes during my last month of pregnancy to learn the techniques of a natural and painless delivery.

During those classes, our teacher asked all husbands and wives to lie on the floor with big comfortable pillows to help us relax. Then we were instructed to close our eyes and empty our minds of everything, focusing on a bright radiance way out in space. We were to focus on this object so profoundly that we would drift closer and closer to its brightness. The benefit of this activity was to learn to block out the reality of pain in childbirth. Pete and I communicated only with our eyes that night, telling each other not to do what she said.

On the way home, we agreed she was promoting and directing meditation and self-hypnosis, which can empty the mind of its own sensibility enough to give Satan an opportunity to fill it with thoughts contrary to our own beliefs. God tells us to be filled with the Spirit, not to empty our minds. The most dangerous thing we can do spiritually is to let our minds go blank. God's Word directs us to take every thought captive in obedience to Christ (see 2 Cor. 10:5) and to think upon those things that are true (see Phil. 4:8).

Pete and I had both spent our time on the floor thinking only about Jesus, praying He would keep our minds in tune with reality and in tune only with Him. Although we hadn't directly participated in the meditation exercise, we renounced our presence there that night. We also renounced any foothold Satan may have gained in our lives or in Jared's life because of the mind games that had been played.

Two weeks after the due date, Jared was born with the umbilical cord wrapped around his neck at least three times. Our Muslim doctor became concerned when Jared didn't start breathing after the cord was unwrapped. He worked on Jared for what seemed like an eternity, until he finally began to cry. What a wonderful sound! But even though we were very thankful for the work the doctor did, we had to renounce the false religion the doctor represented and any false god he may have called upon to help him in Jared's crisis.

With every renunciation, no matter how small, Satan's grip weakened and he lost some of his power. So we kept on searching and renouncing. We daily asked Jared questions to unlock his memory. We asked him if any movies, television shows or video games had caused him to be afraid.

He told us about a video game he had played that was just an excursion into a dangerous jungle, that is until he became proficient enough to experience the last level of the game where he fought a big demonlike alien creature. Jared believed the fear he had experienced in the last level had created a stronghold in his life, so he renounced it.

Jared also had a problem with the G.I. Joe figures, not the kind we remembered when we were children, but the new ones with grotesque, inhuman faces. We had already discarded all the G.I. Joe figures, but now Jared renounced the fear they had produced in his life. Later, we made sure our children realized the G.I. Joe action figures were not evil themselves, nor did any demons live in them, but Satan had merely used those toys to evoke fear in children.

I continued to question Jared about movies or television shows that might have caused him fear. We thought we were discretionary about what we watched. We never allowed the kids to view anything with sexual innuendos and tried to avoid graphic violence and murder scenes. But even with our strict discretionary standards, we still had much to learn about the subtle entrances of evil into our home through movies and television.

We had been deceived to believe it would be all right to see *Batman* because it was one of those fun shows from our own childhood. But we soon learned the innocence of several decades ago had been replaced with the fears of a dark world. The super hero of our childhood had become a dark character in hellish surroundings. And now years later we were discovering the movie had affected Jared.

He finally remembered the opening scene of *Batman*. He recalled how Batman swooped down bigger than life in his sinister surroundings. Then he recalled how something heavy and diabolic had swooped down in front of *him* as he sat there stiff in his seat. This power of darkness brought an incredible fear upon Jared, gripping him in silent terror for years.

It's hard to believe Satan can do his work through movies and television, but we have even known adults who have become involved in the occult after becoming inordinately interested in a show such as "Bewitched." The many avenues of electronic entertainment have opened our minds and our children's lives to evil enticement, fear and seduction.

Many schools deal with the problems of fear, anxiety, violence and anger by teaching students in stress management courses how to meditate or transport their spirits to someplace such as a beautiful clear lake to escape their anxieties.

We met a Christian couple during our vacation whose son had been taught this in school. These Christian parents didn't know he was being taught to do this until they became concerned about his reaction to anger. He would go to his room and get under the covers for long periods of time. When his mother finally confronted this uncharacteristic behavior, he said he had been told to go to the "clear lake" to find peace and calmness during times of stress or anger. He was told to stay there until he felt better.

School children are also being encouraged to "enjoy" the company of an imaginary friend. One group of students was told to handle their difficulties by closing their eyes and thinking about a dead relative whom they had loved very much. They were then instructed to open a door to an elevator in their minds and join that relative in the elevator. What vulnerability this created for these children who were now open to demonic visitations. The door of their minds has been opened to possible spirit guides and "friendly" demons who at first appear to help, but eventually show their hideous nature.

Jared had to renounce one of those "friendly" demons. Along with Gabriel and some of the other obviously destructive demons, Jared admitted there was one demon he liked. We explained to him that demons are deceitful and tricky. They will at first pretend to be nice, but after they have gained our trust, they will always show their evil nature and wicked plan. When Jared renounced in the name of Jesus this demon he liked, and announced he didn't want to be deceived, the demon never bothered him again.

I REMEMBER

Jared also had to renounce voices he had heard. He had to renounce television shows that had made him afraid. But the biggest stronghold in Jared's life came to his remembrance 17 days after the accident had cracked open the fear in his life.

He was still being attacked nightly, and Pete and I were still experiencing near sleepless nights. It was a Tuesday afternoon and Jared was out riding his bike. He came bounding into the house to tell me he had remembered a stronghold. So we sat down right away to renounce it. But disappointment set in quickly when he said, "I remembered it while I was riding my bike on the road, but when I turned up our driveway, I forgot it." I tried to jog his memory, but he just couldn't remember.

It wasn't until the next day when Jared was out riding his bike again that he remembered the incident that had produced the stronghold. Again, he came bounding in the house and said, "I remembered it again, Mom!"

"Hurry and tell me before you forget it again!" I exclaimed. And he began to tell me about an incident several years before when he was about five. He had ridden his bike to the end of our street where an older boy who had often played at our house lived. The boy invited Jared into his house, offering him candy, toys and fun.

We had given him strict instructions never to enter anyone's house without our permission, but the candy and toys were just too appealing. The boy did give him candy and toys, but then he took him upstairs to a room that housed a big stereo with huge speakers attached to the corners of the ceiling. With the stereo turned up very loud, the boy played an audiocassette of Freddy Krueger stalking women and killing them. Through sound only, Jared experienced the fear of someone being stalked by an insane killer who repeatedly verbalized, through his threatening words and his panting and gasping breaths, his intent to kill the screaming woman running from him. Jared heard the desperate running footsteps, the constant threats of murder, the fearful wailing and screaming of the victim, then the sounds of the repeated stabbings and the agonizing cries of pain as the woman died. In the silence of her death, came the shrieking laughter of Freddy Krueger as he delighted in her demise. Then he began to stalk other human prey and they would run away, crying "Here he comes!" "Watch out!" "There he is!"

Why didn't our son tell us about such a traumatic event? Because it was so revolting that his young mind couldn't handle it. He was so scared that he buried it in his deepest memory bank. He had forgotten the incident until that day almost four years later. He had forgotten it, but its effect on him had been actively working on his life all those years.

We are thankful God revealed this painful memory to Jared or he would still be living under the bondage of that fear today, and Satan would be using it against him to weaken him and prevent him from being free in Christ. How Satan loves to terrorize us to the point of helplessness until we bury the events of our past too appalling to remember. And as we get older, the fears grow larger and our minds protect us by pushing those fears and traumas even deeper into our memory banks.

Jared not only renounced the incident with Freddy Krueger, but he also forgave the boy for terrorizing his mind. He broke one of Satan's huge strongholds that day, and he also broke the chains that had bound him in fear to Freddy Krueger and the boy down the street. This breakthrough was monumental; however, Jared's journey was not over, and he continued to persevere in his path to freedom (see Isa. 40:30,31).

13

RETALIATION

FEAR FIGHTS BACK

As fear began to lose its grip on Jared, the kingdom of darkness fought back with a fierce last effort.

One night Jared was again overcome by fear in the early morning hours, so we began pulling Scriptures off the wall to read as we had been doing for quite some time. On this particular night, however, Jared tried to read the verses, but couldn't see the words. His optical perspective had reversed and he could no longer read the verses that had been his sword in every battle. He panicked, so we told him to close his eyes and repeat after us as we read verses from the Bible. He won the battle by repeating verses after us.

The following morning, he could see just fine and went off to school. His inability to focus was limited at first to Scripture reading in the middle of the night. Eventually, the problem with his visual perspective also began happening at approximately 5:00 P.M. every evening, the time of the accident with the tree. When enough truth was proclaimed each time, Jared's eyesight would return to normal.

His perspective only reversed once at school, and because I had informed Jared's Christian teacher about what was happening with his eyes, she took him into the hallway and prayed with him. His eyesight instantly returned to normal.

These battles were not easily won, because footholds were being broken in Jared's life and his adversary was retaliating. Fortunately, God gave us the strength to persist, and Jared's eyesight returned to normal within a week. He has never had a recurrence of eye trouble. In a recent eye exam his vision was 20-20.

We later heard about a young man whose eyes had been affected much like Jared's shortly after a fearful event. His parents took him to an optometrist, and he began wearing glasses, but that didn't take care of his problem. The young man continued to be trapped in fear until he was diagnosed schizophrenic.

If we would only take care of our troubles in the spiritual realm before we attribute our difficulties to a physical or psychological cause, we could often eliminate our problems through the power of God in our lives. That is not to say there aren't legitimate physical problems, but why not go to God *first*, as Scripture directs us? If symptoms disappear in response to prayer and Scripture, then we know the primary problem is not physical.

THE BASEMENT PIANO

It was the end of January before Satan lost his fight to reestablish fear in Jared's life by affecting his eyes. His retaliation attempt had failed.

We were winning the battle and many strongholds had been broken, but we were weary. Life had been fraught with hell's horrors for 13 long months and we craved time in the presence of God. After so much darkness, we sought more of Jesus, the light of the world. He promises that "Whoever follows me will never walk in darkness, but will have the light of life" (John 8:12). We all gloried in the promise that one day Jesus would take us home to heaven where there is no night (see John 14:1-3; Rev. 21:23-25; Ps. 30:5; 1 Thess. 5:5).

One evening after the sun had set, bringing on the darkness we had learned to abhor, I made my way to the basement where I sat on the bench of our big old piano. At first I just sat there, unable to play or sing. I was reminded of Martin Luther's powerful statement about music:

> I wish to see all arts, principally music, in the service of Him who gave and created them. Music is a fair and glorious gift of God. I would not for the world forego my humble share of music. Singers are never sorrowful, but are merry, and smile through their troubles in song. Music makes people kinder, gentler, more staid and reasonable. I am strongly persuaded that after theology there is no art capable of affording peace and joy of heart...the devil flees before the sound of music

almost as much as before the Word of God.[1]

Eventually I started to play some old hymns such as "How Great Thou Art." I love the words to that hymn, but because my voice was so clogged with emotion and fatigue, I could only play the notes.

Then I couldn't help but sing the words to other hymns, because their power just had to be proclaimed that night. Some of those hymns were packed with theological truths and firsthand experience, written by people who had been tested and tried in the furnace and had emerged from the refiner's fire as pure gold:

When peace like a river attendeth my way,
When sorrows like sea-billows roll;
Whatever my lot, Thou hast taught me to say,
"It is well, it is well with my soul."
Though Satan should buffet, tho' trials should come,
Let this blest assurance control,
That Christ has regarded my helpless estate,
And hath shed His own blood for my soul.
It is well...with my soul.
It is well, it is well with my soul.

IN OUR SELF-SUFFICIENCY, WE OFTEN MISS OUT ON EXPERIENCING THE STRENGTH OF GOD. IN OUR SELF-SUFFICIENCY, GOD WILL OFTEN PASS US BY UNTIL WE BECOME DEPENDENT UPON HIM.

Through the pain, I did have to admit that "it was well with my soul." As I sang song after song, the tears flowed like rivers down my face. I was in my hour of greatest weakness, and yet I felt a new sense of God's grace and strength. Even "the weakness of God is stronger than man's strength" (1 Cor. 1:25). I felt comfortable being weak because I was not only experiencing the strength of God, but also the Holy Spirit, who helps us in our weakness (see Rom. 8:26).

I felt free to collapse before God because He said, "'My grace is sufficient for you, for my power is made perfect in weakness.' Therefore I will boast all the more gladly about my weaknesses, so that Christ's power may rest on me. That is why, for Christ's sake, I delight in weaknesses, in insults, in hardships, in persecutions, in difficulties. For when I am weak, then I am strong" (2 Cor. 12:9,10).

How paradoxical that when I am weak, then I am strong! In our own self-sufficiency, we often miss out on experiencing the strength of God. In our self-sufficiency, God will often pass us by until we become dependent upon Him.

There I sat at that old piano with the chipped finish and broken ivories, singing the words of Martin Luther from "A Mighty Fortress Is Our God" in a trembling, weak voice that ironically exuded the power of God through my own frailty:

Did we in our own strength confide,
Our striving would be losing,
Were not the right man on our side
The man of God's own choosing.
Dost ask who that may be?
Christ Jesus, it is He—
Lord Sabaoth His name,
From age to age the same,
And He must win the battle.

I praised almighty God as I never had done before, and He comforted me and lifted me up as I sang "God Leads Us Along." The words spoke of times when our paths do not go through the shady green pastures, but through the darkest valley—how some people only go through the water, but others go through flood and fire.

We were currently in the flood and in the fire, but we were definitely all in the blood—the blood of Jesus Christ—and we were on the winning side!

Note
1. Taken from the Saturday Sacred Concerts program, Ministry of Bible Town Community Church, Boca Raton, Fla.

14

VICTORIES

VICTORIES, ONE AT A TIME

During those winter months as our family tried to relax and enjoy our evenings, we found we couldn't watch television. We tried to watch only wholesome programs, but even the commercials were peppered with filth. Almost every night we were renouncing the media trash that filtered into our home. So we finally stopped turning on the television.

We only listened to Christian radio. We also went to our local Christian bookstore and bought stacks of good historical Christian fiction and children's adventure books for the entire family. When dinner was over and the kids were tired of playing, we had our family time together, then opened our books and read until it was time to go to sleep.

Jared moved back to his own room that he shared with Dave, which gave us all cause to rejoice. He was still having a few bouts with fear each week, but they were mild compared to the battles that had raged in January.

Throughout the winter Pete preached about our identity in Christ, the freedom we can have in Christ and how our old nature has been crucified (see Rom. 6:6,7). He interrupted his theme only once to preach a powerful pro-life sermon on January 24th, the Sanctity of Human Life Sunday. He received much praise for his poignant message, but he also received strong rebukes from two people in the church that day, confirming that the battle over abortion was still raging—even in the church. One man told him if he ever preached a sermon like that again, he would never come back, and another long-time church goer asked him when he was going to get off his "pro-life kick."

FEWER FOOTHOLDS—MORE FREEDOM

Our family was still praying for God to reveal the final lingering footholds of fear in Jared's memory. It had been almost 15 months since our family's ordeal started, and we still wondered when it would end.

Meanwhile, we were beginning to understand how our trials could be considered pure joy (see Jas. 1:2). They taught us priceless lessons. We could see how our sufferings were producing perseverance (see Rom. 5:3), and that without the darkness we would not have been privileged to see the brightness of His light and the glory of His all-surpassing power. We had come to know Him intimately and we had shared in the battle for truth against our common adversary.

We were beginning to say with confidence and honesty that we were "hard pressed on every side, but not crushed; perplexed, but not in despair; persecuted, but not abandoned; struck down, but not destroyed (2 Cor. 4:8,9).

God did faithfully reveal another foothold to Jared. As he was sitting at the kitchen counter one day, he nonchalantly said, "Mom, I remember a dream I've been having every night for as long as I can remember."

In my own unruffled way, I replied, "Oh. Well, renounce it!"

And that's what he did. Right there at the counter he thanked God for helping him remember, and then he renounced the foothold this dream had had in his life for many years, probably since we moved into our house just as he turned two years old.

He described a dream where two men with guns would endlessly chase him in their jeep, stalking him. He even remembered the nights I held him in the rocking chair while he screamed in fear. As soon as he described the dream and renounced its hold on him, the fear of that dream disappeared. He proclaimed there was no truth to the dream and that in Christ there is no fear (see 1 John 4:18).

A few days later, he recalled why he was so afraid Pete and I were going to leave him. Every night he could remember, a plaguing and repetitive thought had tormented his mind after we put him to bed. He had been afraid to go to sleep, fearful that every sound represented the front door closing behind his parents who were never coming back.

By morning, the thought had been pushed way down into the depths of his memory, down where fear sometimes replaces truth. Now he was able to remember that recurring thought and renounce the nightly fear in the name of Christ. He boldly announced the truth to his adversary—the truth that his parents were not going to leave him and that "God has not given us a spirit of fear, but of power, and of love, and of a sound mind" (2 Tim. 1:7, *NKJV*).

Jared gained tremendous freedom that spring, and his middle-of-the-night episodes were occurring less than once a week. We praised God for searching his heart and exposing many of his hidden fears. But we continued to pray, waiting patiently for God to reveal the rest of the footholds that were like crumbs falling from the table—they were small but they still made a mess.

SUMMER FUN

That summer Jared attended a Christian camp with his best friend. Although it was only an hour and a half from our home, we had some apprehension about what might happen at night. So we summoned our faith and entrusted him to God's protection. Jared talked and goofed around so much with his cabin buddies they hardly slept all week! God was faithful.

Our association with the camp became far greater than Jared's camping experience, however. When one of the camp directors discovered that some of his summer college staff had deeply rooted personal problems, Pete introduced him to the Steps to Freedom as a counseling tool. This director began using the Steps with his male staff members and watched them experience great freedom. When several of the female staff members also wanted to go through the Steps, he asked me to take each one through them. Freedom began to permeate the summer staff. A year later we heard that these students had maintained their freedom in Christ.

FREE AT LAST

Almost a year after Jared remembered his recurring dream and tormenting thought about our leaving him, another foothold was revealed. He was still having intermittent fearful incidents in his sleep, when we noticed a pattern. Whenever Jared was exposed to rock music with a heavy metal sound, he would have problems. He began renouncing rock music, and he stayed away from it as much as he could. As his nights became remarkably more peaceful and his attitude during the day became less rebellious, total freedom appeared to be close at hand.

The affirmation that rock music was a foothold in his life came late one night after Pete and I had fallen asleep watching the news. While we were sleeping, Jared entered our room and stood beside our bed—fearful, but not fully awake. Not quite awake ourselves, we began praying for him when he turned suddenly and pointed to the television, shouting, "Turn it off! Turn it off!" As we were pray-

FOR THE CHRISTIAN, FDR'S STATEMENT CAN BE SHORTENED TO "WE HAVE NOTHING TO FEAR!"

ing, a rock group had started singing and he reacted immediately to the music with great fear and apprehension. It was our confirmation that rock music had adversely affected him and caused a foothold of fear. He continued to renounce it, and his nights slowly improved until he was only experiencing fear in his sleep once every two or three months.

The last foothold Jared had to conquer was fear itself. I'm reminded of Franklin Delano Roosevelt's statement, "The only thing we have to fear is fear itself." We often eliminate all our fears except the fear of fear. Jared had taken care of his fear of Freddy Krueger, Batman and GI Joes. He had renounced the fear that his parents were going to leave him, and he had renounced his frightening recurring dream. Now he had nothing to fear but fear itself.

For the Christian, FDR's statement can be shortened to "We have nothing to fear!" We have a position in heaven right next to Jesus, and because we have been given authority over Satan and all his demons, we have nothing to fear!

Last Christmas each person in our family received matching gray sweatshirts. Emblazoned on the front and back are the words, "FEAR NOT." Below those triumphant words is part of a verse from Psalm 23: "I will fear no evil, for you are with me" (v. 4). We all had to learn that fear doesn't have to be a part of the Christian life.

Jared's fear was tested one more time at a Christian wilderness camp in the summer of 1994 when they really roughed it in tents out in the woods. Pete and I were under the impression the leaders would be in the tents with the boys at night, but the state laws prohibited that.

Being alone at night in a tent with three other boys during a violent thunderstorm, as well as getting caught in unexpected rough rapids on the river one day, caused Jared to face fear again. But this time he knew how to conquer it. He knew the truth, and the truth again set him free. Realizing that Christians don't have to live in fear if they are relying on Christ and the authority they have in Him has brought Jared great freedom.

After almost two years of fighting his foes with the truths of Scripture, praying daily for God to search his heart and reveal all of Satan's footholds, Jared is free. Will fear raise its ugly head again in his life? It probably will. But he now knows what to do when it does. He knows that freedom is rightfully his and all he has to do is appropriate it (see Gal. 5:1).

Pete and I rejoice that Jared doesn't sleep as soundly as he used to. Since he began verbally submitting himself to God and resisting the devil every night before bed, he hasn't had any problems. James 4:7 tells us, "Submit yourselves, then, to God. Resist the devil, and he will flee from you." It is a promise that if we *first* submit, *then* resist, the devil *will* flee.

WARRIOR

Pete attended the Moody Pastors' Conference in the spring of 1995 after Jared was totally free. He brought home a poster for each of the kids to hang in their rooms. On Jared's poster boldly stands a beautiful, long, shiny, silver sword, inlaid with gold and glistening on a dark gray background. In the foreground is a silver helmet that radiates strength and invincibility. It looks large enough to cover a person's entire head, including the face below the chin. It is suspended there in front of the sword in all its royalty and authority. Printed in large letters across the poster is the word "WARRIOR" and below that are words that proclaim: "For our fight is not against flesh and blood, but against the rulers, against the authorities, against the powers of this dark world and against the spiritual forces of evil in the heavenly realms. Ephesians 6:12."

That poster now has a prominent place on Jared's closet door. It is a testament to what he has been through. He is a WARRIOR, without a doubt. He fought a long battle on the front lines and emerged victorious in Christ.

Through our family's three-year battle, we *all* became warriors. There were no war casualties—only victors. We delight in our victory every day because Jesus has won our battles and He has won the war!

> Do not be afraid or discouraged because of this vast army. For the battle is not yours, but God's (2 Chron. 20:15).

In ourselves, we didn't win any battles. Only through Jesus Christ were we victorious. Only through Jesus Christ were our enemies defeated. Only through Jesus Christ were we set free.

15

THE CHURCH UNDER ATTACK

CHAOS AND CONFUSION

In the midst of our battle for Jared's freedom (1993), we moved to another town and another church. Our increased contacts with high school and college kids desperately needing to find freedom in Christ constrained us to enter a ministry committed to helping them. Pete accepted a position as youth pastor in a church just an hour and a half away.

Through many tears, we left our dear friends at the Madison church where we had served for nine years. The Lord affirmed our change almost daily by smoothly orchestrating the move. Plans to find a house in our new community and prepare our own house for sale were going well.

We felt at home in this church of about 800 people. It reminded us both of the churches we had attended as children. This church had a history of strong Bible teaching and preaching; and a large portion of its budget was distributed to missionaries—many of whom had been raised in the church.

We had great peace and anticipation that God was leading us to a church where we could minister comfortably and effectively. However, we discovered instead a church under attack.

The church was replete with wonderful programs and members abounding in talent, but many were steeped in pride.

Order had been replaced with confusion and gossip. Many people were angry and bitter toward leadership. The church had been deeply hurt by the sexual sins of a former pastor. As a result, church leaders didn't trust each other, nor did a large segment of the congregation trust the leadership. A lack of respect for leadership in general filtered down to the young adults and teens.

Satan's army was having a field day. A staff member was on medical leave because of a recent nervous breakdown. Decisions were being confirmed through unbiblical practices. Minor issues were catastrophized while major ones were minimized.

Overall, we found a church that had, in many ways, lost its first

---

PETE EXPLAINED THAT DEMONIC STRONGHOLDS ARE NOT DEMON POSSESSION. THEY ARE SINS OR EVENTS THAT ALLOW SATAN TO HAVE A CONTINUING EFFECT IN A PERSON'S LIFE OR IN A CHURCH.

---

love (see Rev. 2:4) and was not allowing Jesus to be the head of the church. So instead of plunging into a joyous youth ministry, Pete found a church in bondage—a body of believers with personal and corporate strongholds.

Many of the elders did not appear to recognize that these problems were "not against flesh and blood, but against the rulers, against the authorities, against the powers of this dark world and against the spiritual forces of evil in the heavenly realms" (Eph. 6:12). For a while Pete met with blank stares and opposition from the 25-member board of elders when he openly attributed the church's problems to unresolved personal and spiritual conflicts resulting in demonic strongholds that needed to be broken with spiritual weapons.

One elder asked Pete if he was accusing people of being demon possessed. Pete explained that demonic strongholds are not demon possession. They are sins or events that allow Satan to have a continuing effect in a person's life or in a church. He explained how a person living with unforgiveness in his or her life has a stronghold of bitterness that weakens the person and keeps him or her in bondage.

Initially, only one lay elder on the board agreed with Pete and believed that 2 Corinthians 10:3-5 could be applied to our church in its present situation:

> For though we live in the world, we do not wage war as the world does. The weapons we fight with are not the weapons of the world. On the contrary, they have divine power to demolish strongholds. We demolish arguments and every pretension that sets itself up against the knowledge of God, and we take captive every thought to make it obedient to Christ.

During our fourth month of ministry there, in the middle of the busy Christmas season, the board began dealing earnestly with the staff member who had been on medical leave for almost six months, as well as alleviating the mistrust among the leadership.

Conflict and confusion were rampant at every board meeting, and gossip and anger flourished as church members and board members tried to clarify the truth. The staff member resigned amidst the bitterness and conflict.

Soon after, board members resigned, volunteer leaders left and within several months hundreds of people walked out on the church many had attended for more than 15 years.

When the board had to deal with a threat of suicide in the church, they finally believed the battle in the church was not against flesh and blood, but against principalities and powers of darkness. They were convinced demonic strongholds existed within this church God had used so mightily in the past.

Finally, with an earnest desire to understand how Satan might be affecting the church, each of the elders accepted a copy of Neil Anderson's 45-page booklet entitled "Winning Spiritual Warfare." They also united, for the first time in many years, for a time of fasting and prayer. For a full week they took turns fasting and praying, joining with other members who also agreed to fast and pray for the church.

God honored the sincerity of the fasting that had accompanied those prayers. He was faithful to remove unbiblical practices and to prevent the suicide. But much more cleansing was needed.

The importance of personal and corporate repentance was stressed, and people were encouraged to read *Victory over the Darkness* and *Setting Your Church Free*. The need for the leaders of the church to be free in Christ before the church could be set free was emphasized, and attending a Freedom in Christ Resolving Spiritual and Personal Conflicts seminar was recommended, as well as personally going through the Steps to Freedom in Christ.

Ten months after the staff member resigned, the senior pastor and a few board members went to a Resolving Spiritual and Personal Conflicts seminar led by Neil Anderson in Rockford, Illinois. The senior pastor and one other board member attended the entire seminar. Some of the wives and a couple of other elders attended a few of the sessions. Two of those who attended were impressed with what it meant to be free in Christ, but the rest were not real interested.

The church purchased the Resolving Spiritual and Personal Conflicts video series. A month later, nearly half of the elder board attended a weekend retreat to view the video series and go through the Steps to Freedom. Those unable to attend watched it on their own. Soon the board agreed that the church needed to go through the process of "Setting Your Church Free."

The year-end, however, brought the end of elected terms for some of those elders and they were unable to participate in this endeavor to gain corporate church freedom. Other elders, who had given of themselves completely in an effort to resolve the problems, resigned and left the church. They felt they could no longer handle the stress and frustration of serving on the board. Consequently, the new year began with a new board of lay elders who were willing to give of themselves to resolve the conflicts in the church.

By mid-February of 1995, God showed them the need to go through a biblical process to release the church from its strongholds and allow God to set it free. A retreat to go through the Steps to Setting Your Church Free was scheduled for the last weekend in March.

16

THE FORTIFICATION PROCESS

ADVANCE PREPARATION

Much planning and preparation preceded the March retreat. The board members began bathing the whole process in prayer. They realized the urgency of the church's situation, and knew their hearts had to be in tune with God before He could do a complete work. They read *Setting Your Church Free* by Neil T. Anderson and Charles Mylander to gain understanding of the tool they would be using to allow God to work. They also began to comprehend the nature of the church's warfare and its biblical defense. As they continued to examine the truths in God's Word, order and unity grew amongst them.

The board then needed to choose a facilitator who would lead them through the Steps to Setting Your Church Free. No one disputed the recommendation of Dr. Gerald W. Gillaspie, a highly respected and trusted former pastor of the church. After leaving the church nearly 30 years before, he had often returned to speak or take part in its missionary conferences. His present position as a missions pastor for United World Mission qualified him to minister to church leaders. Dr. Gillaspie willingly availed himself to help at the retreat.

By the end of March, the elders had gone through the Steps and prepared themselves with prayer and repentance to enter into battle on behalf of the church. They had all committed themselves to being prepared and in attendance at the upcoming retreat.

BEGINNINGS

The retreat began on the last Friday evening of March at a small retreat center only a few miles from the church. The board members had been fasting and praying all day, planning to continue through Saturday evening. Dr. Gillaspie had arrived and they began with a simple, unpretentious song expressing their desire to open up their hearts and their lives to the work of the Holy Spirit.

And that's what they did—they laid their lives before Jesus and

THE BOARD MEMBERS WILLFULLY DISMANTLED THE MASKS OF HYPOCRISY IN THE CHURCH, ASKING GOD TO REMOLD IT AND RESHAPE IT INTO A CHURCH THAT WOULD PLEASE HIM.

became transparent before Him and each other. They sought freedom from past failures and current bondages.

Their search was conducted according to Revelation 2 and 3, by asking God to write a "letter" through the enlightenment of the Holy Spirit to discern God's views about our church. The elders asked themselves, *If God were to write a letter to our church, what would God commend and what would He rebuke?*

They also used Nehemiah 9 as a prototype for restoring worship and God's ordinances. Ezra had encouraged the Jews to "stand up and praise the Lord your God, who is from everlasting to everlasting" (v. 5) for the things He has done. The elders followed that example.

Just as Ezra had grieved and anguished in prayer over the corporate sins of his people, so our elders had agonized over the sins of our church before they arrived that Friday evening, and they would shed tears of repentance as the retreat progressed.

STRENGTHS AND WEAKNESSES

As our own spiritual leaders followed Nehemiah's example, they began by praising God and thanking Him for the church's strengths. One by one, they listed the strong points about the church, the ways God has used them corporately to do His work.

Recalling the church's strengths had been enjoyable. But Saturday morning, the board reviewed the weaknesses and painful memories of the church, objectively asking themselves what were its faults, failures and sins.

They painfully admitted pride, gossip and bitterness over broken relationships. They acknowledged they had left their first love and loved the church more than the head of the Church, Jesus Christ. They confessed that Bible study, prayer and evangelism had taken a backseat to performing and pleasing people. It was difficult to admit these weaknesses and write them down, but they desired truth. They willfully dismantled the masks of hypocrisy in the church, asking God to remold it and reshape it into a church that would please Him.

MEMORIES

Humility and confession were followed with more joyful matters as the leaders recalled the good memories they had experienced in the church.

But with the good memories also came the remembrances of those painful experiences in the church's past. As they made the transition from the good memories to the painful memories, they prayed:

Dear heavenly Father, we thank You for the riches of Your kindness, forbearance and patience, knowing that Your kindness has led us to repentance. We acknowledge that we have not extended that same patience and kindness toward those who have offended us. We have not acted gracefully and wisely in all our past dealings. Sometimes pain has come to others even when we were using our best judgment in following You. The actions and attitudes of others have also deeply wounded us. Show us where we have allowed a root of bitterness to spring up, causing trouble and defiling many. As we wait silently before You, bring to our minds all the painful memories of our church's past. In Jesus' compassionate name we pray. Amen.

Experiencing the emotional core that accompanied this Step of forgiveness was painful. Each person they needed to forgive was named and each offense was listed on a large sheet of paper in the front of the room. Each memory was lifted before the Lord, who gave them the courage to face the pain honestly and the grace to forgive fully. The list of offenses was then destroyed.

CORPORATE SINS

In Revelation 2 and 3, Jesus recalls the corporate sins to the churches and entreats them to repent. Doing the same for our own church was a heart-rending process for both the elders and the staff. A list of 15 corporate sins was agreed upon:

1. A destructive, critical and judgmental spirit (see Matt. 7:1-5).
2. Unsubmissiveness to the Lordship of Christ and the leading of the Holy Spirit (see Luke 6:46-49; 1 Thess. 5:19).
3. Allowing sins to continue and a failure to follow biblical guidelines for conflict resolution (see Matt. 18:15-18).
4. Engaging in gossip and rumors (see Jas. 3:1-12).
5. Unhealthy communication (see Eph. 4:29).
6. Failure to engage in lifestyle evangelism (see Matt. 28:19,20).
7. Apathy and lukewarmness (see Rev. 3:15,16).
8. Pride and arrogance (see 1 Peter 5:5,6).
9. Unwillingness to forgive (see 2 Cor. 2:10,11).
10. Neglecting to meet one another's needs in love (see 1 John 3:16-18).
11. Unrepentant attitude (see 1 John 1:8-10).
12. Loss of our first love (see Rev. 2:4,5).
13. Prayerlessness (see 1 Thess. 5:17,18).
14. Lack of spiritual disciplines (see Heb. 5:11-14).
15. Allowing sexual immorality in all its forms (see 1 Cor. 6:18-20).

The elders and staff prayed:

Heavenly Father, we confess [they named one corporate sin each time] as sinful and displeasing to our Lord Jesus Christ. We ask

Your forgiveness for it. We turn from it, forsake it and renounce it.
In Jesus' name we pray. Amen.

Then they individually asked the Holy Spirit to reveal their own participation in the church's corporate sins, confessing it out loud. The healing and resolution of personal conflicts that occurred was a powerful display of God's reconciling love.

SATAN'S SCHEMES

In Revelation, Jesus revealed to each of the seven churches how they had allowed Satan to attack and defeat them. Likewise, our church leaders acknowledged that Satan had crept into the operations of our church body.

As Dr. Gillaspie put it: "That is a revelation to many of us because we think Satan is only operative in Africa or Irian Jaya, but he is operative here, and he tries to creep into the Church to destroy and devastate it. Often Satan attacks us in our strengths, and causes us to be proud. That defeats our ministry and defeats our service."

PRAYER ACTION PLAN

Toward the end of the day, the board members developed a prayer action plan. They condensed the list of 15 corporate sins to 9, and for each of them said *we renounce* (repentance), *we announce* (remembrance), *we affirm* (hold on to) and *we will* (obedience). For example:

We renounce our destructive, critical, unrepentant
and judgmental spirit.
We announce that in Christ we have love and acceptance
for one another.
We affirm that because we are born of the God of love,
we can love and accept one another (see 1 John 4:7,8).
We will accept and love one another as Christ has
accepted and loves us (see Rom. 15:7).

BREAK-FAST

The board finished the Steps at 6:00 P.M. Saturday feeling exhausted, yet exhilarated. They were physically hungry, but spiritually full. Their wives were at the church waiting to conclude their retreat with an evening break-fast (a meal to break their fast).

The next day (Sunday), a combined worship service had been planned instead of the two customary services, so the elders and staff could share about their weekend together. There would be no sermon, just music and personal testimonies.

17

GOING PUBLIC

CLEANING HOUSE

Early the next morning, the elders and staff arrived at the church to pray together about the combined service, and to dedicate the facility and property to God.

Sins had been committed there, so the elders and staff took their authority in Jesus Christ over any principalities or powers of darkness that may have inhabited the building. Then they dedicated each room to God for His service only. It took a lot of grace and wisdom for these men to admit that the church had given Satan and his workers some space in its facility. They spiritually cleaned up the house of God.

When Sunday School was over, the combined worship service began. It started as it usually did with prelude music and congregational singing. But the service was different that day, because the hearts of most of our leaders were clean and repentant and because they had repented of the corporate sins of the church. As the worship team led the service with singing, the congregation joined in with "The Battle Belongs to the Lord."

Later I was reminded of the powerful Scripture verse associated with that song, the one that tells us: "Do not be afraid or discouraged because of this vast army. For the battle is not yours, but God's" (2 Chron. 20:25).

A MIGHTY FORTRESS

My love for God overflowed with emotion for what He had done that weekend. Then the words to "A Mighty Fortress Is Our God" appeared on the screens as the worship team continued to lead the congregation.

A mighty fortress is our God,
A bulwark...

My mouth continued to form the words, but my emotions clogged any sounds that might follow. I wanted to boldly sing those words of strength and truth. As I stood in church that early spring Sunday morning in 1995, I was oblivious to the hundred of others who stood with me raising their voices to our Creator and Savior.

I was remarkably impervious to anyone's attempt to analyze my grief—or was it my joy—or perhaps my past association with the truths of Martin Luther's great hymn. It probably appeared as though I were still singing as I mouthed the words...

A bulwark never failing.
Our helper, He amid the flood
Of mortal ills prevailing.
For still our ancient foe
Doth seek to work us woe—
His craft and pow'r are great,
And, armed with cruel hate,
On earth is not his equal.

The song reminded Pete and me of the painful yet triumphant memories of our past, both of us sensing God's awesome continuing power and ability to be a "Mighty Fortress."

SPIRITUAL WORSHIP

Our souls worshiped the Lord as the soloist sang "With All My Heart." Pete and I were inwardly singing to our Savior and our God, those words the composer Babbie Mason sings so truthfully from her own heart. The words voiced our own desires to live daily knowing, serving, trusting and obeying Him with all our hearts.

Pete and I continued to worship God from the depths of our spiritual beings, praising Him for our family's victories throughout the past three years and for working so mightily in our church that weekend.

The nine elders, three staff members and Dr. Gillaspie approached the platform as the final song concluded. The way they left their places in the pews and filtered to the front of the sanctuary translated peace. The way they ascended the platform spoke humility. And the expressions on their faces as they sang—"Redeemed through His infinite mercy, His child and forever I am"—uttered freedom in Christ.

SPIRITUAL VOYAGE

The elders took their places in the 13 chairs placed in a semicircle on the platform, a formation that stated unity and invited the congregation to complete the circle. High above the choir loft directly behind them stood a large wooden cross, illuminated by fluorescent lights, declaring in its simplicity the reason for the church and the reason these men sat on the platform. A solitary microphone stood in the center of the platform.

Dr. Gillaspie, the former-pastor-now-facilitator, gently came to the microphone with his Bible in his hand to explain the spiritual voyage from which the 13 had just returned. While summarizing the seven Steps to Setting Our Church Free, he conveyed the painfulness of the process and the depth of commitment these men had experienced. He explained the corporate sins of our church and how these men not only repented of them before God, but also personally repented of their own involvements in these sins.

Dr. Gillaspie told how the leaders had developed, by God's grace, a prayer action plan. He told how they had renounced or repented of their failures and then asked for God's forgiveness. He summarized the weekend as a "time of holiness before God, a day of glorious liberation." He characterized the church leaders as different men now, men who had made a covenant with one another, and a covenant with God that they would obey.

SOUL BARING

One by one the elders poured out their hearts before the congregation.

When the elders finished their testimonies, very few dry eyes remained. People were deeply moved by the Holy Spirit, and they were unquestionably changed by the humble repentance of most of their spiritual leaders.

Although the people were moved by what many of the elders experienced, the fire of revival did not ignite among the people. They did not let that spark begun by the elders become a conflagration that would spread throughout the church. I was disappointed,

COMPLETE FREEDOM DOES NOT ALWAYS COME INSTANTANEOUSLY. GOD OFTEN REMOVES JUST ONE LAYER AT A TIME; AND WHILE WE WAIT, OUR FAITH GROWS AS WE TRUST THE HOLY SPIRIT TO SEARCH HEARTS AND CONVICT OUR SOULS.

but I had to remember that this was all new to many people. Some were overwhelmed and possibly confused by the depth of confession the leaders had experienced. And I reminded myself that our family's journey to freedom started more than three years before. Layers of bondage were still being peeled off by God. I knew I had to show patience and grace as the congregation began to digest this tidbit of freedom.

We rejoice in those leaders who experienced complete freedom in Christ that weekend, and we trust God to continue to work. God is working in the church and we are praying He will bring each person, one by one, to freedom. We are excited to watch God slowly work in people's lives. God removed one huge layer of sin and bondage from the church that weekend and He will complete the work—in His time.

We learned in our own family that complete freedom does not always come instantaneously. God often removes just one layer at a time; and while we wait, our faith grows as we trust the Holy Spirit to search hearts and convict our souls. God will honor the fervent, consistent prayer of the righteous (see Jas. 5:16).

We won't stop praying for God's Church, because the head of the Church is Jesus Christ. The Church is Jesus' Body, and He is the Savior of that Body (see Eph. 5:23; Col. 1:24).

Many elders are committed to the flock God has given them and they are faithfully waiting for God to do a complete work within the church. "Keep watch over yourselves and all the flock of which the Holy Spirit has made you overseers. Be shepherds of the church of God, which he bought with his own blood" (Acts 20:28).

THE TRUTH WILL SET YOU FREE

*"THEN YOU WILL KNOW THE TRUTH,
AND THE TRUTH WILL SET YOU FREE."*
—JOHN 8:32

After three years of spiritual warfare in our family and three years of serving in a church under attack, we can say God has truly blessed us with freedom. "So if the Son sets you free, you will be

> **WAR IS NEVER PRETTY, NOR IS IT SOMETHING WE DESIRE; BUT WHEN OUR FREEDOM IS AT STAKE, WE WILLINGLY GO INTO BATTLE.**

free indeed" (John 8:36). We have seen God's glory and known that He has also been glorified.

I still occasionally ask myself, *Why did all this happen? Why was our family so fiercely attacked? Why were we subsequently put in a church so desperately needing freedom?* I don't have an answer to these questions except that God was incredibly glorified through it all. The battle belongs to Him and we are called only to be faithful.

War is never pretty, nor is it something we desire; but when our freedom is at stake, we willingly go into battle. We trust our General to sufficiently arm us and outstrategize the enemy. We believe our army is stronger than the enemy's because our General has already eternally defeated the leader of the opposing side. We enter war as boys and girls—we emerge as men and women, strong and focused. Though wounded in battle, we are never defeated. And not until we experience war, do we really experience freedom.

NOT UNTIL

Not until we saw the depth of evil's darkness,
...did we truly comprehend the glory of God's light.
Not until we walked through the valley of the shadow of death,
...did we fully value the life we have in Christ.
Not until we were visited by the inhabitants of hell,
...did we understand the glory of the presence of God.
Not until we buffeted the principalities and powers of darkness,
...did we really feel the precious loving arms of Jesus.
Not until we were hard pressed on every side,
...did we fathom the wholeness found in Jesus Christ.
Not until we totally repented of our sins,
...did we realize the amazing joy of living a holy life.
Not until we had a small taste of hell,
...did we crave the promise of heaven.
Not until we experienced incredible fear,
...did we appreciate the amazing peace of God.
Not until we saw Satan's agenda of death,
...did we truly glory in Christ's victory over death.
Not until we saw Satan's power,
...did we realize how incredibly more powerful is our God.
Not until we knew Satan was powerless over the believer,

...did we experience the abundant life found in Christ.
Not until we experienced war,
...did we really experience freedom.

We rejoice that greater is He that is in us than he that is in the world (see 1 John 4:4). We rejoice that through Christ "we are hard pressed on every side, but not crushed; perplexed, but not in despair; persecuted, but not abandoned; struck down, but not destroyed" (2 Cor. 4:8,9). We rejoice that the time is short for Satan and his demons who will one day be cast into the lake of burning sulfur where they will be tormented day and night forever and ever (see Rev. 20:10). We rejoice that someday Jesus will come again and we will live forever in the place He has prepared for us—a place without evil, without sin, without fear and without darkness—a place where we will rejoice forever with Jesus, our Savior and our Light. And we rejoice that this message of truth is being proclaimed, even through our family's story, all to His honor and glory.

But the Lord stood at my side and gave me strength, so that through me the message might be fully proclaimed...And I was delivered from the lion's mouth. The Lord will rescue me from every evil attack and will bring me safely to his heavenly kingdom. To him be glory for ever and ever. Amen (2 Tim. 4:17,18).

PART II

LEADING YOUR CHILDREN TO FREEDOM IN CHRIST

18

OVERCOMING
DECEPTION AND FEAR

Pete and Sue Vanderhook are to be commended for sharing their story. I know firsthand the risk of "coming out of the evangelical Christian closet" with the truth about the reality of the spiritual world in which we live. Walking in the light (see 1 John 1:7), and "speaking the truth in love" (Eph. 4:15) carries an element of risk if our friends, family and community don't understand or prefer to live in denial. But that is precisely the problem. Listen to the sober warning of the prophet Hosea in the Old Testament:

> My people are destroyed for lack of knowledge. Because you have rejected knowledge, I also will reject you from being My priest. Since you have forgotten the law of your God, *I also will forget your children* (Hos. 4:6, *NASB*, emphasis mine)

Ignorance is not bliss—it is defeat. Paul was able to say, "For we are not ignorant of his [Satan's] schemes" (2 Cor. 2:11, *NASB*). Are we able to echo Paul's words in our present Western world? This is not a time to live in denial, and ignorance of the truth is no excuse. We must know the truth that will set us free in Christ. We must strive for a balanced answer for ourselves and our children. So where do we start?

Dear mother and father, uncle and aunt, brother and sister, pastor and minister to children, Sunday School teacher and playground director, neighbor and friend, we start with ourselves.

This is what Pete and Sue discovered as they desperately sought for biblically-based material and a Christ-centered answer for their children. Parents often bring their children to our conferences hoping we will "fix" them. Without exception we schedule an appointment with the parents first.

We are not blaming the mother and father, nor are we suggesting they are the primary cause for their child's problem. But we are saying that a major factor in the recovery and growth of every child is a Christ-centered home where the parents are free in Christ. We

---

CHRISTIANS CAN BE UNDER ATTACK, NOT BECAUSE THEY ARE DOING ANYTHING WRONG, BUT BECAUSE THEY ARE DOING SOMETHING VERY RIGHT.

---

could potentially help some children apart from their parents, but how much has been accomplished in the long run if we have to put them back into dysfunctional homes?

Included in appendix A are the Steps to Freedom in Christ for adults. We at Freedom in Christ Ministries estimate that 85 percent of people in the Christian community can work through this process on their own. The possibility of that happening and the assurance of staying free will be greatly enhanced if they first read *Victory over the Darkness* and *The Bondage Breaker*. The other 15 percent need the help of a biblically trained facilitator/encourager.

The theological rationale and practical process of counseling others is provided in my book *Helping Others Find Freedom in Christ* and in its youth edition (title forthcoming). Please see appendix B for a full listing of resources for yourself and your church. Understand that the Steps to Freedom in Christ do not set people free. Let me repeat: *Who* sets us free is Christ, and *what* sets us free is our response to Him in repentance and faith. There is no substitute for the Word of God. It is the truth of God's Word that sets us free.

Once you have secured your own freedom in Christ, I strongly recommend that you read *The Seduction of Our Children*. The book is devoted to parenting, understanding our children and the world to which they are being exposed. Some of the following instructions for helping your children find their freedom in Christ have been adapted from Part 3 in *The Seduction of Our Children*. Another helpful book for a family experiencing spiritual attack is *Reclaiming Surrendered Ground* by my dear friend Jim Logan. Before we turn our attention to that, however, let me clarify two important issues from Pete and Sue's story.

The first concerns their house. Could it have been "haunted"? That is a difficult question to answer after the fact. Establishing cause is not always easy. For instance, Pete and Sue had personal issues to resolve as we all have, and their strong stand for the sanctity of life could also have been a factor in their spiritual battle.

Christians can be under attack, not because they are doing anything wrong, but because they are doing something very right. It is similar to the problem of suffering. We will certainly suffer the consequences of our own sin and irresponsible behavior, but we can also suffer for righteousness sake as Job and many other courageous saints have done throughout church history. Paul says, "All who desire to live godly in Christ Jesus will be persecuted" (2 Tim. 3:12, *NASB*).

It should not surprise us when we experience opposition to the gospel and a message of truth. John records: "The light is come into the world, and men loved the darkness rather than the light; for their deeds were evil. For everyone who does evil hates the light, and does not come to the light, lest his deeds should be exposed" (John 3:19,20, *NASB*). Those who will not repent and choose the truth must flee from the light or try to discredit the light source. Only "in Christ" can we live in the light and speak the truth in love. What is so insidious about the devil is his relentless pursuit of those who are most vulnerable, such as our children.

The house Pete and Sue moved into *could* have been a factor. Who knows what the previous owners or occupants did in that house? They could have dedicated the house to Satan, or performed satanic rituals in it. They could have used the home as a base for selling drugs or holding séances. Do demons inhabit inanimate objects such as houses or items in our homes? To be honest, I'm not sure, but Scripture does indicate the possibility. We read in Acts 19:18,19:

> Many also of those who had believed kept coming, confess-
> ing and disclosing their practices. And many of those who
> practiced magic brought their books together and [began]
> burning them in the sight of all (*NASB*).

In Revelation 2:13, Jesus said to the church at Pergamum, "I know where you dwell, where Satan's throne is" (*NASB*).

We do know that "The Son of God appeared for this purpose, that He might destroy the works of the devil" (1 John 3:8, *NASB*). Recapturing lost ground, setting captives free and restoring the years that the locusts have eaten is part of the continuing work of Christ. Pete and Sue were the legal owners of the house; therefore, they were and still are under the authority of the laws of the land God established for our protection (see Rom. 13:1-7). We are required to be good stewards of all God has entrusted to us (see 1 Cor. 4:1,2).

Why not walk through your newly acquired property and ver-
bally renounce any prior use of property that would not please the Lord, or renounce any prior commitment of that property to anyone other than the Lord? Then commit the property and all that is in it to the Lord. Ask for His divine protection, and resist the devil. Scripture clearly says, "Submit therefore to God. Resist the devil and he will flee from you" (Jas. 4:7, *NASB*). You have nothing to lose by doing this and potentially much to gain. I would personally cleanse my house of anything that could hinder my walk with God, or cast doubt on my identity in Christ.

On the other hand, I personally resent the notion that God-creat-
ed objects must be shunned simply because they are used by the occult. A goat's head may be symbolic of Satanism, but God created goats and they are not evil. Neither is a pumpkin evil just because the forerunners of Halloween carved them into jack-o'-lanterns to frighten off evil spirits. "For everything created by God is good, and nothing is to be rejected, if it is received with gratitude; for it is sanctified by means of the word of God and prayer" (1 Tim. 4:4,5, *NASB*). All God has created and entrusted to us can be committed to the Lord.

When seeking to resolve personal and spiritual conflicts in our homes, we must consider all reality and every possible cause. Parents should resolve their issues individually and as a couple. We have discovered that individuals can resolve their own personal issues, but still have unresolved issues that must be faced as a couple.

Consequently, in the *The Christ-Centered Marriage*, which I coauthored with Charles Mylander, we have presented an effective process for setting marriages free. God's intention is that the two become one in Christ and be a visible model of the relationship the Church has with Christ. Because parents are the God-established authorities in the home over their children, they need to exercise that authority in godly ways. One way to do that is by committing all that has been entrusted to them, including their properties, ministries and families to the Lord.

We have discovered the same phenomena in our churches. Individual staff and board members can resolve their own personal issues and leave unresolved corporate issues. Many church leaders throughout the world have resolved their corporate conflicts by going through the process provided in our book *Setting Your Church Free*, as did the church where Pete and Sue Vander Hook served. Ungodly decisions made by former spiritual leaders must be resolved by those who are now in positions of authority of the same corporate body.

The same applies for couples in marriage. If they have made decisions or done things as a couple that are wrong, they need to face the truth and resolve the issues as a couple.

In providing a balanced answer for our families, we must also consider the possibility of health issues. Children can become "wired" by eating junk food or overdosing on sweets. A father asked if I would talk to his 19-year-old son. The young man appeared quite normal although he was educationally handicapped and unable to read. I asked if he had ever been checked for dyslexia. I was surprised when his father said no even though he had undergone almost every other medical test.

Some problems are clearly physical; others are clearly spiritual. The difficult cases are those that could be one or the other, or both. When I began my ministry 25 years ago, the big issue was hypoglycemia. I got caught up in it. I suggested to every fourth person I counseled as a pastor to get a glucose tolerance test. Most reported back that they tested borderline. Now we rarely hear about low blood sugar. What happened to hypoglycemia? Did all Americans change their eating habits?

Then came Epstein-Barr or chronic fatigue syndrome. Now people claim to have attention deficit disorder (ADD).

Of course, we should consider a physical explanation for these disorders, but in too many cases that is the only aspect of health being considered. In our society, every possible physical explanation must be exhausted. When no physical connection is found, people say, "There is nothing left to do now but pray."

Why not seek first the kingdom of God (see Matt. 6:33), especially if the symptoms relate to the mind? If nothing is resolved by first submitting to God and resisting the devil (see Jas. 4:7), then visit the doctor. Because we are both physical and spiritual beings, we need both the church and the hospital.

The Steps to Freedom in Christ are a safe way to "check it out." But we are doing far more than just checking it out. We are trying to help people get radically right with God so the Great Physician can bring healing and wholeness to the Body of Christ. We have nothing to lose and potentially a lot to gain.

A mother of two boys heard me speak about the battle for the mind at a writers' conference. She bought *The Bondage Breaker* and worked through the Steps herself that evening. As a result, a whole new possibility opened up for her children who had been diagnosed as having an obsessive compulsive disorder (OCD). Medication had only made their problems worse. She had never even considered asking her sons if they had thoughts or voices telling them what to do. When she finally did ask them what was going on inside, they readily admitted to a battle for their minds. She was then able to lead them through modified Steps to Freedom for children, which we will discuss in the next chapter. Both of the boys experienced immediate resolution and freedom.

In Peter and Sue's case and in many similar cases, we must consider the possibility of coming under attack for taking a strong stand for the sake of righteousness. We should not be surprised when we experience spiritual opposition for taking a public stand for Christ. Paul said, "For we wanted to come to you—I, Paul, more than once—and yet Satan thwarted us" (1 Thess. 2:18, *NASB*). How did he do that? I don't know, and I don't think there is any one way Satan operates. Satan is too clever to limit himself to only one form of attack. But I do know that we are to:

Be of sober spirit, be on the alert. Your adversary, the devil, prowls about like a roaring lion, seeking someone to devour. But resist him, firm in your faith, knowing that the same experiences of suffering are being accomplished by your brethren who are in the world (1 Pet. 5:8,9, *NASB*).

I think it is safe, however, to say that the primary strategies of Satan are deception and fear. A lion roars to paralyze its prey in fear. Then he consumes it. Most of Satan's work is achieved by deceived people who believe his lies. "The father of lies" (John 8:44) has blinded the minds of "the unbelieving" (2 Cor. 4:4, *NASB*), and such people oppose the work of God. Satan cannot stand against a united Church. Therefore, much of his effort is to deceive Christian workers and family members so they turn against each other. Look at James 3:13-16:

Who among you is wise and understanding? Let him show by his good behavior his deeds in the gentleness of wisdom. But if you have bitter jealously and selfish ambition in your heart, do not be arrogant and so lie against the truth. This wisdom is not that which comes from above, but is earthly, natural, demonic. For where jealousy and selfish ambition exist, there is disorder and every evil thing (*NASB*).

The first advice I give to parents who are struggling with their children is, "Don't let this pull you apart. That is exactly what Satan wants by attacking your children. You must combat this with a united front." A house divided against itself cannot stand. Pointing fingers and casting blame is to play right into the hands of your adversary.

Now suppose the mother and father have sufficiently dealt with all their issues, committed their home to the Lord and stood against the attacks of the enemy. Each child would still need to assume personal responsibility, which involves the second issue. Why did it take so long to resolve the night terrors of Pete and Sue's second child, Jared?

One reason was blocked memories, which I will discuss later. The other reason was his struggle with fear and anxiety. In my book *Walking in the Light* (the youth edition is entitled *Know Light, No Fear*), I analyze and offer a biblical response to both fear and anxiety. Let me summarize the key points.

Anxiety is a fear of the unknown, or fear without an adequate cause. The basis for anxiety is uncertainty and a lack of trust. According to Scripture we worry about what we treasure in our hearts (see Matt. 6:19-24), and we worry about tomorrow (see vv. 25-34) because we don't know what will happen. Jesus said, "Do not be anxious for tomorrow" (v. 34, *NASB*), because your heavenly Father will take care of you.

SPIRITUAL LIFE IS THE ULTIMATE VALUE. IT WILL BE HEAVEN WHEN OUR SOULS SEPARATE FROM OUR BODIES; IT WILL BE HELL IF OUR SOULS ARE SEPARATED FROM GOD.

To be anxious is to be double-minded. That is why Jesus said, "No one can serve two masters; for either he will hate the one and love the other, or he will hold to one and despise the other. You cannot serve God and mammon. For this reason I say to you, do not be anxious for your life" (vv. 24,25, *NASB*). A mind that is free and pure is single-focused.

James wrote that if we are experiencing trials in life, we should ask the Lord in faith for wisdom. But if we are overcome by doubting thoughts, we will be overcome by the storms of life. "Let not that man expect that he will receive anything from the Lord, being a double-minded man, unstable in all his ways" (Jas. 1:7,8, *NASB*). God is the antidote for anxiety. Therefore, cast "all your anxiety upon Him, because He cares for you" (1 Pet. 5:7, *NASB*). We have to choose to trust Him and turn to Him in prayer. "Be anxious for nothing, but in everything by prayer and supplication with thanksgiving let your requests be made known to God" (Phil. 4:6, *NASB*).

Unlike anxiety, fear has an object. Fears are even categorized by their objects. For instance, claustrophobia is a fear of closed places. Xenophobia is a fear of strangers or foreigners. Agoraphobia is a generalized fear of the "market place" or public places where people seem to close in on them. A fear object must have two attributes to be legitimate: It must be perceived as potent (having some power), and it must be imminent (present).

For instance, I have what I think is a healthy fear of rattlesnakes. But as I am writing this, I sense no fear for them at all because none are in the room. If you were to throw one into my room, I would have an immediate fear response because it is now both imminent and potent in my own mind. If I didn't see it, I wouldn't be afraid either, even though I should be.

A fear object can be eliminated by removing just one of its attributes. For instance, death is no longer a legitimate fear object for us because God has removed one of the attributes. Although death is still imminent, it is no longer potent, because "death is swallowed up in victory" (1 Cor. 15:54, NASB). Therefore, Paul could write, "For to me, to live is Christ, and to die is gain" (Phil. 1:21).

Some would believe the worst thing that could happen to them is to die; but physical death is not the ultimate value. We would just be in the presence of our heavenly Father and in far better shape than we are now. Spiritual life is the ultimate value. It will be heaven when our souls separate from our bodies; it will be hell if our souls are separated from God. "And do not fear those who kill the body, but are unable to kill the soul; but rather fear Him who is able to destroy both soul and body in hell" (Matt. 10:28, NASB).

That is not a license to commit suicide nor an excuse for being a poor steward of the physical life God has given to us. It is a liberating truth, however. Those who are free from the fear of death are free to live their lives in responsible ways. We are also not to fear humankind. "Even if you should suffer for the sake of righteousness, you are blessed. And do not fear their intimidation, and do not be troubled, but sanctify Christ as Lord in your hearts, always being ready to make a defense to everyone who asks you to give an account for the hope that is in you, yet with gentleness and reverence" (1 Pet. 3:14,15, NASB).

Why is "the fear of the Lord...the beginning of wisdom" (Prov. 9:10)? Because the fear of the Lord is the one fear that expels all other fears. "Do not fear what they fear, and do not dread it. The Lord Almighty is the one you are to regard as holy, he is the one you are to fear, he is the one you are to dread, and he will be a sanctuary" (Isa. 8:12-14). What two attributes of God make Him the ultimate fear object? He is omnipotent (all powerful), and omnipresent (everywhere present).

We don't worship God because He needs His ego stroked, and He doesn't need you and me to tell Him who He is. God is totally sufficient in and of Himself. We worship God because we need to keep His divine attributes constantly before us. If we did, the following scenario could occur:

Our child comes screaming into our bedroom shouting, "There is something in my room!"

We could calmly respond. "I know honey, God is there."

Your child would likely say, "No! Something else!" The child did sense something else, but also needs to know that God is always present. And because He is, we can submit to Him and resist the devil.

I have asked Christian congregations throughout the world if they have had fearful encounters with a spiritual force that frightened them—at least 50 percent have responded affirmatively. I have found that percentage to be higher among Christian leaders, which shouldn't surprise us. At least 35 percent of the same audiences have awakened either terrorized or alertly awake at a precise time in the morning, such as 3:00 A.M.

Such a terror attack may feel as though pressure is being exerted on the person's chest or something is grabbing his or her throat. When the person tries to respond physically, he or she can't. The person wants to call upon the Lord, but can't even say the name "Jesus." Why not?

Remember, "The weapons of our warfare are not of the flesh, but divinely powerful for the destruction of fortresses" (2 Cor. 10:4, NASB). Trying to physically respond may prove fruitless. Because God is "able to judge the thoughts and intentions of the heart" (Heb. 4:12, NASB), we can always call upon Him in our hearts and minds. As soon as we acknowledge Him and His authority in the inner person, we will be free to say "Jesus." And that is all we have to say.

Please don't assume that every time you awaken in the middle of the night you are experiencing a spiritual attack. In most cases you probably need to go to the bathroom or your stomach is not reacting well to something you ate. You could also be rudely awakened by a burglar trying to enter your house, or a gust of wind causing a shutter to bang. But if a definite pattern exists, such as a certain time and the awakening is abrupt as opposed to a gradual awareness, then it could be a spiritual attack.

I must confess I am not a timid person, but I have felt the terror of a spiritual attack at night. In each instance, I have experienced immediate victory by turning to God in the inner man, and then verbally resisting the devil.

Persistent attacks are usually because of some unresolved issues either in your life or in your home. Panic attacks may also occur during the day. Usually they can be traced to deceiving thoughts. Have you ever been driving your car and become suddenly overwhelmed by impulsive thoughts such as, *Drive into that car beside you* or *Jump out of the car*? Have you ever felt panic stricken as you looked over a cliff and thought, *Jump*?

Many people who struggle with agoraphobia have mitral valve prolapse. It usually is not a serious condition of the heart; however, it does cause the heart to flutter, often causing people to panic. These people don't want to panic in a social setting so they live in avoidance of having a reaction in public. The most common remedy is to stay at home, but that is not the Lord's solution. They are letting the fear control their lives. These kinds of fears need to be faced and overcome. Some wise sage said, "Do the thing you fear the most and the death of fear is certain."

I have talked to several ladies who struggled with postpartum depression. A woman may have just given birth to a third child who is crying for attention. The other two children are fighting over a toy. In her weak and vulnerable condition, she suddenly has the thought, *Kill your baby! How can I possibly think that? What kind of a mother am I that I would even think of killing my own child?* That kind of attack on the mind by the accuser of the brethren has left many people questioning their salvation or paralyzed in fear.

If we shared some of these experiences with secular doctors or counselors, they would call it an anxiety attack or a panic attack. Why don't they call it what it is—a fear attack. Because they can't identify the fear object, it falls under the definition of anxiety. I can identify the object of their fear, however, and so should you.

Every child of God should be taught to discern a spiritual attack and know how to resolve it. Unfortunately, many Christians are not mature enough to discern the nature of the battle they are in, as the writer of Hebrews clearly stated: "For everyone who partakes only of milk is not accustomed to the word of righteousness, for he is a babe. But solid food is for the mature, who because of practice have their senses trained to discern good and evil" (Heb. 5:13,14, *NASB*).

A major difference exists between fears developed over time and those that are essentially attacks. The latter can be dealt with at the time. When people "hear" or "see" something that frightens them, which they discern to be a spiritual attack, they can exercise their authority in Christ by submitting to Him and resisting the devil.

IT IS IMPORTANT TO UNDERSTAND THAT AUTHORITY DOES NOT INCREASE WITH VOLUME. WE DON'T SHOUT OUT THE DEVIL.

Taking our place in Christ may require us to verbally express the truth of 1 John 5:18: "He who was born of God keeps him and the evil one does not touch him" (*NASB*). I could share many illustrations of Christians who have stood their ground under attack by deceived people saying, "I'm a child of God, you cannot touch me." This requires discernment, however. The person could be mentally retarded or desperate enough to steal for food.

A large lady who was deeply in spiritual bondage suddenly rose from her chair in my office and began walking toward me with menacing eyes. What would you do? I calmly said out loud, "I'm a child of God, the evil one cannot touch me." She stopped in her tracks. Understand that I was not addressing the lady, but the spiritual forces she had given in to.

It is important to understand that authority does not increase with volume. We don't shout out the devil. It is no different from exercising parental authority. If you are trying to gain control of your children by screaming at them, you are not exercising your God-given authority, you are undermining it. All you are doing is operating in the flesh, which is precisely what the devil wants you to do. Fear of anything other than God is mutually exclusive of faith in God.

Irrational fears learned through time and repetition must be unlearned, and that will take time. First, legitimate fears necessary for survival must be differentiated from irrational fears (phobias). Phobias either compel us to do something irresponsible, or prevent us from doing that which is responsible.

Pete and Sue's second child struggled with irrational fears. It took much prayer and time to root out the causes. Some children may be reluctant to share with their parents the experiences they had that led them to fear the unknown. They could be intimidated by the dark side not to share anything. Others may be afraid to tell their parents because they were specifically instructed not to do whatever it was that created the fear.

Some may not recall what they did to open the door for the evil one. In such cases we must do what Pete and Sue did. They continued to establish all their children in Christ, helping them to realize the truth that "greater is He who is in you, than he who is in the world" (1 John 4:4, *NASB*). "For God has not given us a spirit of timidity, but of power and love and discipline" (2 Tim. 1:7, *NASB*).

When we don't humanly know what is keeping people in bondage, we instruct them to ask the Lord. Sometimes they receive an immediate response to their prayers. In other cases the answers come as they continue to grow in Christ. That is why Paul wrote: "Therefore do not go on passing judgment before the time, but wait until the Lord comes who will both bring to light the things hidden in darkness and disclose the motives of men's hearts; and then each man's praise will come to him from God" (1 Cor. 4:5, *NASB*).

When I was a child, the villains in horror movies were King Kong, Godzilla and the Blob. They were things we could see. Today the horror movies are *Poltergeist*, *The Exorcist*, *Omen*, etc. Hollywood has moved from physical monsters to spiritual entities scaring the daylights out of a gullible public. Consequently, the vast majority of Americans are deathly frightened of things that go bump in the night, and have no fear of God. That is the exact opposite of Scripture. Not one verse in the Bible instructs us to fear Satan. God is the only legitimate fear object.

We have all heard the computer lingo, garbage in—garbage out. Our children are most vulnerable to this well-known axiom. All parents have the responsibility to protect their children from harmful movies and television programs. Hollywood is incapable of giving a balanced biblical answer for the world in which we live.

Children can have nightmares after watching horror movies because they are easily scared. But it is difficult to establish an authoritative answer to combat the fear once it has been established. Before Paul warned us about the need to put on the armor of God in Ephesians 6, he assured us of our rich heritage and position in Christ in chapters 1 and 2. We need to observe the same order.

During a conference, a mother talked to me about her daughter who was having nightmares and visitations. Little did this mother know the conference would have such an impact on herself. She had no idea how much she was living in bondage until she found her freedom in Christ. She then began to help her four-year-old daughter realize all she is in Christ and all Satan is not. One night she heard her daughter say, "You have to leave me alone, I belong to Jesus." Neither the mother nor the daughter are having any more problems. Both are free to be all God has called them to be.

19

STEPS TO SETTING YOUR CHILD FREE

Whenever I travel by air, I hear the flight attendants dutifully point out the safety features of the aircraft and instruct us in the proper use of the oxygen masks should they lose cabin pressure. They always tell the parents to place their own oxygen masks on first before attempting to help their children. Panic-stricken parents gasping for air are in no position to help their children. Although the air is thin, the children are in no immediate danger. They can wait until the parents have resolved their own issues.

The same follows for spiritually helping our children. They need us to be strong and confident in the Lord. We cannot impart what we don't possess. If the parents are not free in Christ, they will have a difficult, if not impossible, time leading their children to freedom. Let's examine from a parental perspective the most definitive passage in the New Testament for helping others find freedom in Christ:

> And the Lord's bond-servant must not be quarrelsome, but be kind to all, able to teach, patient when wronged, with gentleness correcting those who are in opposition, if perhaps God may grant them repentance leading to the knowledge of the truth, and they may come to their senses and escape from the snare of the devil, having been held captive by him to do his will (2 Tim. 2:24-26, NASB).

As you can see this is a kind, gentle, able-to-teach, patient-when-wronged model that requires the presence of God to set a captive free. The passage also clearly teaches that freedom comes from knowing the truth. The battle is shown to be in the mind because when they come to their senses they escape from the snare of the devil. It also establishes the fact that the one who is going to help the child must be the Lord's bond servant.

Christian counseling should be understood as an encounter with God rather than a technique we learn. Jesus is the wonderful counselor and only He can grant repentance and set a captive free. Pastors, counselors, teachers and parents must be totally dependent upon the Lord to be effective in helping children.

Have you been patient when wronged by your child? Have you been kind or harsh? Have you corrected your child's opposition with gentleness? Have you known the truth well enough to teach him or her what to do when he or she is under attack? You may need to start by asking your child to forgive you for the times you have not disciplined in love or understood the true nature of his or her problem.

If a parent has severely disciplined a child without knowing what is going on inside, the child has probably written the parent off, and any other authority figure that has tried to shape only his or her behavior without understanding the battle that may be going on for the child's mind. Can you imagine the frustration of hearing voices or experiencing a frightening presence in a room and not having anyone to talk to about it? And how would you feel if you tried to share what was going on with another person and they wouldn't accept it? What a relief it would be for a person to know he or she is not going crazy, but a battle is raging for his or her mind and the problem is resolvable!

In this chapter I am going to share how you can help your preteen and preschool child. If you are trying to help another adult or teenager, we recommend that you read the following books and in the order given:

Adult	Teenage
Victory over the Darkness	*Stomping Out the Darkness*
The Bondage Breaker	*The Bondage Breaker Youth Edition*
Helping Others Find Freedom in Christ	*Helping Young People Find Freedom in Christ* (tentative)
Walking in the Light	*Know Light, No Fear*
A Way of Escape	*Purity Under Pressure*

In addition to our adult Steps to Freedom we have developed youth (ages 12 to 18) and single adult (ages 18 to 25) Steps. If those who are trying to help children find freedom in Christ have already gone through the Steps themselves, they will have a greater awareness of what must be resolved and how to do it. Their experience will also qualify them to be examples to follow rather than people who are judging or condemning. Children will want to experience the same joy and freedom they witness in the one helping them.

My book *Helping Others Find Freedom in Christ* provides much more theological truth and practical application than can be covered in this book. In the majority of cases, however, the following will be sufficient for parents:

LEADING YOUR CHILD TO FREEDOM IN CHRIST AGES 9–12

Without sounding redundant let me say again, the parent, pastor, teacher or counselor working with the child must be sure of his or her own identity and freedom in Christ before trying to help another. Understand that obtaining spiritual freedom is not spiritual maturity. All other aspects of normal development are still in process. Be careful to use terms a child of this age can understand. The prayers and doctrinal statement have been modified from the adult Steps to Freedom to accommodate younger children. We will share later what to do if the child is too young to read.

If children are going to cooperate, they must be told that they are not the problem, but that they have a problem for which they must assume their own responsibility. If our attitude is, "What's wrong with you anyway," they will probably become defensive.

We asked one young boy if he had thoughts in his head telling him what to do. He said he did, and we asked what the thoughts were saying. "I'm no good!" he replied. The frustrated parents of this adopted child had all but thrown in the towel trying to control his behavior. The message he was receiving internally and externally was "I am incorrigible."

The goal is to resolve the child's personal and spiritual conflicts in Christ and find the peace of God that passes all understanding. But for the rest of his or her life the child needs to know that he or she must be responsible for what he or she thinks. For this process to work, we must have the child's cooperation to share with us any mental opposition or thoughts he or she is having that are in direct opposition to what we are attempting to do.

THE POWER OF SATAN IS IN THE LIE. AS SOON AS THE LIE IS EXPOSED, THE POWER IS BROKEN.

The power of Satan is in the lie. As soon as the lie is exposed, the power is broken. The control center is the mind, and if Satan can get the child to believe a lie he can control that child's life. Thoughts such as, *This isn't going to work,* or *God doesn't love you,* etc., can interfere only if the child believes the lies. We tell people it doesn't make any difference if the thoughts they are hearing are coming from a loud speaker on the wall or inside their own heads—in either case, don't pay attention to them.

Two reasons prevent most people, including our children, from sharing what is going on inside. First, if they even remotely suspect we won't receive the information appropriately, they won't share it. Patronizing responses such as, "You're just having a bad day," or "It will go away," or "You have an overactive imagination," or judgmental statements such as, "You need to see a shrink!" keep people from revealing what they are thinking.

The last response is feared the most. These people already fear they are going crazy; therefore, anything we do to suggest that possibility will only drive them away. Many adults fear they are going crazy and are frightened by the prospects of being drugged. We have assured many people that nothing they could share would surprise us. The thoughts are often threatening or vulgar. Once they know we understand that those thoughts are not their own thoughts, they are more free to share what is going on inside.

Second, they may be threatened by the voices. Usually they are threats to harm them when they get home or back in their bedrooms. The threat can be directed toward others such as their fathers or siblings. They believe they have to obey the voices to save someone else. Much of the intimidation threatens them not to share what is really going on inside. Demons are like cockroaches. They only come out in the safety of darkness. They fear being exposed. When we turn on the lights they scurry for the shadows.

All this intimidation is to keep children from sharing what must be shared to be free in Christ. The problem isn't at home or in their rooms, it's in their minds. So if they resolve their problems in our offices, they will be resolved in their homes. And if the problems are resolved in the parents' bedrooms they will be resolved in the children's bedrooms. One person called hours later and said with a great deal of delight, "They're not here either!" They never were "there."

Children will be set free by what they do, not what we do. Because Satan is under no obligation to obey our thoughts, children must pray the prayers out loud, and assume personal responsibility to resolve the issues standing between themselves and God. Interference is common during the early stages of the Steps to Freedom, but we can gain enough control by exercising our authority to assist the person in becoming free enough to do what he or she must do to get right with God.

Even though people struggle through the Steps, a valuable lesson is learned in the process. They learn the nature of the spiritual battle, and how to win it whenever they are under attack. If we try to "cast out" a demon for them, they will believe it is necessary to call us whenever they are under future attacks. They need to learn how to call upon the Lord. He is the deliverer.

Parents, pastors, teachers or counselors are the facilitators in the process. Children under attack must pray the prayers themselves. It is not what we do that sets them free; it is what they choose to renounce, confess, forgive, etc.

It is important to watch them closely throughout the Steps, especially their eyes. If they start to mentally drift, ask them what they are hearing. In some cases they may be seeing something. The moment they share it, the lie is exposed, and the power is broken. If they experience much interference, slow down or you may lose them. We sometimes instruct them to get up and walk around the room to refocus their minds and to ensure them of their volitional control, which they must choose to exercise.

Children commonly experience severe headaches or feel as though they are becoming sick. Some will say they are going to throw up. Usually the physical symptoms stop when they share them. If not, pray again that Satan stop harassing them. If they say they have to leave, let them go—they will be back within minutes. Never try to physically restrain them. In the midst of a battle they will feel violated if anyone touches them. The weapons of warfare are not of the flesh (see 2 Cor. 10:3-5). Prayer is our weapon against such attacks.

Trust is an essential prerequisite. If children trust us they will believe what we say. Trust must be preceded by our assurance that they are accepted, significant and secure. The more we explain and reassure them, the more they will believe and trust us. They have a greater chance of finding freedom from all of the lies they have believed when they feel safe.

Don't get into a shouting match. Authority does not increase with volume. If you as the facilitator find yourself shouting, you are probably responding in the flesh. God does everything decently and in order. You may copy the following Steps, or have an extra book for the child to use. It is important that you follow along as the child reads to make sure words are not being misread or left out that might change the meaning.

STEPS TO FREEDOM IN CHRIST
AGES 9–12

Footnotes, which are found at the end of the Steps, are for the parent, pastor, teacher or counselor. They give additional help and explanation.

Jesus wants you to be free! Free from the sins of your past, free from the problems you have right now, and free from any fear you may have of the future. If you have received Jesus as your Savior, He has already won your battles for you through His death on the cross. If you haven't been living free in Christ, maybe you just haven't understood what Jesus can do for you.

Here's the good news for you! You may be young, but you don't have to live with sin and evil in your life! Satan wants you to think he is stronger than he really is. But he really is an enemy who has been defeated by Jesus Christ. And you are in Christ, the winner!

Satan doesn't really want you to be free in Christ. So be sure to tell me how you are feeling and what you are thinking as we go along. If you get any bad thoughts or feel sick in any way, please tell me. It's usually the enemy trying to scare you or distract you. If we stop and pray, we can tell him to go away. I can pray with you at any time.

We're going to start now. I'm going to read this prayer out loud with you.

Dear heavenly Father, thank You for Your presence in this room and in our lives. You are everywhere, all powerful and You know all things. We need You, and know that we can do nothing without You. We believe the Bible because it tells us what is really true. We refuse to believe the lies of Satan. We ask You to rebuke Satan, and place a hedge of protection around this room so we can do Your will. Because we are children of God, we take authority over Satan and command Satan not to bother (name) so (name) can know and choose to do the will of God. In the name and authority of the Lord Jesus Christ, we command Satan and all His forces to be bound and silenced so they cannot inflict any pain or in any way prevent God's will from being accomplished in (name's) life. We ask the Holy Spirit to fill us and direct us into all truth. In Jesus' name we pray. Amen.

STEP ONE

RENOUNCING INVOLVEMENT WITH SPIRITUAL COUNTERFEITS

Now we are ready to start. We're going to go through seven Steps to help you be free in Christ. Remember, you can only win your battles when you *personally* choose to believe and confess. Confession is simply agreeing with God. Satan cannot read your mind (see Job 1:11; 2:5; compare with 1:20-22; 2:10); only God can do that (1 Sam. 16:7; Pss. 44:21; 139:1-6; Jer. 11:20; 17:10; Rom. 8:27). Therefore, it is recommended that you read each prayer *out loud*. This tells Satan we really mean what we say.

You are about to take a close-up look at your life, so you can have a great relationship with God. It is important you go through all seven Steps, so don't get discouraged and give up. Remember, the freedom Christ purchased for all believers on the cross is meant for *you*!

The first step is to turn your back on anything you have done that is spiritually wrong or against Christianity or God. Satan can and does use past experiences to draw us away from God and to control the way we think and behave. We need to be honest about these experiences with God so Satan will not have permission to bother us anymore. Begin by reading the following prayer out loud:

> Dear heavenly Father, I ask You to help me remember anything I have done that is spiritually wrong. If someone has done something to me that is wrong, would You also help me to remember it? I want to be free and able to do Your will. I ask this in Jesus' name. Amen.

Even if you did something as a game or a joke, you need to turn your back on it. Satan will try to take advantage of us in any way he can. Even if you were just watching others do it, you need to turn your back on it. Even if you had no idea it was evil, you need to turn your back on it.

Put a check by anything you have been involved in (this is only a partial list):

____Out of body experience

____Bloody Mary

____Magic Eight Ball

____Automatic writing
      (in a trance)

____Fortune telling

____Palm reading

____Hypnosis

____Black or white magic

____Dungeons & Dragons

____Video or computer games

____Movies or TV shows that
      are anti-Christian

____Martial Arts

____Light as a feather

____ Ouija board

____ Table lifting

____ Putting spells or curses
      on people

____ Spirit guides

____ Tarot cards

____ Astrology/ horoscopes

____ Seances

____ Meditation

____ Blood pacts

____ Music that is anti-
      Christian that suggests
      occult powers or cruel
      violence

____ Books, magazines,
      comics that
      are anti-Christian

____ Non-Christian religions

____ Believing in special
      powers from toys
      (Care Bears, Trolls,
      Power Rangers, etc.)

____Other experiences _____

1. Have you ever heard or seen a spiritual being in your room?
2. Have you had an imaginary friend that talks to you?
3. Do you hear voices in your head that tell you what to do?
4. Have you ever made a promise to the devil?
5. What other non-Christian experiences have you had?
6. Have you ever been involved in the worship of Satan or attended a concert where they sang about Satan?
7. Are you afraid to go to bed at night because of nightmares?

Now that you have completed the checklist, pray the following prayer for each experience:

Dear heavenly Father, I confess that I have been involved in _____. Thank You for Your forgiveness. I turn my back on _____.

(Note to parent, pastor or counselor: If the child has been subjected to satanic rituals or has any eating disorders, please go to "Special Renunciations" at the end of these Steps.)

STEP TWO

CHOOSING TRUTH

God's Word is true, and we need to accept that truth deep in our hearts (see Psalm 51:6). King David wrote, "How blessed is the man...in whose spirit there is no deceit" (32:2, *NASB*). Start this important step by praying the following prayer out loud:

> Dear heavenly Father, I know You want the truth from me, and I must be honest with You. I have been fooled by the father of lies, and I have fooled myself. I thought I could hide from You, but You see everything and still love me. I pray in the name of the Lord Jesus Christ, and ask You heavenly Father to rebuke all of Satan's demons by Your power. Because I have asked Jesus into my life I am now Your child. Therefore, I command all evil spirits to leave me alone. I ask the Holy Spirit to lead me into all truth. I ask You to look right through me and know my heart. Show me if there is anything in me that I am trying to hide, because I want to be free. In Jesus' name I pray. Amen.

(For parents: I just want to remind you how much I love you and how thankful I am that God has given you to me as my child. I want our relationship to be honest, and I want us to be able to trust each other as we go through these Steps. Speaking the truth in love is important because we are members of one another (see Eph. 4:25). We can walk in the light so we can have fellowship or friendship with each other (see 1 John 1:5-9). Only the truth can set us free, and we have to speak that truth to each other in love.

Read the following statements of faith out loud:

1. I believe there is only one true God who is the Father, Son and Holy Spirit. I believe He made all things and holds all things together.

2. I believe Jesus Christ is the Son of God who defeated Satan and all his demons.

3. I believe God loves me so much He had His own Son go to the Cross and die for all my sins. Jesus delivered me from Satan, because He loves me, not because of how good or bad I am.

4. I believe I am spiritually strong because Jesus is my strength. I have the authority to stand against Satan because I am God's child. In order to stay strong, I am going to obey God and believe His Word. I put on the armor of God so I can stay strong in the Lord.

5. I believe I cannot win spiritual battles without Jesus so I choose to live for Him. I resist the devil and command him to leave me alone.

6. I believe the truth will set me free. If Satan tries to put bad thoughts into my mind, I will not pay any attention to them. I will not listen to Satan's lies and I will not do what he wants me to do. I believe the Bible is true and I choose to believe it. I choose to speak the truth in love.

7. I choose to use my body to do only good things. I will not let Satan into my life by using my body in a wrong way. I believe what God wants me to do is the best thing for me, and I choose to do it.

8. I ask my heavenly Father to fill me with His Holy Spirit, guide me into all truth and make it possible for me to live a good Christian life. I love the Lord my God with all my heart, soul and mind.

Some very important decisions for truth have just been made that will have a lasting impact. (Parents or counselor: This is a good time to share with each other how you are feeling and what you are thinking.)

STEP THREE

FORGIVING OTHERS

When you do not forgive those who have hurt you, you become a target for Satan. God commands us to forgive others as we have been forgiven (see Eph. 4:31). You need to obey this command so

Satan can't take advantage of you (see 2 Cor. 2:11). Ask God to bring to your mind the names of the people you need to forgive by praying the following prayer out loud:

> Dear heavenly Father, I thank You for Your kindness, patience and love for me. I know at times I have not been very loving and patient toward others, especially those I don't like. I have been thinking bad thoughts about other people, and holding onto bad feelings. I ask You to bring to my mind those people I need to forgive. I ask this in the wonderful name of Jesus who will heal me from my hurts. Amen.

On a sheet of paper, list the names of everyone you have bad feelings toward. The Lord will bring them to your mind. It's okay to put Mom and Dad on your list if you need to forgive them for something. Forgiving people who have hurt you is God's way of setting you free from painful past experiences. Unless we forgive, the past will continue to cause us pain and have a hold on us. (Take time to finish the list of names.)

Now that you have finished your list, let's think about the meaning of real forgiveness. Read out loud the statements in dark print.

Forgiveness is not forgetting. You may not be able to forget your past, but you can be free from it by forgiving others. Once you forgive someone, you don't need to bring up the past and use it against them ever again.

Forgiveness is my choice. Forgiveness seems difficult because we all naturally want revenge for the things done to us. But God tells us to never take our own revenge (see Rom. 12:19).

Forgiveness is like removing a painful fish hook. Forgiving is like removing fish hooks others have put in us. It is a painful process, but when we forgive people we are no longer hooked to them. As long as those fish hooks are still in us, we are still bound to those people.

When I let someone off my hook, they aren't off God's hook. We must trust Jesus to deal with the other person justly, fairly and mercifully. That is something we cannot do. "It is mine to avenge, I will repay," says the Lord (Deut. 32:35).

Forgiveness is to accept that we can't change what happened. If someone steals your bike or calls you a name, you can't change that. You can be mad for a long time, or you can forgive them and let God deal with them. People do bad things and we can't always stop them, but we can choose not to let what they did control us.

To forgive from your heart, you need to admit the hurt and the hate. Go through your list of names one at a time. Stay with each person until all the pain is out. Then go on to the next person. Say the following prayer out loud for each name:

> Lord, I forgive (name the person) for (say what they did to hurt you). It made me feel (say how you felt).

STEP FOUR

REBELLION

We live in rebellious times. Some children don't respect people in positions of authority. But God has placed these people in authority over us (parents, teachers, church leaders, policemen, God). It's easy to think those in authority over us are robbing us of our freedom. Actually, God has placed them there for our protection so we can enjoy our freedom. God assures us that living under authority is for our good.

Rebelling against God and His authorities is serious business. Rebellion comes from Satan. It gives Satan an opportunity to attack us. Obedience to God is the only answer. He wants us to submit to our authorities. The following is a list of different authority figures God has placed over us.

If any of these people are asking you to do something that is wrong, you need to tell someone. God cannot tell you to do something wrong or to obey someone telling you to do something morally wrong. If any of these people are telling you to do something bad, ask for help from someone you trust. If these people are telling you to do something that is not morally wrong— even if you don't like it—you are to obey. If you have disobeyed anyone in the list below, put a check by them and pray the following prayer out loud:

____ Parents		____ Grandparents
____ School teachers		____ Policemen
____ Sunday School teachers		____ Church leaders
____ God		____ Others

Dear heavenly Father, You have said in the Bible that rebellion is the same thing as witchcraft, and disobedience is like honoring other gods. I know I have disobeyed and rebelled in my heart against You and (name of others). I ask for Your forgiveness for my rebellion. By the shed blood of the Lord Jesus Christ, I resist all evil spirits who took advantage of my rebellion. I now choose to be obedient and submissive to those in authority over me. In Jesus' precious name I pray, Amen.

STEP FIVE

PRIDE

Pride says, "I am better than everyone else." It also says, "I can do this all by myself, without God or anyone else!" Oh no we can't! We absolutely need God, and we desperately need each other. Paul wrote, "Do nothing out of selfish ambition or vain conceit, but in humility consider others better than yourselves" (Phil. 2:3). He also said we are to be "strong in the Lord and in the strength of His might" (Eph. 6:10, *NASB*). We will have spiritual problems when we are proud (see James 4:6-10; 1 Peter 5:1-10). Pride is what caused Satan to be cast out of heaven. The following is a list of ways we are prideful. If any of them are true of you, place a check mark next to them and use the following prayer to promise you will live humbly before God.

____ I don't need God or anybody else to help me!
____ I never do anything wrong!
____ I'm better than others!

Dear heavenly Father, I confess I often think only of myself. Sometimes I think I am better than others. I have believed I am the only one who cares about me, so I have to take care of myself. I have turned away from You, and not let You love me. I am tired of living for myself and by myself. I turn my back on the self life, and ask that You fill me with Your Holy Spirit so I can do Your will. By giving my heart to You, I stand against all the ways Satan would attack me. I ask You to show me how to live for others. I now choose to make others more important than myself, and make You the most important of all. I ask this in the name of Jesus Christ. Amen.

STEP SIX

SIN

The next step to freedom deals with sins in our lives. Many sins can control us. The Bible says, "Let us put aside the deeds of darkness and put on the armor of light...Rather, clothe yourselves with the Lord Jesus Christ, and do not think about how to gratify the desires of the sinful nature." (Rom. 13:12,14). Pray the following prayer out loud:

> Dear heavenly Father, I agree with You that I have done some bad things. I ask You to help me know all the things I have done that are wrong.

The following list contains some common sins. Put a check by the sins you have committed and then pray the following prayer for each sin:

____ stealing (shop lifting)	____ lying
____ fighting	____ jealousy
____ envying	____ outbursts of anger
____ complaining	____ desire for sexual pleasures
____ cheating	____ swearing (cussing)
____ greed	____ laziness
____ vandalism (damaging someone else's property)	
____ other _____	

> Lord, I have committed the sin of _____.
> Thank You for Your forgiveness and cleansing. I turn away from this sin and turn to You, Lord. In Jesus' name. Amen.

God has completely forgiven you of those sins. Don't ever let Satan put you down or make you think you are still guilty of them. Whenever sin creeps back into your life, remember 1 John 1:9: "If we confess our sins, He is faithful and righteous to forgive us our sins and to cleanse us from all unrighteousness" (NASB).

Pray the following prayer:

Lord, I thank You for forgiving me for all my sins. I ask You
to fill me with Your Holy Spirit so I will not sin anymore. I
now command Satan to leave, and I choose to live the right
kind of life so I can be free. In Jesus' name I pray. Amen.

(Note to parent, pastor or counselor: If the child has been subjected to sexual sins, satanic ritual abuse or eating disorders, please
refer to "Special Renunciations" at the end of these Steps.)

STEP SEVEN

SINS OF THE FATHERS

The last Step to freedom is to turn your back on the sins of your parents and grandparents. The Bible says God brings "the punishment
for the fathers' sins into the laps of their children after them" (Jer.
32:18). You are not guilty for the sins of other family members, but
because of their sins, Satan may have gained a foothold in the doorway to your family. To be free from the influence of the sins of your
ancestors, pray the following prayer out loud:

Dear heavenly Father, I come to You as Your child, bought by
the blood of the Lord Jesus Christ. I turn my back on all the
sins that have been committed in my family. I have been set
free from the power of darkness and I am now in the kingdom of Jesus. Jesus has broken all ties and workings of Satan
passed on to me from my ancestors. I am spiritually alive in
Christ, and united with Him. Because I am owned by Jesus, I
reject any and all ways Satan may claim ownership of me. I
announce to all the forces of evil, that I am forever and completely committed and signed over to the Lord Jesus Christ. I
now command every evil spirit that is familiar with my family, and every enemy of the Lord Jesus Christ to leave my
presence forever. I now ask You, heavenly Father, to fill me
with Your Holy Spirit. I present my body to You so people
will know You live in me. All this I do in the name of the Lord
Jesus Christ. Amen.

STAYING FREE

Becoming free and staying free in Christ are two different issues. The battle for your mind will continue. You will still be tempted to do wrong things. Consider the following suggestions to stay free in Christ:

1. Make sure you have the right kind of friends.
2. Always think and speak the truth in love.
3. Read your Bible daily.
4. Honor your mother and your father.
5. Obey all those who have authority over you.
6. Don't let problems build up. Share your struggles with someone you can trust.
7. Don't try to live the Christian life by yourself.
8. Always call upon God when you think you are under attack.
9. If something tries to scare you, tell it to leave in the name of Jesus.
10. Enjoy the wonderful life God has given you, and all He has created. Christ will meet all your needs according to His riches in glory.

Read together the following:

IN CHRIST I AM ACCEPTED

John 1:12	I am God's child.
John 15:15	I am Christ's friend.
Romans 5:1	I have been justified (made good in God's eyes).
1 Corinthians 6:17	I am united with the Lord and one with Him in spirit.
1 Corinthians 6:20	I have been bought with a price. I belong to God.
1 Corinthians 12:27	I am a member of Christ's body.
Ephesians 1:1	I am a saint.
Ephesians 1:5	I have been adopted (chosen) as God's child.
Ephesians 2:18	I can go right to God through the Holy Spirit.

| Colossians 1:14 | I have been redeemed (bought by God) and forgiven of all my sins. |
| Colossians 2:10 | I am complete in Christ. |

IN CHRIST I AM SECURE

Romans 8:1,2	I am free from condemnation.
Romans 8:28	I am assured that all things work together for good.
Romans 8:33,34	I am free from any condemning charges against me.
Romans 8:35-39	I cannot be separated from the love of God.
2 Corinthians 1:21,22	I have been established, anointed, and sealed by God.
Colossians 3:3	I am hidden with Christ in God.
Philippians 1:6	I am confident that the good work that God has begun in me will be perfected.
Philippians 3:20	I am a citizen of heaven.
2 Timothy 1:7	I have not been given a spirit of fear, but of power, love and a sound mind.
Hebrews 4:16	I can find grace and mercy in time of need.
1 John 5:18	I am born of God and the evil one cannot touch me.

IN CHRIST I AM SIGNIFICANT

Matthew 5:13,14	I am the salt and light of the earth.
John 15:1,5	I am a branch of the true vine, a channel of His life.
John 15:16	I have been chosen and appointed to bear fruit.
Acts 1:8	I am Christ's personal witness.
1 Corinthians 3:16	I am God's temple.
2 Corinthians 5:17-21	I am a minister of reconciliation (bringing others to God).
2 Corinthians 6:1	I am God's co-worker (1 Cor. 3:9).

Ephesians 2:6	I am seated with Christ in the heavenly realm.
Ephesians 2:10	I am God's workmanship.
Ephesians 3:12	I may approach God with freedom and confidence.
Philippians 4:13	I can do all things through Christ who strengthens me.

Note 1: Binding Satan does not ensure total release for the victim. If it could, the entire instruction in the Epistles would be to bind Satan throughout the world and cast him to some far away planet. The Lord will cast him into the abyss in the final days, but until then he roars around. We do, however, have all the authority in Christ we need to live a righteous life and fulfill the ministry to which God has called us. Binding Satan is an agreement with Scripture, an acknowledgment of God's sovereignty and an announcement to the enemy of our authority in Christ.

Note 2: Our children will be genetically predisposed to certain strengths and weaknesses. And the environment they were raised in will also affect them for good and evil. Could there also be an unrighteous inheritance? We think the answer is yes. Look at the words of Jeremiah 32:17,18: "Ah Lord God! Behold, Thou hast made the heavens and the earth by Thy great power and by Thine out-stretched arm! Nothing is too difficult for Thee, who showest lov-ingkindness to thousands, but repayest the iniquity of fathers into the bosom of their children after them, O great and mighty God. The Lord of Hosts is His name" (*NASB*).

In our experience, sins passed on from one generation to anoth-er is the second most common ground Satan has for gaining access to our children. In little children that is about all it can be because they haven't yet had the opportunity to become involved in sex and drugs, etc.

SPECIAL RENUNCIATIONS

SPECIAL RENUNCIATIONS FOR SEXUAL SINS

A child who has unfortunately been subjected (voluntarily or involuntarily) to sexual sins will need to renounce his or her participation. It is important to explain to the child that renouncing any unwilling participation does not mean he or she was at fault. However, the child needs to understand that even forced participation needs to be renounced because Satan has brought bondages into the child's life through that involvement. The child also needs to understand that any threats made by his or her perpetrator should not stop him or her from renouncing these acts.

(Caution: Children are highly susceptible to adult suggestions and often have creative imaginations. Do not ask leading questions. Some children are clever enough to tell us what they think we want to hear and lead us down a wrong path. They might also fabricate a story to abdicate themselves from their own responsibilities.)

If children are paying attention to deceiving spirits, those voices could be giving them false memories. False memories usually come from dreams, hypnosis or counterfeit "words of knowledge" given to them by others. Never use such "evidence" against another person unless you have some hard core external evidence to substantiate the accusations. Such accusations should not even be made against an elder in the church unless two or three witnesses can substantiate the accusations.

It is our responsibility not to allow sin to reign in our mortal bodies by not using our bodies as instruments of unrighteousness (see Rom. 6:12,13). If the child has struggled with sexual sins or has been subjected involuntarily to sexual acts, have the child read or repeat the following prayer:

Dear heavenly Father, I ask You to help me remember every sexual use of my body. In Jesus' precious name I pray. Amen.

As the Lord brings to the child's mind every sexual use of his or her body, whether it was done unwillingly (rape, incest or other sexual abuse) or willingly, have the child read or repeat the following renunciation for each occasion:

Dear heavenly Father, I renounce (name the specific sexual participation) with (name the person) and ask You to break that bond. In Jesus' name I pray. Amen.

Now have the child read or repeat the following prayer:

Dear heavenly Father, I turn my back on all these uses of my body. I ask You to break all bondages Satan has brought into my life through these involvements. I confess my participation. I now present my body to You as a living sacrifice, holy and acceptable to You. I reserve the sexual use of my body only for marriage. I renounce Satan's lie that my body is not clean or that it is dirty or unacceptable because of my sexual experiences. Lord, I thank You that You have totally cleansed and forgiven me, that You love and accept me no matter what. Therefore, I accept myself and my body as clean. In Jesus' name I pray. Amen.

SPECIAL RENUNCIATIONS FOR SATANIC-RITUAL ABUSE

A child who has had the horrible experience of being involuntarily subjected to satanic rituals will need to renounce his or her forced participation.

Sarah was an 11-year-old girl who had been raised the first five years of her life in a coven. Sarah's mother had given her life to Christ several months before she came for counseling. Her children had also prayed to receive Christ. But they were still being harassed. They were experiencing nightmares, dreams of snakes, banging noises, etc.

We took Sarah through the spiritual inventory, renouncing all the practices of the coven to which she had been subjected. She had three "spirit guides" because she was three years old. After renouncing them by name, the voices stopped. Forgiveness was a big Step for her (Step three) because many people had deeply hurt her. After we finished, we asked her how she felt. She replied, "Like I'm sitting in the lap of God!"

There are specific activities satanists use in all their rituals. When we encounter people who recall satanic ritual involvement, we have them repeat the following renunciations. (Caution: Children are highly susceptible to adult suggestions and often have creative imaginations. Do not ask leading questions. Some children are clever enough to tell us what we want to hear and lead us down a wrong path. They could also be fabricating a story to abdicate themselves from their own responsibility.)

If children are paying attention to deceiving spirits, those voices could be giving them false memories. False memories usually come from dreams, hypnosis or counterfeit "words of knowledge" others have given them. Never use such "evidence" against another person unless you have some hard core external evidence to substantiate the accusations. Such accusations should not even be made against an elder in the church unless there are two or three witnesses.

Notice in the following list that satanic rituals counterfeit Christian acts of worship. Have the child read across the page, renouncing the first item in the column under "Kingdom of Darkness." Then affirm the first truth in the column under "Kingdom of Light." Continue through the list to the end.

Kingdom of Darkness	Kingdom of Light
I renounce ever signing my name over to Satan or having my name signed over to Satan.	I announce that my name is now written in the Lamb's Book of Life.
I renounce any ceremony where I may have been married to Satan.	I announce that I am the Bride of Christ.
I renounce any and all covenants (agreements) with Satan.	I announce that I have a new covenant with Christ.
I renounce any sacrifices that were made for me where Satan would claim ownership of me.	I announce that I belong to God because of the sacrifice of Jesus on the cross for me.
I renounce ever giving of my blood in satanic ritual.	I trust only in the shed blood of Jesus for my salvation.
I renounce ever eating of flesh or drinking of blood for satanic worship.	By faith, I take communion which represents Jesus' body and blood which was given for me.

Kingdom of Darkness	Kingdom of Light
I renounce all guardians and surrogate parents that were assigned to me by satanists.	I announce that God is my heavenly Father and the Holy Spirit is my guardian.
I renounce every sacrifice made on my behalf by satanists whereby they may claim ownership of me.	I announce that Christ is my sacrifice and I belong to Him because I have been bought and purchased by the blood of the Lamb.
I renounce any ceremony where I was assigned to be a high priestess for satanic service, and I renounce Satan's lie that he owns me.	I announce that in Christ I am a chosen race, a royal priesthood, a holy nation, a person for God's own possession. I belong to Him.

Donny was only two and a half years old and extremely hyperactive. He left destruction in his wake. He couldn't sleep at night and screamed in fear whenever he attended anything Christian. His family had recently left witchcraft and were trusting in Christ. His mother, sister and brother had gone through the Steps and were growing in their relationship and freedom in Christ.

Donny's problems, however, seemed to worsen after his family went through the Steps. We prayed over him, with his mother claiming stewardship over his life. We renounced his involvement in witchcraft, and took authority over all the spirit guides assigned to him. When we finished, Donny slept for the better part of two days. Two weeks later when he returned for a visit, he was calm—his whirlwind behavior had stopped, and he had developed regular sleeping patterns.

SPECIAL RENUNCIATIONS FOR EATING DISORDERS

People with eating disorders are driven by compulsive thoughts to eliminate things from their bodies by defecating, vomiting or cutting themselves. Many believe they are purging themselves of evil. It is not uncommon to see cuts on the arms of those struggling with anorexia. Many cut themselves in secretive ways. One young lady would meticulously cut herself under her pants in the groin area so others wouldn't see. Suicidal thoughts are a given for these people.

Another young lady had starved herself down to 78 pounds. By the time I had a chance to talk with her, she was taking 75 laxatives a day. I asked her about her thought life—if she had ever shared fully what was going on inside her mind. She hadn't, of course, and was intimidated by thoughts threatening her that worse things would happen when she got home if she ever did. I suggested, "This isn't about food, is it?"

"No, but everybody thinks it is," she responded. Every attempt to control her behavior had only resulted in the problem getting worse. She had no idea who she was in Christ, and no understanding about the nature of the spiritual battle going on for her mind. Years of counseling and hospitalizations ended when she finally understood. She responded in tears after finding her freedom in Christ saying, "I can't believe all the lies I have been listening to."

Typically, those with eating disorders are physically attractive. From the time they were very little, they have received strokes for their looks. Their self-concepts are based on appearance. They become so body-conscious that their minds are fertile ground for the enemy. Instead of buffeting their bodies and making them their slaves (see 1 Cor. 9:27), they have become enslaved to their bodies. Many have been sexually abused. They also think their bodies are evil or something evil exists in them that they have to get rid of. The evil is spiritual, not physical. These people need to establish their identities in Christ, and develop their characters to obtain a legitimate sense of worth. Have them renounce as follows:

Kingdom of Darkness	Kingdom of Light
I renounce as lies from Satan, cutting myself to clean myself of evil.	I announce that only the blood of Jesus can cleanse me (Heb. 9:14).
I renounce throwing up to clean myself of evil and reject the lie that I am fat or that my self-worth is found in my physical appearance.	I announce that all food created by God is good, and nothing is to be rejected by those who know the truth (1 Tim. 4:1-5).
I renounce taking laxatives to clean myself of evil by going to the bathroom.	I announce that it is not what enters into the mouth that defiles me, but what comes from the heart (Matt. 15:10-20).

LEADING YOUR CHILD TO FREEDOM IN CHRIST AGES 5-8

Younger children in this age group can't read the Steps, so the parent, pastor, teacher or counselor must share with them what they must do. The best thing going for us is "childlike faith." Children at this age seldom question what a responsible adult shares with them. They have not yet learned to be defensive about the thoughts they are thinking.

....

WE NEED TO UNDERSTAND THAT CHILDREN

IN THE LORD HAVE THE SAME AUTHORITY

WE DO AS ADULTS.

....

You cannot overemphasize the love of God and His powerful presence in their lives. Children can accept the fact that God is in them and bigger than Satan. And we need to understand that children in the Lord have the same authority we do as adults. Therefore, they can resist the devil.

If the child has not yet trusted in Christ as his Savior, this might be a good opportunity for you to lead that child to Christ, then proceed through the Steps. If the child does not trust in Christ at this time, refer to the following chapter on "Praying For Your Child."

Take seriously the fearful comments of children. If they complain of horrible nightmares, or see frightening things in their rooms, encourage them to share all their experiences without judgment. If we make light of their experiences, they will conclude that we don't care or understand. In either case, they may never share again, which is the worst thing that can happen.

Many children have imaginary "friends" they play with. It can be harmless unless the imaginary friend is talking back. Then it is no longer imaginary. New Age proponents are actually encouraging children to have spirit friends or spirit guides.

A child's dependence on spirit "friends" will eventually result in spiritual bondage. This must be identified as soon as possible. Satan disguises himself as an angel of light, so young children probably won't see the danger. They might even be reluctant to give it up. As harmless as it may initially appear, it won't be as the relationship progresses.

Young children don't understand the term renounce, so we have them say no to Satan and yes to Jesus. For instance, if they have been sexually molested, have them say, "I say no to the way (name) touched me and I give my body to Jesus." As much as possible, we have the child assume his or her responsibility.

The following is a modified version of the Steps to Freedom to accommodate children ages 5-8. They may read the prayers themselves or repeat them after you.

Because of the suggestibility of younger children, the following section is open-ended. You may discover that your child has dabbled in some of these things, or your child may in the future mention them to you in casual conversation. Helping ourselves and our children to maintain freedom in Christ is not simply a one-time event, but a matter of watching for and capturing teachable moments when our children are ready and willing to listen. As Deuteronomy 6:4-7 says:

> Hear, O Israel: The Lord our God, the Lord is one. Love the Lord your God with all your heart and with all your soul and with all your strength. These commandments that I give you today are to be upon your hearts. Impress them on your children. Talk about them when you sit at home and when you walk along the road, when you lie down and when you get up.

STEPS TO FREEDOM IN CHRIST
AGES 5–8

(Note: Anything in parentheses is instructive material for the parent or counselor and should not be read to the child.)

Jesus wants you to be free—free from any sins and free from any fears. If you have received Jesus as your Savior, He has already won your battles for you on the cross.

Here's the good news for you: You don't have to live with sin and evil in your life! Satan wants you to think he is stronger than he really is. But he has been defeated by Jesus. And you have Jesus, the winner, with you all the time!

Satan doesn't really want you to be free in Christ. So be sure to tell me how you are feeling and what you are thinking as you go along. I can pray with you whenever you need to.

We're going to start now. I'm going to pray this prayer out loud.

Dear heavenly Father, we thank You for Your presence in this room and in our lives. You are everywhere, all powerful and You know all things. We need You, and know that we can do nothing without You. We believe the Bible because it tells us what is really true. We refuse to believe the lies of Satan. We ask You to silence and bind Satan, and place a hedge of protection around this room so we can do Your will. Because we are children of God, we take authority over Satan and command Satan not to bother (name) so (name) can know and choose to do the will of God. In the name of Jesus and His authority, we command Satan and all His forces to be bound and silenced so they cannot inflict any pain or in any way prevent God's will from being accomplished in (name's) life. We ask the Holy Spirit to fill us and direct us into all truth. In Jesus' name we pray. Amen.

STEP ONE

SAYING NO TO THINGS THAT ARE SPIRITUALLY WRONG

Now we are ready to start. We're going to proceed through seven Steps to help you be free in Christ. God can hear your prayer, whether you pray your prayer out loud or not. But because Satan cannot read your mind, it is important that you say each prayer out loud. I'll help you with each prayer.

The first step is to say no to anything you have done that is spiritually wrong. Read or repeat this prayer after me:

Dear heavenly Father, please help me remember anything I have done or been a part of that is spiritually wrong. If someone has done something to me that is wrong, would You also help me remember that? I ask this in Jesus' name. Amen.

The Bible teaches that God has an evil enemy, Satan, who fights against God. Satan is a liar and tries to trick us so he can get us to worship and obey him rather than the one true God.

If we listen to or obey any spirit other than God, that is wrong. God wants the best for us and He will protect us from the evil one.

(Parent or counselor: At this point, talk with the child about any experiences he or she has had with things that are spiritually wrong. The following list is for you to use as a resource so you can be aware of things children are exposed to. This is only a partial list. If some of these things come up in the course of your conversation, be sure the child says no to each involvement (see prayer at end of list). Be sensitive to the extent of their involvement without creating in them a desire to become more involved in something. Put a check by anything the child mentions, even if he or she only watched someone else do it or had no idea it was evil.)

____ Video or computer games that suggest occult powers or cruel violence
____ Inappropriate books, magazines or comics
____ Inappropriate movies or TV shows

____ Music that is anti-Christian
____ Dungeons & Dragons
____ Out of body experience
____ Bloody Mary
____ Table lifting
____ Ouija board
____ Magic eight ball
____ Putting curses or spells on people
____ Blood pacts
____ Fortune telling, tarot cards, palm reading
____ Astrology/horoscopes
____ Hypnosis
____ Table lifting
____ Seances
____ White or black magic
____ Martial Arts (The false beliefs that they may teach)
____ Meditation
____ Writing in a trance
____ Non-Christian religions
____ Other_____

(Have the child read or repeat the following prayer for each experience):

Dear heavenly Father, I confess that I have been involved in
_____. Thank You for Your forgiveness.
I say no to _____. I say yes to God.

(Parent or counselor: Again, be sensitive to the child's involvement as you ask the following questions.)

1. Have you ever been afraid of something you heard or saw in your room?
2. Have you had an imaginary friend that talks to you?
3. Do you hear voices in your head that tell you what to do?
4. Have you ever made a promise to the devil?
5. Has anyone ever told you to close your eyes and imagine you are going to a different place?
6. Have you had any other experiences that would hurt your relationship with God?
7. Are you afraid to go to bed at night because of nightmares?

(Now have the child read or repeat the following prayer):

Dear heavenly Father, I confess that I have been involved in
_____. Thank You for Your forgiveness.
I say no to _____. I say yes to God.

(Parent or counselor: If the child has been subjected to satanic rituals or has any eating disorders, please refer to "Special Renunciations" at the end of the Steps for children ages 9-12.)

STEP TWO

CHOOSING TRUTH

The Bible is true, and we need to accept that truth deep in our hearts (see Ps. 51:6). King David wrote, "How blessed is the man...in whose spirit there is no deceit" (Ps. 32:2, *NASB*). Start this important Step by reading or repeating the following prayer out loud:

Dear heavenly Father, I know that you want me to tell the truth. You know everything about me and You still love me. Because I have asked Jesus into my life I am now Your child. I command all evil spirits to leave me alone. Show me if there is anything I am trying to hide, because I want to be free. I choose to believe the truth about who You are and who I am as Your child. In Jesus' name I pray. Amen.

(For parents to read to their children): I just want to remind you how much I love you and how thankful I am that God has given you to me as my child. I want us to trust each other as we go through these Steps. Speaking the truth in love is important because we are partners together in Christ (see Eph. 4:25).

(Have the child read or repeat the following statements of faith out loud):

1. I believe there is only one true God who is the Father, Son and Holy Spirit.
2. I believe Jesus is the Son of God who defeated Satan and all his demons.
3. I believe God loves me so much that He had His own Son die on the Cross for all my sins.
4. I have the authority to stand against Satan because I am God's child. I put on the armor of God so I can stay strong in the Lord.
5. I believe the truth will set me free.
6. I choose to use my body to do only good things.
7. I ask God to fill me with His Holy Spirit. I love God with all my heart, soul and mind.

STEP THREE
FORGIVING OTHERS

God tells us to forgive others just like He has forgiven us (see Eph. 4:32). Ask God to bring to your mind the names of the people you need to forgive by praying the following prayer out loud:

Dear heavenly Father, help me remember who the people are that I need to forgive. I know Jesus will heal me from my hurts. In Jesus' name I pray. Amen.

I'll help you make a list of all the people you need to forgive. Remember that forgiving people who have hurt you is God's way of setting you free from painful past experiences. (Take time to make a list.)

Now that you have finished your list, you can forgive them as Jesus has forgiven you. Pray about each person until all the pain is out. Then go on to the next person. Read or repeat the following prayer out loud for each name:

Lord, I forgive (name the person) for (say what they did to hurt you). It made me feel (say how you felt).

STEP FOUR

REBELLION

Many children today don't respect people who tell them what to do. But God has placed these people in authority over us—parents, teachers, church leaders, policemen, God. God has placed them there for our protection. God assures us that living under authority is for our good.

Ignoring or fighting against God and the people he puts over us is wrong. It gives Satan an opportunity to bother us. Obedience to God is the only answer. He wants you to obey your parents, grandparents, teachers, church leaders and policemen. If any of these people are asking you to do something that is wrong, you need to tell someone that you trust. Have you ever disobeyed your parents? grandparents? teachers? church leaders? policemen? Then read or repeat the following prayer out loud:

> Dear heavenly Father, the Bible teaches that rebellion is the same thing as witchcraft, and disobedience is like honoring other gods. I know I have disobeyed and rebelled in my heart against You. I have also disobeyed (name of person). I ask for Your forgiveness for my disobedience and rebellion. By the shed blood of Jesus, I resist all evil spirits who took advantage of my rebellion and disobedience. I now choose to be obedient to those in authority over me. In Jesus' precious name I pray, Amen.

STEP FIVE

PRIDE

Pride says, "I am better than everyone else." It also says, "I can do this all by myself, without God or anyone else!" Oh no we can't! We absolutely need God, and we desperately need each other. Paul wrote, "Do nothing out of selfish ambition or vain conceit, but in humility consider others better than yourselves" (Phil. 2:3). He also said we are to be "strong in the Lord and in the strength of His might" (Eph. 6:10, *NASB*). We will have spiritual problems when we are proud (see Jas. 4:6-10; 1 Pet. 5:1-10). Read or repeat the following prayer to promise that you will live humbly before God.

Dear heavenly Father, I have often thought only of myself. Sometimes I think I am better than others. Please forgive me for my pride. I need You and I need other people to help me live right. I now choose to make others more important than myself, and make You the most important of all. I ask this in the name of Jesus Christ. Amen.

STEP SIX

SIN

The next step to freedom deals with sins in our lives. Many sins can control us. The Bible says, "Let us put aside the deeds of darkness and put on the armour of light...Rather, clothe yourselves with the Lord Jesus Christ, and do not think about how to gratify the desires of the sinful nature" (Rom. 13:12,14). Read or repeat the following prayer out loud:

Dear heavenly Father, I agree with You that I have done some bad things. I ask You to help me know all the things I have done that are wrong.In the name of Jesus, Amen.

The following list contains some of the more common sins. I will read a list of sins—if you have done these sins in your life, tell me so I can put a check mark by them.

_____ stealing (shoplifting)
_____ lying
_____ fighting
_____ calling names
_____ anger
_____ bad thoughts
_____ cheating
_____ swearing

_____ laziness
_____ wishing you had what someone else has
_____ other _____

Then read or repeat the following prayer for each sin.

Lord, I have committed the sin of _____.
Thank You for Your forgiveness and cleansing. I say no to this
sin and say yes to You. In Jesus' name I pray. Amen.

God has completely forgiven you of those sins. Don't ever let
Satan put you down or make you think you are still guilty of them.
Whenever sin creeps back into your life, remember 1 John 1:9: "If we
confess our sins, he is faithful and just and will forgive us our sins
and purify us from all unrighteousness." "Faithful" means that God
always does what He says He will do.

Read or repeat the following prayer:

Lord, I thank You for forgiving me for all my sins. I now
command Satan to leave me. I choose to live the right kind of
life so that I can be free. In Jesus' name I pray. Amen.

(Note to parent or counselor: If the child has been subjected to sexual sins, satanic ritual abuse or eating disorders, please refer to "Special
Renunciations" at the end of the Steps for children ages 9 to 12.)

STEP SEVEN

SINS OF THE FATHERS

The last Step to freedom is to say no to the sins of your parents and
grandparents. The Bible says God brings "the punishment for the
fathers' sins into the laps of their children after them" (Jer. 32:18).
You are not guilty for the sins of any other family member, but
because of their sin, Satan may have gotten a foot in the doorway of
your family. Read or repeat the following prayer out loud:

Dear heavenly Father, I say no to all the sins of my family.
Jesus has broken all the works of Satan passed on to me from
my parents and grandparents. Because I am owned by Jesus,

I reject any ways Satan may claim ownership of me. I announce to all the forces of evil, that I am forever and completely committed and signed over to the Lord Jesus Christ. I now ask You, heavenly Father, to fill me with Your Holy Spirit. I present my body to You. In the name of Jesus, Amen.

STAYING FREE

Now that you are free in Christ, let's talk about staying free in Christ. (Review the following points with your child.)

1. Make sure you have the right kind of friends.
2. Always think and speak the truth in love.
3. Read your Bible daily (or have someone read it to you).
4. Obey your mother and your father.
5. Obey all those who have authority over you.
6. Don't let problems build up. Share your struggles with someone you can trust.
7. Don't try to live the Christian life by yourself.
8. Always call upon God when you think you are under attack.
9. If something tries to scare you, tell it to leave in the name of Jesus.
10. Enjoy the wonderful life God has given you, and all He has created. Christ will meet all your needs according to His riches in glory.

Read or repeat the following together:

IN CHRIST I AM ACCEPTED

John 1:12	I am God's child.
John 15:15	I am Jesus' friend.
1 Corinthians 6:20	I have been bought with a price. I belong to God.
Ephesians 1:5	I have been adopted as God's child.
Colossians 1:14	I have been redeemed and forgiven of all my sins.

IN CHRIST I AM SAFE AND SECURE

Romans 8:28	I am assured that all things work together for good.
Romans 8:35	I cannot be separated from the love of God.
Philippians 3:20	I am a citizen of heaven.
2 Timothy 1:7	I have not been given a spirit of fear, but of power, love and a sound mind.
1 John 5:18	I am born of God and the evil one can not touch me.

IN CHRIST I AM SIGNIFICANT

Matthew 5:13,14	I am the salt and light of the earth.
2 Corinthians 6:1	I am God's co-worker (1 Cor. 3:9).
Ephesians 2:6	I am seated with Christ in the heavenly realm.
Ephesians 3:12	I may come to God with freedom and confidence.
Philippians 4:13	I can do all things through Christ who strengthens me.

STEPS TO FREEDOM IN CHRIST
AGES 0-4

Because children in this age group cannot read, parents must assume responsibility for them and exercise their authority in Christ. Children of these ages can understand the love and power of Jesus in their lives, however. Their childlike faith will be an encouragement to you as you pray for them, and what they learn in your prayers may lead them to put their trust in Christ someday. This is the only time we encourage you to place your hands on your children, if they will allow you, and pray for them.

After I finished a conference, a pastor shared with me how he was finally able to help his three-year-old daughter. She was waking up every night terrified and complaining something was in her room. He and his wife initially did what most parents would do. They accompanied her to the room and declared nothing was there after looking in the closet and under the bed. This had been occurring for three months. The child hadn't seen any bad movies, or lived long enough to commit any major sins.

During the week of the conference, the parents began to understand what was happening. Friday evening they sat down with her and explained that she had Jesus in her heart (she had trusted in Christ at an early age), and because Jesus was in her heart she could tell whatever was in her room to leave because Jesus was bigger than they were. She didn't come into their room that night, and the next morning she proclaimed boldly, "They came into my room last night, and I told them to get out in Jesus' name, and they left!"

A veteran missionary attending my class at seminary shared that his child had been having nighttime visitations. He and his wife personally confessed all their sins and then laid their hands on their child, commanding Satan to leave their child in the name of Jesus. The nightmares ended.

You can adapt for your child any of the prayers in the other Steps to Freedom for children, or you can pray something such as the following:

Dear heavenly Father, I bring my child (name) before You. I declare myself and my family to be under Your authority. I acknowledge my dependency upon You, for apart from

Christ I can do nothing. I ask for Your protection during this time of prayer. I assume my responsibility for all that You have entrusted to me, and I now commit my life, my marriage and my family to You. I declare my child to be eternally signed over to the Lord Jesus Christ. Because I am in Christ, and seated with Him in the heavenlies, I take authority over the enemy by renouncing any and all assignments Satan has on my child (name). I accept only the will of God for myself and my family. I now command Satan and all his demons to stop bothering my child (name) and to leave. I ask for a hedge of protection around him/her and my home. I submit myself to You and ask You to fill me with Your Holy Spirit. I dedicate myself and my child (name) as temples of the living God. I ask this in the precious name of Jesus, my Lord and Savior. Amen.

Our children are precious gifts from God. We must do everything we can to protect them from the god of this world. We can do that by being the parents He wants us to be, by surrounding them with a Christ-centered home and by lifting them up in prayer such as the one that follows. Suggestions for praying more specifically for our children are offered in the next chapter.

Praying for Your Child

Daily Prayer:

Dear heavenly Father, I ask that (name) may be filled with the knowledge of Your will in all spiritual wisdom and understanding so (name) may walk in a manner worthy of Your name. May he/she please You in all respects, bearing fruit in every good work and increase in the knowledge of You. I pray that (name) be strengthened with all power according to Your glorious might so he/she may be steadfast and patient. I ask, heavenly Father, that (name) would see Your mighty work and joyfully give thanks to You who has qualified us to share in the inheritance of the saints (see Col 1:9-12). I pray that (name) will continue to grow in wisdom and stature and in favor with God and others (see Luke 2:52) In Jesus' precious name I pray, Amen.

20

PRAYING FOR YOUR CHILD

Paul concluded his teaching about the armor of God by saying, "With all prayer and petition pray at all times in the Spirit, with this in view, be on the alert with all perseverance and petition for all the saints" (Eph. 6:18, *NASB*). Certainly this includes our children. Forces we don't see leave us totally dependent upon the Lord. Some battles can't be fought with our own limited resources. Again we are dependent upon the Lord. Paul says we don't really know how or for what to pray (see Rom. 8:26,27). That is why we must pray in the Spirit, because the prayer God the Holy Spirit prompts us to pray is a prayer God the Father will always answer.

Prayer is the most tangible demonstration of our dependence upon God. I have a tendency not to pray when I think I can do it all by myself. I become a prayer warrior when I know that apart from Christ I can do nothing (which is all the time). We don't need to wait for some unusual leading of the Holy Spirit to pray effectively, however. Because that same Holy Spirit is the means by which the Word of God was given to us. We can then pray with confidence if our prayers of intercession and petition are consistent with Scripture. The following are scriptural prayers for your children.

GIVING YOUR CHILD TO GOD

Paul wrote, "Let a man regard us in this manner, as servants of Christ, and stewards of the mysteries of God. In this case, moreover, it is required of stewards that one be found trustworthy" (1 Cor. 4:1,2, *NASB*). A steward is a manager or superintendent of another's household. As Christians, we own nothing in the kingdom of God.

Everything we possess belongs to God; we are to be trustworthy stewards of what He has given to us.

Our children are the most valuable possession God has entrusted to our care. God allows us to enter into only one creative act, and

---

WE CALL THEM OURS BUT,

LIKE EVERYTHING ELSE WE POSSESS,

OUR CHILDREN BELONG TO GOD.

---

that is procreation. We call them ours but, like everything else we possess, our children belong to God. He knew them from the foundations of the world. We are merely stewards of the precious human lives God has allowed us to bring into the world.

A PRAYER FOR A CHILD'S DEDICATION

Baby dedication is a public declaration of parental stewardship. In this declaration we are saying, "This child belongs to God. We dedicate our child to God and commit ourselves to be faithful stewards of that which He has entrusted to us." The account of Hannah is often read in conjunction with baby dedication (see 1 Sam. 1:1-28). For some reason God had closed Hannah's womb and she was childless. Greatly distressed, she prayed asking God to give her a son, vowing to give the boy to the Lord (see v. 11). God answered Hannah's prayer, and she fulfilled her vow. After Samuel was weaned Hannah presented him to the Lord: "So I have also dedicated him to the Lord; as long as he lives he is dedicated to the Lord" (v. 28, *NASB*).

Joseph and Mary also modeled the importance of giving our children to God. "When the days for their purification according to the law of Moses were completed, they brought Him up to Jerusalem to present Him to the Lord" (Luke 2:22, *NASB*). Like Joseph and Mary, we need to purify ourselves as trustworthy, obedient stewards and bring our children to the Lord.

Reformed churches and most liturgical churches combine the formal dedication of the child with infant baptism. Other churches that hold to believer's baptism by immersion see baby dedication as a separate act. Either way, the parents' act of presenting their children to God is based on a solid scriptural principle.

Baby dedication or baptism is too often regarded as little more than an opportunity for the proud parents to show off their new child. We act as though nothing of spiritual significance is expected to happen. But what takes place in the spiritual realm is the only thing significant that can happen. Satan has something spiritually significant in mind for your child, and it's not what you would want. Presenting your child to God through public dedication is the first step in protecting the child from Satan's destructive plans.

Let me suggest a prayer which the head of the home or the husband and wife could publicly say as they dedicate their child to the Lord:

> Dear heavenly Father, I thank You for loving me and giving me eternal life in Christ Jesus. I am Your child, purchased by the blood of the Lord Jesus Christ, who gave His life for me. I renounce any claim of personal ownership over anything I have, and I announce my responsibility to be a good steward of that which You have entrusted to me. I dedicate myself to You as a living sacrifice, and I commit myself to know You and do Your will. I commit myself to bring up Your child (name) in the discipline and instruction of the Lord. I know this child belongs to You and is a gift from You, and I dedicate him/her to You for as long as he/she shall live. I reject any claim Satan may have on (name); he/she belongs to the Lord Jesus Christ. I announce that Jesus paid the price for my child and he/she belongs to Him. As for me and my house, we will serve the Lord. I do all this in the wonderful name of Christ Jesus my Lord. Amen.

A PRAYER FOR A CHILD'S SALVATION

In no way are we more dependent on God as parental stewards than for the salvation of our children. We cannot cause them to be born again. But we can and must do all within our power to lead them to

Christ by being the witnesses God wants us to be. In addition, we must pray for their salvation. The apostle John wrote about the importance of prayer in bringing others to Christ:

> This is the confidence which we have before Him, that, if we ask anything according to His will, He hears us. And if we know that He hears us in whatever we ask, we know that we have the requests which we have asked from Him. If anyone sees his brother committing a sin not leading to death, he shall ask and God will for him give life to those who commit sin not leading to death (1 John 5:14-16, *NASB*).

The context of these verses is the assurance of eternal life (vv. 11-13) and assurance of answered prayer (vv. 14,15). The word "life" in this passage is clearly spiritual life. A "brother committing a sin not leading to death" refers to a non-Christian who has not totally rejected the conviction of the Holy Spirit, which is the sin of unbelief or the "unpardonable sin." John is saying that God will give spiritual life to unbelievers in response to our prayers of faith.

This passage does not teach that we can choose the people we want to be saved, pray for them and they will automatically be saved. But it does teach that prayer plays an integral part in the process of God bringing people to Himself. We know that the salvation of unbelievers is God's desire because He "desires all men to be saved and to come to the knowledge of the truth" (1 Tim. 2:4, *NASB*). God promises to respond to our prayers for the unbeliever in some fashion if the person has not hardened his or her heart.

Your child should be at the top of your prayer list. One of your primary roles as God's steward is to intercede for his or her salvation. Let me suggest a prayer you can use for the salvation of your child:

> Dear heavenly Father, I bring Your child (name) before You. I stand against the blinding of Satan that would keep him/her from seeing the light of the gospel of the glory of Christ and from believing the truth that leads to salvation (2 Cor. 4:4). I take my position in Christ, and I exercise His authority over Satan in regard to (name) whom You have entrusted to me. In the name of Jesus, I take authority over speculations and every lofty thing raised up against the knowledge of God in

the mind of my child (2 Cor. 10:5). I stand against the strong-holds in his/her mind that keeps him/her from obeying Christ. By the authority that I have in Christ and in obedience to the Great Commission to make disciples, I ask You to free the mind of (name) so he/she may obey God. I declare myself and all You have entrusted to me to be eternally signed over to the Lord Jesus Christ. Based on Your Word in 1 John 5:16, I ask You to give eternal life to (name). I pray You will enable me to be the parent You want me to be. May I never be a stumbling block to this child You have entrusted to me. Enable me to be a positive witness and a living epistle to him/her. I ask this in the name and authority of the Lord Jesus Christ. Amen.

COMMITTING YOUR CHILDREN TO GOD DAILY

Even as a faithful steward over your child you don't always know what he or she is thinking and you can't be everywhere the child goes. You must depend on the Lord for your child's daily protection, direction and growth. You may have dedicated your child to the Lord and prayed with him or her to receive Christ as his Savior; but your ministry of prayer for your child doesn't stop there. You are responsible to lift him or her to the Lord daily.

Job apparently understood the importance of daily prayer for his children, because he would "consecrate them, rising up early in the morning and offering burnt offerings according to the number of them all" (Job 1:5, *NASB*). When God pointed out to Satan Job's righteousness, Satan pointed to the hedge God had placed around Job, his family and his possessions (see vv. 8-10), inferring that Job wouldn't be so righteous if God didn't protect him so well. Perhaps the reverse is true: The hedge of protection was the result of Job's godly life and his willingness to pray daily for his family. Of course, God then removed the protection and allowed Satan to do a number on Job and his family. Yet even without the hedge "Job did not sin nor did he blame God" (v. 22, *NASB*).

The story of Job provides several important principles about parenting and prayer. Satan is actively looking for ways to destroy your family: you and your children. And the more righteous you are, the more interested he is in attacking you. You and your children are utterly dependent on God for your spiritual protection.

God will put a hedge of protection around your family in response to your godly living and dependent prayer. But God may also remove your protection if it will serve a greater purpose. Suffering is the result of sin. However, as I pointed out earlier, even the righteous may suffer for doing what is right, but never without a purpose (see 2 Tim. 3:12). Should suffering come to your family, you must continue to trust the Lord, pray and refuse to justify yourself. God will make everything right in the end for parents who trust and love Him as He did Job.

A PRAYER FOR PROTECTION

How did you feel when your first child walked out of the house for the first day at school? If your children are still at home, how do you think you will feel on that special day? You may lament, "There goes my child, off into the hostile world without me!" You're excited about the child's potential and growing awareness but fearful about the godless world he or she is about to encounter. You know you can't keep the child home forever, and yet you wish you could for his or her own protection.

Your child doesn't go anywhere alone. The God to whom you have presented him or her is omnipresent. He will never leave nor forsake your child. You can call on Him daily for your child's protection. Here's a prayer you can use to ask for God's hedge of protection around your child:

Dear heavenly Father, I ask for Your divine protection for (name) as he/she is absent from me. I pray You will put a hedge of protection around him/her so all harmful influences cannot affect him/her. I commit (name) to You for Your care, and I assume all my responsibility for training him/her in the Lord. I also assume the responsibility for the attitudes and actions in him/her that are the result of my training. I ask that Your Holy Spirit guard (name's) heart and bring to his/her mind all he/she has learned from your Word. I thank You that when he/she is tempted You will provide him/her with a way of escape, and he/she will not be tempted beyond his/her ability in You to endure (1 Cor. 10:13). I ask that the way he/she lives may be a witness to Your presence in his/her life. May whatever (name) does be done to the glory of God. I ask this in the precious name of my Lord and Savior Jesus Christ. Amen.

PRAYER FOR A REBELLIOUS CHILD

Have you ever tried to reason with a rebellious child? You can't do it! In fact, we are told not to: "He who corrects a scoffer gets dishonor for himself, and he who reproves a wicked man gets insults for himself. Do not reprove a scoffer, lest he hate you" (Proverbs 9:7,8, *NASB*). What can you do?

First, you must maintain a standard of personal godliness in your home. You can't compromise your convictions and expect God to bless your efforts. Being out of the will of God yourself and expecting your child to get into the will of God won't work!

Second, rebellion is a spiritual problem that requires a spiritual solution (see 1 Sam. 15:23). Allowing a child who is out of fellowship with God to control your home is allowing someone other than the Spirit of God to control your home, and that's wrong. Spiritual problems like rebellion can only be resolved by exercising the fruits of the Spirit and going to the Lord in prayer. Consider using the following prayer for a rebellious child:

Dear heavenly Father, I ask in the name of the Lord Jesus Christ and through His shed blood that You will rebuke Satan and prohibit him from having any harmful influence on (name). Forgive me for any negative influence I may have had on him/her that prompted him/her to choose to rebel against You. I pray that You will give me grace to ask (name's) forgiveness for my negative influence. I ask for the wisdom and grace to be the kind of parent that You created me to be. I acknowledge the sins of (name, and then list all known sins) and I assume my responsibility for the part I played in his/her actions. I pray that You will build a hedge around him/her so that all harmful influences will lose interest. I pray that he/she will come to his/her senses and return to righteous living and loving relationships. I pray for grace to welcome (name) home or guidance to find a place of refuge for his/her good. Teach me to love my child but hate his/her sin. I ask this in the precious name of Jesus. Amen.

A PRAYER FOR YOUR CHILD'S FUTURE

You cannot determine your child's future; only God is the author and finisher of life and faith. James wrote: "Come now, you who say, 'Today or tomorrow, we shall go to such and such a city, and spend a year there and engage in business and make a profit.' Yet you do not know what your life will be like tomorrow. You are just a vapor that appears for a little while and then vanishes away. Instead, you ought to say, 'If the Lord wills, we shall live and also do this or that'" (Jas. 4:13-15, *NASB*).

> YOU CAN'T MOLD YOUR CHILD INTO WHAT YOU WANT HIM OR HER TO BE; YOU CAN ONLY HELP HIM OR HER BECOME WHAT GOD WANTS THE CHILD TO BE.

This is not license to be irresponsible about your child's future or your own. But you don't know what God has planned for your child or yourself. You can't mold your child into what you want him or her to be; you can only help him or her become what God wants the child to be. The following prayer is an example of how to pray for your child's future:

Dear heavenly Father, I ask for divine guidance for (name). I trust that You have already gone before him/her and prepared a place for him/her. You have known (name) from the foundation of the world. I commit him/her into Your hands and pray for wisdom as to how I should relate to him/her in the future. I release (name) from all my expectations and entrust him/her to be what You want him/her to be. I pray

You will give (name) wisdom in choosing a life partner. I pray for his/her future spouse. Should You bless them with children, I pray they will train their children according to Your Word and teach them how to trust in Jesus as their Savior. May I be the grandparent You want me to be. I pray as Jesus prayed that You keep (name) from the evil one and sanctify him/her in Your Word, for Your Word is truth. I ask this in the name of my Lord and Savior Jesus Christ. Amen.

PRAYER FOR AN ADOPTED CHILD

Adopted children are extremely vulnerable to demonic influence. Most of them are available for adoption because their single mothers or fathers are unable to raise them or because their natural parents did not want them. Some children are adopted because their parents abused them or because they were poor stewards for the time the children were in their homes.

Satan attempts to claim ownership of anyone not committed to Jesus Christ and brought under His authority. Because these children are not spiritually under the protective care of loving parents, they come to their adopted parents with spiritual problems even as infants. We have counseled many godly couples who have adopted children only to see them all but destroy their families.

If you are thinking of adopting a child, we recommend that you work with an agency that locates adoptive parents before the child is born. If at all possible you should be present at the time of birth and bring the child home from the hospital. You should dedicate your adopted child to the Lord immediately to assume stewardship and negate any demonic influence.

If you already have an adopted child, lead the child through the Steps to Freedom as explained in chapter 19. Then pray over the child as follows:

Dear heavenly Father, I thank You for entrusting (name) to me as my adopted child. I declare (name) to be under Your authority. I dedicate this child to You and ask for Your protection and guidance as I commit myself to do all I can to lead him/her to an understanding of Your saving grace. I stand against all the devices of Satan that would keep (name) in bondage. I renounce the sins of this child's ancestors and all

curses that have been passed on from generation to generation. I announce that Christ became a curse for (name) when
He was crucified on the cross. I renounce all satanic sacrifices
that have been made on behalf of (name) and any claim of
ownership that Satan may have. I announce that only the
Lord Jesus Christ has any claim of ownership on him/her. I
pray for a hedge of protection around (name) all the days of
his/her life. I ask this in the strong name of Jesus, who reigns
supreme as the sovereign Lord of the universe. Amen.

PRAYER FOR BEDTIME

The following is an example of a prayer you can teach your children
to pray at bedtime. You may lead them in saying the prayer line by
line until they can say it on their own. This prayer is based on Psalm
91:

Dear God, I thank You that You are my heavenly Father. I
thank You for being in my life, in my room and everywhere I
go. I know that You are always with me and will never leave
me. I commit myself to You and ask for Your protection. I
choose to trust You. I know that if I'm ever afraid I can always
call on You to rescue me. I ask You to protect my mind tonight
as I am sleeping. Please bless and protect my home and parents. I love You. I pray this in the name of Jesus. Amen.

TEACHING YOUR CHILD TO PRAY AGAINST A SPIRITUAL ATTACK

Every child needs to know how to stand when he or she senses a
presence in his or her room or has some direct confrontation with
evil. In the Scriptures, Satan or his demons always submit to the
spoken Word. There is no Scriptural case in which Satan is defeated
simply by believers' thoughts. Therefore, we believe it is important
for your child to take a stand verbally when under spiritual attack
and express his or her faith out loud.

For the small child, communicate something such as: "Honey,
Jesus is in your life and He is bigger than they are, so you can tell
them to leave in Jesus' name." If your child can't say anything

because of fear, let the child know that he or she can always talk to God in his or her mind, and God will help the child say what he or she needs to say. Encourage the child to memorize this paraphrase of 1 John 5:18: "I am a child of God, and the evil one cannot touch me." If nothing else, all the child really needs to say is "Jesus."

A PRAYER FOR DAILY LIFE

As you prepare to send your child out into the world each day, consider using a prayer similar to the following. The goal is to teach your child the basic concepts of the prayer so he or she can learn to pray them independently:

Dear heavenly Father, You are my Lord. I know You love me and will never leave me nor forsake me. You are the only true and living God. You are worthy of worship. You are kind and loving in all Your ways. I love You and I thank You that I am alive in Christ. I submit myself to You and ask You to fill me with Your Holy Spirit so I can live my life free from sin. I choose to believe the truth which You have given in the Bible, and I reject all the lies of Satan. I refuse to be discouraged because You are the God of all hope. I believe You will meet my needs as I seek to obey You. I know I can do everything You want me to do, because Jesus is my strength. I submit to God and resist the devil. I stand against Satan and all his lies, and I command him and all his demons to leave me. I put on the armor of God and commit myself to believe and speak the truth. I believe Jesus is my protection. He never sinned, and He took my sin on Himself. I commit myself to be a peacemaker and to take the truth of the Bible and use it against all of Satan's dirty tricks. I submit my body as a living sacrifice to God. I will keep studying the truth so I can prove what God wants me to do is good and perfect for me. I do all this in the name of Jesus. Amen.

As you pray for your children daily through the problems and crises of their lives, you may feel at times like you are standing alone against the world, the flesh and the devil. But you're really not. When you pray for your children you are in good company. God's

Word tells us that the Lord Jesus Himself and His Holy Spirit are committed to intercede for your children and for you (see Rom. 8:27; Heb. 7:25). You never pray alone.

Everything in life needs to be renewed. What would our homes look like if we never repainted them? How well would our cars run if we never changed the oil? We need to periodically renew our faith and commitment to the Lord. Four years after Pete and Sue led their oldest son to freedom in Christ, I received this note from Sue:

Dear Neil,

I just took my oldest son through the Steps again last night using the youth edition. What a joy it was! He had been building up anger, rebellion and pride in his life. So when he was well rested, I asked him if he wanted to go through the Steps. He eagerly wanted to. It wasn't a judgmental thing on my part to ask him because he knows that the truth sets you free-it doesn't condemn. So there is a gentleness and a love already built into repentance because of its liberating result! The frustration of trying to "get through" to your children when they're angry or rebellious is replaced with a tender time of sharing together through repentance and prayer. David prayed when we were done, after breathing out a sigh of relief, "Thank you that I am free again."

Appendix

A

STEPS TO FREEDOM IN CHRIST

It is my deep conviction that the finished work of Jesus Christ and the presence of God in our lives are the only means by which we can resolve our personal and spiritual conflicts. Christ in us is our only hope (see Col. 1:27), and He alone can meet our deepest needs of life, acceptance, identity, security and significance. The discipleship counseling process upon which these steps are based should not be understood as just another counseling technique we learn. It is an encounter with God. He is the Wonderful Counselor. He is the one who grants repentance that leads to a knowledge of the truth that sets us free (see 2 Tim. 2:24-26).

The Steps to Freedom in Christ do not set you free. *Who* sets you free is Christ, and *what* sets you free is your response to Him in repentance and faith. These steps are just a tool to help you submit to God and resist the devil (see Jas. 4:7). Then you can start living a fruitful life by abiding in Christ and becoming the person He created you to be. Many Christians will be able to work through these steps on their own and discover the wonderful freedom Christ purchased for them on the cross. Then they will experience the peace of God that surpasses all comprehension, and it shall guard their hearts and their minds (see Phil. 4:7).

Before You Begin

The chances of that happening and the possibility of maintaining that freedom will be greatly enhanced if you read *Victory over the Darkness* and *The Bondage Breaker* first. Many Christians in our Western world need to understand the reality of the spiritual world and our relationship to it. Some can't read these books or even the

Bible with comprehension because of the battle that is going on for their minds. They will need the assistance of others who have been trained. The theology and practical process of discipleship counseling is presented in my book *Helping Others Find Freedom in Christ*, and the study guide that accompanies it. The book attempts to biblically integrate the reality of the spiritual and the natural world so we can have a whole answer for a whole person. In doing so, we cannot polarize into psychotherapeutic ministries that ignore the reality of the spiritual world or attempt some kind of deliverance ministry that ignores developmental issues and human responsibility.

You May Need Help

Ideally, it would be best if everyone had a trusted friend, pastor or counselor who would help them go through this process because it is just applying the wisdom of James 5:16: "Therefore, confess your sins to one another, and pray for one another, so that you may be healed. The effective prayer of a righteous man can accomplish much." Another person can prayerfully support you by providing objective counsel. I have had the privilege to help many Christian leaders who could not process this on their own. Many Christian groups throughout the world are using this approach in many languages with incredible results because the Lord desires for all to come to repentance (see 2 Pet. 3:9), and to know the truth that sets us free in Christ (see John 8:32).

Appropriating and Maintaining Freedom

Christ has set us free through His victory over sin and death on the cross. Appropriating our freedom in Christ through repentance and faith and maintaining our life of freedom in Christ, however, are two different issues. It was for freedom that Christ set us free, but we have been warned not to return to a yoke of slavery that is legalism in this context (see Gal. 5:1) or to turn our freedom into an opportunity for the flesh (see Gal. 5:13). Establishing people as free in Christ makes it possible for them to walk by faith according to what God says is true, and to live by the power of the Holy Spirit and not carry out the desires of the flesh (see Gal. 5:16). The true Christian life avoids both legalism and license.

If you are not experiencing freedom, it may be because you have not stood firm in the faith or actively taken your place in Christ. It is every Christian's responsibility to do whatever is necessary to maintain a right relationship with God and humankind. Your eternal destiny is not at stake. God will never leave you nor forsake you (see Heb. 13:5), but your daily victory is at stake if you fail to claim and maintain your position in Christ.

Your Position in Christ

You are not a helpless victim caught between two nearly equal but opposite heavenly superpowers. Satan is a deceiver. Only God is omnipotent, omnipresent and omniscient. Sometimes the reality of sin and the presence of evil may seem more real than the presence of God, but that's part of Satan's deception. Satan is a defeated foe and we are **in Christ**. A true knowledge of God and knowing our identity and position in Christ are the greatest determinants of our "mental health." A false concept of God, a distorted understanding of who we are as children of God and the misplaced deification of Satan are the greatest contributors to "mental illness."

Many of our illnesses are psychosomatic. When these issues are resolved in Christ, our physical bodies will function better and we will experience greater health. Other problems are clearly physical, and we need the services of the medical profession. Please consult your physician for medical advice and prescriptions. We are both spiritual and physical beings who need the services of both the church and the hospital.

Winning the Battle for Your Mind

The battle is for the mind, which is the control center of all that we think and do. The opposing thoughts you may experience as you go through these steps can control you only if you believe them. If you are working through these steps alone, don't be deceived by any lying, intimidating thoughts in your mind. If a trusted pastor or counselor is helping you find your freedom in Christ, he or she must have your cooperation. You must share any thoughts you are having in opposition to what you are attempting to do. As soon as you expose the lie, the power of Satan is broken. The only way you can lose control in this process is if you pay attention to a deceiving spirit and believe a lie.

You Must Choose

The following procedure is a means of resolving personal and spiritual conflicts that have kept you from experiencing the freedom and victory Christ purchased for you on the cross. Your freedom will be the result of what *you* choose to believe, confess, forgive, renounce and forsake. No one can do that for you. The battle for your mind can only be won as you personally choose truth. As you go through this process, understand that Satan is under no obligation to obey your thoughts. Only God has complete knowledge of your mind because He is omniscient (all-knowing). So we can submit to God inwardly, but we need to resist the devil by reading aloud each prayer and by verbally renouncing, forgiving, confessing, etc.

This process of reestablishing our freedom in Christ is nothing more than a fierce moral inventory and a rock-solid commitment to truth. It is the first step in the continuing process of discipleship. There is no such thing as instant maturity. It will take you the rest of your life to renew your mind and conform to the image of God. If your problems stem from a source other than those covered in these steps, you may need to seek professional help.

May the Lord grace you with His presence as you seek His face and help others experience the joy of their salvation.

Neil T. Anderson

PRAYER

Dear heavenly Father,

We acknowledge Your presence in this room and in our lives. You are the only omniscient (all knowing), omnipotent (all powerful) and omnipresent (always present) God. We are dependent upon You, for apart from You we can do nothing. We stand in the truth that all authority in heaven and on earth has been given to the resurrected Christ, and because we are in Christ, we share that authority in order to make disciples and set captives free. We ask You to fill us with Your Holy Spirit and lead us into all truth. We pray for Your complete protection and ask for Your guidance. In Jesus' name, Amen.

DECLARATION

In the name and authority of the Lord Jesus Christ, we command Satan and all evil spirits to release (name) in order that (name) can be free to know and choose to do the will of God. As children of God seated with Christ in the heavenlies, we agree that every enemy of the Lord Jesus Christ be bound to silence. We say to Satan and all your evil workers that you cannot inflict any pain or in any way prevent God's will from being accomplished in (name's) life.

PREPARATION

Before going through the Steps to Freedom, review the events of your life to discern specific areas that might need to be addressed.

Family History

_____ Religious history of parents and grandparents

_____ Home life from childhood through high school

_____ History of physical or emotional illness in the family

_____ Adoption, foster care, guardians

Personal History

_____ Eating habits (bulimia, binging and purging, anorexia, compulsive eating)

_____ Addictions (drugs, alcohol)

_____ Prescription medications (what for?)

_____ Sleeping patterns and nightmares

_____ Rape or any sexual, physical, emotional abuse

_____ Thought life (obsessive, blasphemous, condemning, distracting thoughts, poor concentration, fantasy)

_____ Mental interference in church, prayer or Bible study

_____ Emotional life (anger, anxiety, depression, bitterness, fears)

_____ Spiritual journey (salvation: when, how and assurance)

Now you are ready to begin. The following are seven specific steps to process in order to experience freedom from your past. You will address the areas where Satan most commonly takes advantage of us and where strongholds have been built. Christ purchased your victory when He shed His blood for you on the cross. Realizing your freedom will be the result of what you choose to believe, confess, forgive, renounce and forsake. No one can do that for you. The battle for your mind can only be won as you personally choose truth.

As you go through these Steps to Freedom, remember that Satan will only be defeated if you confront him verbally. He cannot read your mind and is under no obligation to obey your thoughts. Only God has complete knowledge of your mind. As you process each step, it is important that you submit to God inwardly and resist the devil by reading aloud each prayer—verbally renouncing, forgiving, confessing, etc.

You are taking a fierce moral inventory and making a rock-solid commitment to truth. If your problems stem from a source other than those covered in these steps, you have nothing to lose by going through them. If you are sincere, the only thing that can happen is that you will get very right with God!

STEP 1: COUNTERFEIT VERSUS REAL

The first Step to Freedom in Christ is to renounce your previous or current involvement with satanically inspired occult practices and false religions. You need to renounce any activity and group that denies Jesus Christ, offers guidance through any source other than the absolute authority of the written Word of God or requires secret initiations, ceremonies or covenants.

In order to help you assess your spiritual experiences, begin this Step by asking God to reveal false guidance and counterfeit religious experiences.

Dear heavenly Father,

I ask You to guard my heart and my mind and reveal to me any and all involvement I have had either knowingly or unknowingly with cultic or occult practices, false religions or false teachers. In Jesus' name, I pray. Amen.

Using the "Non-Christian Spiritual Experience Inventory" on the following page, carefully check anything in which you were involved. This list is not exhaustive, but it will guide you in identifying non-Christian experiences. Add any additional involvement you have had. Even if you "innocently" participated in something or observed it, you should write it on your list to renounce, just in case you unknowingly gave Satan a foothold.

Non-Christian Spiritual Experience Inventory
(Please check those that apply.)

Occult

____ Astral-projection

____ Ouija board

____ Table or body lifting

____ Dungeons and Dragons

____ Speaking in trance

____ Automatic writing

____ Magic eight ball

____ Telepathy

____ Using spells or curses

____ Seance

____ Materialization

____ Clairvoyance

____ Spirit guides

____ Fortune-telling

____ Tarot cards

____ Palm reading

____ Astrology/horoscopes

____ Rod and pendulum (dowsing)

____ Self-hypnosis

____ Mental manipulations or attempts to swap minds

____ Black and white magic

____ New Age medicine

____ Blood pacts (or cutting yourself in a destructive way)

Cult

____ Christian Science Unity

____ The Way International

____ Unification Church

____ Mormonism

____ Church of the Living Word

____ Jehovah's Witnesses

____ Children of God (Love)

____ Swedenborgianism

____ Unitarianism

____ Masons

____ New Age

____ The Forum (EST)

____ Spirit worship

____ Other _____

Other Religions

____ Buddhism

____ Hare Krishna

____ Bahaism

____ Rosicrucian

____ Science of the Mind

____ Science of Creative Intelligence

____ Transcendental Meditation

____ Hinduism

____ Yoga

____ Eckankar

____ Roy Masters

____ Silva Mind Control

____ Father Divine

____ Theosophical Society

____ Islam

____ Black Muslim

____ Religion of Martial Arts

____ Other_____

____ Fetishism (objects of worship, crystals, good-luck charms

____ Incubi and succubi (sexual spirits)

____ Other_____

1. Have you ever been hypnotized, attended a New Age or parapsychology seminar, consulted a medium, Spiritist or channeler? Explain.

   _____

2. Do you or have you ever had an imaginary friend or spirit guide offering you guidance or companionship? Explain.

   _____

3. Have you ever heard voices in your mind or had repeating and nagging thoughts condemning you or that were foreign to what you believe or feel, as though a dialog was going on in your head? Explain.

   _____

4. What other spiritual experiences have you had that would be considered out of the ordinary?

   _____

5. Have you ever made a vow, covenant or pact with any individual or group other than God?

   _____

6. Have you been involved in satanic ritual or satanic worship of any form? Explain.

When you are confident that your list is complete, confess and renounce each involvement, whether active or passive, by praying aloud the following prayer, repeating it separately for each item on your list:

> Lord,
>   I confess that I have participated in _____,
> and I renounce_____. Thank You that in
> Christ I am forgiven.

If you have had any involvement in satanic ritual or heavy occult activity, you need to state aloud the following special renunciations that apply. Read across the page, renouncing the first item in the column of the Kingdom of Darkness and then affirming the first truth in the column of the Kingdom of Light. Continue down the page in this manner.

All satanic rituals, covenants and assignments must be specifically renounced as the Lord allows you to recall them. Some who have been subjected to satanic ritual abuse may have developed multiple personalities to survive. Nevertheless, continue through the Steps to Freedom in order to resolve all you consciously can. It is important that you resolve the demonic strongholds first. Every personality must resolve his/her issues and agree to come together in Christ. You may need someone who understands spiritual conflict to help you maintain control and not be deceived into false memories. Only Jesus can bind up the broken-hearted, set captives free and make us whole.

Special Renunciations for Satanic Ritual Involvement

Kingdom of Darkness	Kingdom of Light
I renounce ever signing my name over to Satan or having had my name signed over to Satan.	I announce that my name is now written in the Lamb's Book of Life.
I renounce any ceremony where I may have been wed to Satan.	I announce that I am the bride of Christ.
I renounce any and all covenants that I made with Satan.	I announce that I am a partaker of the New Covenant with Christ.
I renounce all satanic assignments for my life, including duties, marriage and children.	I announce and commit myself to know and do only the will of God and accept only His guidance.
I renounce all spirit guides assigned to me.	I announce and accept only the leading of the Holy Spirit.
I renounce ever giving of my blood in the service of Satan.	I trust only in the shed blood of my Lord Jesus Christ.
I renounce ever eating of flesh or drinking of blood for satanic worship.	By faith I eat only the flesh and drink only the blood of Jesus in Holy Communion.
I renounce any and all guardians and satanist parents that were assigned to me.	I announce that God is my Father and the Holy Spirit is my Guardian by which I am sealed.
I renounce any baptism in blood or urine whereby I am identified with Satan.	I announce that I have been baptized into Christ Jesus and my identity is now in Christ.
I renounce any and all sacrifices that were made on my behalf by which Satan may claim ownership of me.	I announce that only the sacrifice of Christ has any hold on me. I belong to Him. I have been purchased by the blood of the Lamb.

STEP 2: DECEPTION VERSUS TRUTH

Truth is the revelation of God's Word, but we need to acknowledge the truth in the inner self (see Ps. 51:6). When David lived a lie, he suffered greatly. When he finally found freedom by acknowledging the truth, he wrote: "How blessed is the man...in whose spirit there is no deceit" (Ps. 32:2). We are to lay aside falsehood and speak the truth in love (see Eph. 4:15,25). A mentally healthy person is one who is in touch with reality and relatively free of anxiety. Both qualities should characterize the Christian who renounces deception and embraces the truth.

Begin this critical step by expressing aloud the following prayer. Don't let the enemy accuse you with thoughts such as: "This isn't going to work" or "I wish I could believe this but I can't" or any other lies in opposition to what you are proclaiming. Even if you have difficulty doing so, you need to pray the prayer and read the Doctrinal Affirmation.

> Dear heavenly Father,
>
> I know that You desire truth in the inner self and that facing this truth is the way of liberation (John 8:32). I acknowledge that I have been deceived by the father of lies (John 8:44) and that I have deceived myself (1 John 1:8). I pray in the name of the Lord Jesus Christ that You, heavenly Father, will rebuke all deceiving spirits by virtue of the shed blood and resurrection of the Lord Jesus Christ. By faith I have received You into my life and I am now seated with Christ in the heavenlies (Eph. 2:6). I acknowledge that I have the responsibility and authority to resist the devil, and when I do, he will flee from me. I now ask the Holy Spirit to guide me into all truth (John 16:13). I ask You to "Search me, O God, and know my heart; try me and know my anxious thoughts; and see if there be any hurtful way in me, and lead me in the everlasting way" (Ps. 139:23,24). In Jesus' name, I pray. Amen.

You may want to pause at this point to consider some of Satan's deceptive schemes. In addition to false teachers, false prophets and deceiving spirits, you can deceive yourself. Now that you are alive in Christ and forgiven, you never have to live a lie or defend yourself. Christ is your defense. How have you deceived or attempted to defend yourself according to the following?

Self-deception
_____ Hearing God's Word but not doing it (see Jas. 1:22; 4:17)
_____ Saying we have no sin (see 1 John 1:8)
_____ Thinking we are something when we aren't (see Gal. 6:3)
_____ Thinking we are wise in our own eyes (see 1 Cor. 3:18,19)
_____ Thinking we will not reap what we sow (see Gal. 6:7)
_____ Thinking the unrighteous will inherit the Kingdom (see 1 Cor. 6:9)
_____ Thinking we can associate with bad company and not be corrupted (see 1 Cor. 15:33)

Self-defense
(defending ourselves instead of trusting in Christ)
_____ Denial (conscious or subconscious refusal to face the truth)
_____ Fantasy (escaping from the real world)
_____ Emotional insulation (withdrawing to avoid rejection)
_____ Regression (reverting back to a less threatening time)
_____ Displacement (taking out frustrations on others)
_____ Projection (blaming others)
_____ Rationalization (making excuses for poor behavior)

For those things that have been true in your life, pray aloud:

Lord,
I agree that I have been deceived in the area of
_____.
Thank You for forgiving me. I commit myself to know and follow Your truth. Amen.

Choosing the truth may be difficult if you have been living a lie (been deceived) for many years. You may need to seek professional help to weed out the defense mechanisms you have depended upon to survive. The Christian needs only one defense—Jesus. Knowing that you are forgiven and accepted as God's child is what sets you free to face reality and declare your dependence on Him.

Faith is the biblical response to the truth, and believing the truth is a choice. When someone says, "I want to believe God, but I just can't," he or she is being deceived. Of course you can believe God. Faith is something you decide to do, not something you feel like doing. Believing the truth doesn't make it true. It's true; therefore, we believe it. The New Age movement is distorting the truth by saying we create reality through what we believe. We can't create reality with our minds; we face reality. It is what or who you believe in that counts. Everybody believes in something, and everybody walks by faith according to what he or she believes. But if what you believe isn't true, then how you live (walk by faith) won't be right.

Historically, the Church has found great value in publicly declaring its beliefs. The Apostles' Creed and the Nicene Creed have been recited for centuries. Read aloud the following affirmation of faith, and do so again as often as necessary to renew your mind. Experiencing difficulty in reading this affirmation may indicate where you are being deceived and under attack. Boldly affirm your commitment to biblical truth.

DOCTRINAL AFFIRMATION

I recognize that there is only one true and living God (Exod. 20:2,3) who exists as the Father, Son and Holy Spirit and that He is worthy of all honor, praise and glory as the Creator, Sustainer and Beginning and End of all things (Isa. 43:1,7,21; Rev. 4:11; 5:9,10).

I recognize Jesus Christ as the Messiah, the Word who became flesh and dwelt among us (John 1:1,14). I believe that He came to destroy the works of Satan (1 John 3:8), that He disarmed the rulers and authorities and made a public display of them, having triumphed over them (Col. 2:15).

I believe that God has proven His love for me because when I was still a sinner, Christ died for me (Rom. 5:8). I believe that He delivered me from the domain of darkness and transferred me to His kingdom, and in Him I have redemption, the forgiveness of sins (Col. 1:13,14).

I believe that I am now a child of God (1 John 3:1-3) and that I am seated with Christ in the heavenlies (Eph. 2:6). I believe that I was saved by the grace of God through faith, that it was a gift, and not the result of any works on my part (Eph. 2:8,9).

I choose to be strong in the Lord and in the strength of His might (Eph. 6:10). I put no confidence in the flesh (Phil. 3:3) for the weapons of warfare are not of the flesh (2 Cor. 10:4). I put on the whole armor of God (Eph. 6:10-20), and I resolve to stand firm in my faith and resist the evil one.

I believe that apart from Christ I can do nothing (John 15:5), so I declare myself dependent on Him. I choose to abide in Christ in order to bear much fruit and glorify the Lord (John 15:8). I announce to Satan that Jesus is my Lord (1 Cor. 12:3), and I reject any counterfeit gifts or works of Satan in my life.

I believe that the truth will set me free (John 8:32) and that walking in the light is the only path of fellowship (1 John 1:7). Therefore, I stand against Satan's deception by taking every thought captive in obedience to Christ (2 Cor. 10:5). I declare that the Bible is the only authoritative standard (2 Tim. 3:15,16). I choose to speak the truth in love (Eph. 4:15).

I choose to present my body as an instrument of righteousness, a living and holy sacrifice, and I renew my mind by the living Word of God in order that I may prove that the will of God is good, acceptable and perfect (Rom. 6:13; 12:1,2). I put off the old self with its evil practices and put on the new self (Col. 3:9,10), and I declare myself to be a new creature in Christ (2 Cor. 5:17).

I trust my heavenly Father to fill me with His Holy Spirit (Eph. 5:18), to lead me into all truth (John 16:13) and to empower my life that I may live above sin and not carry out the desires of the flesh (Gal. 5:16). I crucify the flesh (Gal. 5:24) and choose to walk by the Spirit.

I renounce all selfish goals and choose the ultimate goal of love (1 Tim. 1:5). I choose to obey the two greatest commandments: to love the Lord my God with all my heart, soul and mind, and to love my neighbor as myself (Matt. 22:37-39).

I believe that Jesus has all authority in heaven and on earth (Matt. 28:18) and that He is the head over all rule and authority (Col. 2:10). I believe that Satan and his demons are subject to me in Christ since I am a member of Christ's Body (Eph. 1:19-23). Therefore, I obey the command to submit to God and to resist the devil (Jas. 4:7), and I command Satan in the name of Christ to leave my presence.

STEP 3: BITTERNESS VERSUS FORGIVENESS

We need to forgive others in order to be free from our pasts and to prevent Satan from taking advantage of us (see 2 Cor. 2:10,11). We are to be merciful just as our heavenly Father is merciful (see Luke 6:36). We are to forgive as we have been forgiven (see Eph. 4:31,32). Ask God to bring to mind the names of those people you need to forgive by expressing the following prayer aloud:

> Dear heavenly Father,
>   I thank You for the riches of Your kindness, forbearance and patience, knowing that Your kindness has led me to repentance (Rom. 2:4). I confess that I have not extended that same patience and kindness toward others who have offended me, but instead I have harbored bitterness and resentment. I pray that during this time of self-examination You would bring to my mind those people I need to forgive in order that I may do so (Matt. 18:35). I ask this in the precious name of Jesus. Amen.

As names come to mind, make a list of only the names. At the end of your list, write "myself." Forgiving yourself is accepting God's cleansing and forgiveness. Then write "thoughts against God." Thoughts raised up against the knowledge of God will usually result in angry feelings toward Him. Technically, we can't forgive God because He cannot commit any sin of commission or omission. But you need to specifically renounce false expectations and thoughts about God and agree to release any anger you have toward Him.

Before you pray to forgive these people, stop and consider what forgiveness is, what it is not, what decision you will be making and what the consequences will be.

In the following explanation, the main points are highlighted in bold print:

Forgiveness is not forgetting. People who try to forget find they cannot. God says He will remember our sins "no more" (see Heb. 10:17), but God, being omniscient, cannot forget. Remember our sins "no more" means that God will never use the past against us (see Ps. 103:12). Forgetting may be the result of forgiveness, but it is never the means of forgiveness. When we bring up the past against others, we are saying we haven't forgiven them.

Forgiveness is a choice, a crisis of the will. Since God requires us to forgive, it is something we can do. However, forgiveness is difficult for us because it pulls against our concept of justice. We want revenge for offenses suffered. We are told, however, never to take our own revenge (see Rom. 12:19). You say, "Why should I let them off the hook?" That is precisely the problem. You are still hooked to them, still bound by your past. You will let them off your hook, but they are never off God's. He will deal with them fairly, something we cannot do.

You say, "You don't understand how much this person hurt me!" But don't you see, they are still hurting you! How do you stop the pain? **You don't forgive someone for their sake; you do it for your own sake so that you can be free. Your need to forgive isn't an issue between you and the offender; it's between you and God.**

Forgiveness is agreeing to live with the consequences of another person's sin. Forgiveness is costly. You pay the price of the evil you forgive. You're going to live with those consequences whether you want to or not; your only choice is whether you will do so in the bitterness of unforgiveness or the freedom of forgiveness. Jesus took the consequences of your sin upon Himself. All true forgiveness is substitutionary because no one really forgives without bearing the consequences of the other person's sin. God the Father "made Him who knew no sin to be sin on our behalf, that we might become the righteousness of God in Him" (2 Cor. 5:21). Where is the justice? It is the Cross that makes forgiveness legally and morally right: "For the death that He died, He died to sin, once for all" (Rom. 6:10).

Decide that you will bear the burdens of their offenses by not using that information against them in the future. This doesn't mean that you tolerate sin. You must set up scriptural boundaries to prevent future abuse. Some may be required to testify for the sake of justice, but not for the purpose of seeking revenge from a bitter heart.

How do you forgive from your heart? You acknowledge the hurt and the hate. If your forgiveness doesn't visit the emotional core of your life, it will be incomplete. Many feel the pain of interpersonal offenses, but they won't or don't know how to acknowledge it. Let God bring the pain to the surface so He can deal with it. This is where the healing takes place.

Don't wait to forgive until you feel like forgiving; you will

never get there. Feelings take time to heal after the choice to forgive is made and Satan has lost his place (see Eph. 4:26,27). Freedom is what will be gained, not a feeling.

As you pray, God may bring to mind offending people and experiences you have totally forgotten. Let Him do it even if it is painful. Remember, you are doing this for your sake. God wants you to be free. Don't rationalize or explain the offender's behavior. Forgiveness is dealing with your pain and leaving the other person to God. Positive feelings will follow in time; freeing yourself from the past is the critical issue right now.

Don't say, "Lord, please help me to forgive," because He is already helping you. Don't say, "Lord, I want to forgive," because you are bypassing the hard-core choice to forgive, which is your responsibility. Stay with each individual until you are sure you have dealt with all the remembered pain—what they did, how they hurt you, how they made you feel (rejected, unloved, unworthy, dirty).

You are now ready to forgive the people on your list so that you can be free in Christ; those people no longer having any control over you. For each person on your list, pray aloud:

Lord,
    I forgive (name the person) for (verbally share every hurt and pain the Lord brings to your mind and how it made you feel).

After you have forgiven every person for every painful memory, then finish this step by praying:

Lord,
    I release all these people to You, and my right to seek revenge. I choose not to hold on to my bitterness and anger, and I ask You to heal my damaged emotions. In Jesus' name, I pray. Amen.

Step 4: Rebellion Versus Submission

We live in rebellious times. Many believe it is their right to sit in judgment of those in authority over them. Rebelling against God and His authority gives Satan an opportunity to attack. As our commanding general, the Lord says, "Get into ranks and follow Me. I will not lead you into temptation, but I will deliver you from evil" (see Matt. 6:13).

We have two biblical responsibilities regarding authority figures: Pray for them and submit to them. The only time God permits us to disobey earthly leaders is when they require us to do something morally wrong before God or attempt to rule outside the realm of their authority. Pray the following prayer:

Dear heavenly Father,

You have said that rebellion is as the sin of witchcraft and insubordination is as iniquity and idolatry (1 Sam. 15:23). I know that in action and attitude I have sinned against You with a rebellious heart. I ask Your forgiveness for my rebellion and pray that by the shed blood of the Lord Jesus Christ all ground gained by evil spirits because of my rebelliousness will be canceled. I pray that You will shed light on all my ways that I may know the full extent of my rebelliousness. I now choose to adopt a submissive spirit and a servant's heart. In the name of Christ Jesus, my Lord. Amen.

Being under authority is an act of faith. You are trusting God to work through His established lines of authority. There are times when employers, parents and husbands are violating the laws of civil government that are ordained by God to protect innocent people against abuse. In these cases, you need to appeal to the state for your protection. In many states, the law requires such abuse to be reported.

In difficult cases, such as continuing abuse at home, further counseling help may be needed. And in some cases, when earthly authorities have abused their position and are requiring disobedience to God or a compromise in your commitment to Him, you need to obey God, not man.

We are all admonished to submit to one another as equals in Christ (see Eph. 5:21). Specific lines of authority in Scripture, however, are provided for the purpose of accomplishing common goals:

Civil Government (see Rom. 13:1-7; 1 Tim. 2:1-4; 1 Pet. 2:13-17)
Parents (see Eph. 6:1-3)
Husband (see 1 Pet. 3:1-4) or Wife (see Eph. 5:21; 1 Pet. 3:7)
Employer (see 1 Pet. 2:18-23)
Church Leaders (see Heb. 13:17)
God (see Dan. 9:5,9)

Examine each area and ask God to forgive you for those times you have not been submissive, and pray:

Lord,
I agree I have been rebellious toward _____.
I choose to be submissive and obedient to Your Word. In Jesus' name. Amen.

STEP 5: PRIDE VERSUS HUMILITY

Pride is a killer. Pride says, "I can do it! I can get myself out of this mess without God or anyone else's help." Oh no, we can't! We absolutely need God, and we desperately need each other. Paul wrote: "We worship in the Spirit of God and glory in Christ Jesus and put no confidence in the flesh" (Phil. 3:3). Humility is confidence properly placed. We are to be "strong in the Lord and in the strength of His might" (Eph. 6:10). James 4:6-10 and 1 Peter 5:1-10 reveal that spiritual conflict follows pride. Use the following prayer to express your commitment to live humbly before God:

Dear heavenly Father,

You have said that pride goes before destruction and an arrogant spirit before stumbling (Prov. 16:18). I confess that I have lived independently and have not denied myself, picked up my cross daily and followed You (Matt. 16:24). In so doing, I have given ground to the enemy in my life. I have believed that I could be successful and live victoriously by my own strength and resources. I now confess that I have sinned against You by placing my will before Yours and by centering my life around myself instead of You. I now renounce the self-life and by so doing cancel all the ground that has been gained in my members by the enemies of the Lord Jesus Christ. I pray that You will guide me so that I will do nothing from selfishness or empty conceit, but with humility of mind I will regard others as more important than myself (Phil. 2:3). Enable me through love to serve others and in honor prefer others (Rom. 12:10). I ask this in the name of Christ Jesus, my Lord. Amen.

Having made that commitment, now allow God to show you any specific areas of your life where you have been prideful, such as:

_____ Stronger desire to do my will than God's will

_____ More dependent upon my strengths and resources than God's

_____ Too often believe that my ideas and opinions are better than others'

_____ More concerned about controlling others than developing self-control

_____ Sometimes consider myself more important than others
_____ Tendency to think I have no needs
_____ Find it difficult to admit that I was wrong
_____ Tendency to be more of a people-pleaser than a God-pleaser
_____ Overly concerned about getting the credit I deserve
_____ Driven to obtain the recognition that comes from degrees, titles and positions
_____ Often think I am more humble than others
_____ Other ways _____

For each of these that has been true in your life, pray aloud:

Lord,
    I agree I have been prideful by _____.
I choose to humble myself and place all my confidence in You. Amen.

STEP 6: BONDAGE VERSUS FREEDOM

The next Step to Freedom deals with habitual sin. People who have been caught in the trap of sin-confess-sin-confess may need to follow the instructions of James 5:16, "Confess your sins to one another, and pray for one another, so that you may be healed. The effective prayer of a righteous man can accomplish much." Seek out a righteous person who will hold you up in prayer and to whom you can be accountable. Others may only need the assurance of 1 John 1:9: "If we confess our sins, He is faithful and righteous to forgive us our sins and to cleanse us from all unrighteousness." Confession is not saying "I'm sorry"; it is saying "I did it." Whether you need the help of others or just the accountability to God, pray the following prayer:

Dear heavenly Father,
  You have told us to put on the Lord Jesus Christ and make no provision for the flesh in regard to its lust (Rom. 13:14). I acknowledge that I have given in to fleshly lusts that wage war against my soul (1 Pet. 2:11). I thank You that in Christ my sins are forgiven, but I have transgressed Your holy law and given the enemy an opportunity to wage war in my physical body (Rom. 6:12,13; Eph 4:27; Jas. 4:1; 1 Pet. 5:8). I come before Your presence to acknowledge these sins and to seek Your cleansing (1 John 1:9) that I may be freed from the bondage of sin. I now ask You to reveal to my mind the ways I have transgressed Your moral law and grieved the Holy Spirit. In Jesus' precious name, I pray. Amen.

The deeds of the flesh are numerous. Many of the following issues are taken from Galatians 5:19-21. Check those that apply to you and any others you have struggled with that the Lord has brought to your mind. Then confess each one with the concluding prayer. Note: sexual sins, eating disorders, substance abuse, abortion, suicidal tendencies and perfectionism will be dealt with later.

_____ stealing
_____ lying
_____ fighting
_____ jealousy
_____ envying

_____ outbursts of anger
_____ complaining
_____ criticizing
_____ lusting
_____ cheating
_____ gossiping
_____ controlling
_____ procrastinating
_____ swearing
_____ greediness
_____ laziness
_____ divisiveness
_____ other_____

Dear heavenly Father,
I thank You that my sins are forgiven in Christ, but I have walked by the flesh and therefore sinned by _____. Thank You for cleansing me of all unrighteousness. I ask that You would enable me to walk by the Spirit and not carry out the desires of the flesh. In Jesus' name, I pray. Amen.

It is our responsibility not to allow sin to reign in our mortal bodies by not using our bodies as instruments of unrighteousness (see Rom. 6:12,13). If you are or have struggled with sexual sins (pornography, masturbation, sexual promiscuity) or are experiencing sexual difficulty in your marriage, pray as follows:

Lord,
I ask You to reveal to my mind every sexual use of my body as an instrument of unrighteousness. In Jesus' precious name, I pray. Amen.

As the Lord brings to your mind every sexual misuse of your body, whether it was done to you (rape, incest or other sexual abuse) or willingly by you, renounce every occasion:

Lord,
I renounce (name the specific misuse of your body) with (name the person) and ask You to break that bond.

Now commit your body to the Lord by praying:

Lord,

I renounce all these uses of my body as an instrument of unrighteousness and by so doing ask You to break all bondages Satan has brought into my life through that involvement. I confess my participation. I now present my body to You as a living sacrifice, holy and acceptable unto You, and I reserve the sexual use of my body only for marriage. I renounce the lie of Satan that my body is not clean, that it is dirty or in any way unacceptable as a result of my past sexual experiences. Lord, I thank You that You have totally cleansed and forgiven me, that You love and accept me unconditionally. Therefore, I can accept myself. And I choose to do so, to accept myself and my body as cleansed. In Jesus' name, amen.

SPECIAL PRAYERS FOR SPECIFIC PROBLEMS

Homosexuality

Lord,

I renounce the lie that You have created me or anyone else to be homosexual, and I affirm that You clearly forbid homosexual behavior. I accept myself as a child of God and declare that You created me a man (woman). I renounce any bondages of Satan that have perverted my relationships with others. I announce that I am free to relate to the opposite sex in the way that You intended. In Jesus' name, amen.

Abortion

Lord,

I confess that I did not assume stewardship of the life You entrusted to me and I ask your forgiveness. I choose to accept Your forgiveness, and I now commit that child to You for Your care in eternity. In Jesus' name, amen.

Suicidal Tendencies

Lord,

I renounce suicidal thoughts and any attempts I have made to take my own life or in any way injure myself. I renounce the lie that life is hopeless and that I can find peace and freedom by taking my own life. Satan is a thief, and he comes to steal, kill and destroy. I choose to be a good steward of the physical life You have entrusted to me. In Jesus' name, I pray. Amen.

Eating Disorders or Self-Mutilation

Lord,

I renounce the lie that my value as a person is dependent upon my physical beauty, my weight or size. I renounce cutting myself, vomiting, using laxatives or starving myself as a means of cleansing myself of evil or altering my appearance. I announce that only the blood of the Lord Jesus Christ cleanses me from sin. I accept the reality that there may be sin present in me due to the lies I have believed and the wrongful use of my body, but I renounce the lie that I am evil or that any part of my body is evil. My body is the temple of the Holy Spirit and I belong to You, Lord. I receive Your love and acceptance of me. In Jesus' name, amen.

Substance Abuse

Lord,

I confess that I have misused substances (alcohol, tobacco, food, prescription or street drugs) for the purpose of pleasure, to escape reality or to cope with difficult situations—resulting in the abuse of my body, the harmful programming of my mind and the quenching of the Holy Spirit. I ask Your forgiveness. I renounce any satanic connection or influence in my life through my misuse of chemicals or food. I cast my anxiety onto Christ Who loves me, and I commit myself to no longer yield to substance abuse, but to the Holy Spirit. I ask You, heavenly Father, to fill me with Your Holy Spirit. In Jesus' name, amen.

Drivenness and Perfectionism

Lord,

I renounce the lie that my self-worth is dependent upon my ability to perform. I announce the truth that my identity and sense of worth are found in who I am as Your child. I renounce seeking the approval and acceptance of other people, and I choose to believe that I am already approved and accepted in Christ because of His death and resurrection for me. I choose to believe the truth that I have been saved, not by deeds done in righteousness, but according to Your mercy. I choose to believe that I am no longer under the curse of the law, because Christ became a curse for me. I receive the free gift of life in Christ and choose to abide in Him. I renounce striving for perfection by living under the law. By Your grace, heavenly Father, I choose from this day forward to walk by faith according to what You have said is true by the power of Your Holy Spirit. In Jesus name, amen.

Plaguing Fears

Dear heavenly Father,

I acknowledge You as the only legitimate fear object in my life. You are the only omnipresent (always present) and omniscient (all knowing) God and the only means by which all other fears can be expelled. You are my sanctuary. You have not given me a spirit of timidity, but of power and love and discipline. I confess that I have allowed the fear of man and the fear of death to exercise control over my life, instead of trusting in You. I now renounce all other fear objects and worship You only. I pray that You would fill me with Your Holy Spirit that I may live my life and speak Your word with boldness. In Jesus' name, I pray. Amen.

After you have confessed all known sin, pray:

I now confess these sins to You and claim my forgiveness and cleansing through the blood of the Lord Jesus Christ. I cancel all ground that evil spirits have gained through my willful involvement in sin. I ask this in the wonderful name of my Lord and Savior, Jesus Christ. Amen.

STEP 7: ACQUIESCENCE VERSUS RENUNCIATION

Acquiescence is passively giving in or agreeing without consent. The last Step to Freedom is to renounce the sins of your ancestors and any curses that may have been placed on you. In giving the Ten Commandments, God said: "You shall not make for yourself an idol, or any likeness of what is in heaven above or on the earth beneath or in the water under the earth. You shall not worship them or serve them; for I, the Lord your God, am a jealous God, visiting the iniquity of the fathers on the children, on the third and fourth generations of those who hate Me" (Exod. 20:4,5).

Familiar spirits can be passed on from one generation to the next if not renounced and if your new spiritual heritage in Christ is not proclaimed. You are not guilty for the sin of any ancestor, but because of their sin, Satan may have gained access to your family. This is not to deny that many problems are transmitted genetically or acquired from an immoral atmosphere. All three conditions can predispose an individual to a particular sin. In addition, deceived people may try to curse you, or satanic groups may try to target you. You have all the authority and protection you need in Christ to stand against such curses and assignments. Ask the Lord to reveal to your mind the sins and iniquities of your ancestors by praying the following prayer:

Dear heavenly Father,

I thank You that I am a new creation in Christ. I desire to obey Your command to honor my mother and my father, but I also acknowledge that my physical heritage has not been perfect. I ask You to reveal to my mind the sins and iniquities of my ancestors in order to confess, renounce and forsake them. In Jesus' name, I pray. Amen.

Now claim your position and protection in Christ by making the following declaration verbally, and then by humbling yourself before God in prayer.

DECLARATION

I here and now reject and disown all the sins and iniquities of my ancestors, including (name them). As one who has been delivered from the power of darkness and translated into the kingdom of God's dear Son, I cancel out all demonic working that has been passed on to me from my ancestors. As one who has been crucified and raised with Jesus Christ and who sits with Him in heavenly places, I renounce all satanic assignments that are directed toward me and my ministry, and I cancel every curse that Satan and his workers have put on me. I announce to Satan and all his forces that Christ became a curse for me (Gal. 3:13) when He died for my sins on the cross. I reject any and every way in which Satan may claim ownership of me. I belong to the Lord Jesus Christ who purchased me with His own blood. I reject all other blood sacrifices whereby Satan may claim ownership of me. I declare myself to be eternally and completely signed over and committed to the Lord Jesus Christ. By the authority I have in Jesus Christ, I now command every familiar spirit and every enemy of the Lord Jesus Christ that is in or around me to leave my presence. I commit myself to my heavenly Father to do His will from this day forward.

PRAYER

Dear heavenly Father,

I come to You as Your child purchased by the blood of the Lord Jesus Christ. You are the Lord of the universe and the Lord of my life. I submit my body to You as an instrument of righteousness, a living sacrifice, that I may glorify You in my body. I now ask You to fill me with Your Holy Spirit. I commit myself to the renewing of my mind in order to prove that Your will is good, perfect and acceptable for me. All this I do in the name and authority of the Lord Jesus Christ. Amen.

Once you have secured your freedom by going through these seven Steps, you may find demonic influences attempting reentry, days or even months later. One person shared that she heard a spirit say to her mind, "I'm back" two days after she had been set free. "No, you're not!" she proclaimed aloud. The attack ceased immediately. One victory does not constitute winning the war. Freedom must be maintained. After completing these Steps, one jubilant lady asked, "Will I always be like this?" I told her that she would stay free as long as she remained in right relationship with God. "Even if you slip and fall," I encouraged, "you know how to get right with God again."

One victim of incredible atrocities shared this illustration: "It's like being forced to play a game with an ugly stranger in my own home. I kept losing and wanted to quit, but the ugly stranger wouldn't let me. Finally I called the police (a higher authority), and they came and escorted the stranger out. He knocked on the door trying to regain entry, but this time I recognized his voice and didn't let him in."

What a beautiful illustration of gaining freedom in Christ. We call upon Jesus, the ultimate authority, and He escorts the enemy out of our lives. Know the truth, stand firm and resist the evil one. Seek good Christian fellowship, and commit yourself to regular times of Bible study and prayer. God loves you and will never leave or forsake you.

AFTERCARE

Freedom must be maintained. You have won a very important battle in an ongoing war. Freedom is yours as long as you keep choosing truth and standing firm in the strength of the Lord. If new memories should surface or if you become aware of "lies" you have believed or other non-Christian experiences you have had, renounce them and choose the truth. Some have found it helpful to go through the Steps again. As you do, read the instructions carefully.

For your encouragement and further study, read *Victory over the Darkness* (adult or youth version), *The Bondage Breaker* (adult or youth version) and *Released from Bondage*. If you are a parent, read *The Seduction of Our Children*. *Walking in the Light* (formerly *Walking Through the Darkness*) was written to help people understand God's guidance and discern counterfeit guidance. To maintain your freedom, we also suggest the following:

1. Seek legitimate Christian fellowship where you can walk in the light and speak the truth in love.
2. Study your Bible daily. Memorize key verses.
3. Take every thought captive to the obedience of Christ. Assume responsibility for your thought life, reject the lie, choose the truth and stand firm in your position in Christ.
4. Don't drift away! It is very easy to get lazy in your thoughts and revert back to old habit patterns of thinking. Share your struggles openly with a trusted friend. You need at least one friend who will stand with you.
5. Don't expect another person to fight your battle for you. Others can help, but they can't think, pray, read the Bible or choose the truth for you.
6. Continue to seek your identity and sense of worth in Christ. Read *Living Free in Christ* and the devotional, *Daily in Christ*. Renew your mind with the truth that your acceptance, security and significance is in Christ by saturating your mind with the following truths. Read the entire list of who you are "in Christ" and the Doctrinal Affirmation (in Step 2) aloud morning and evening during the next several weeks (and look up the verses referenced).
7. Commit yourself to daily prayer. You can pray the following suggested prayers often and with confidence:

DAILY PRAYER

Dear heavenly Father,

I honor You as my sovereign Lord. I acknowledge that You are always present with me. You are the only all-powerful and wise God. You are kind and loving in all Your ways. I love You and thank You that I am united with Christ and spiritually alive in Him. I choose not to love the world, and I crucify the flesh and all its passions.

I thank You for the life that I now have in Christ, and I ask You to fill me with Your Holy Spirit that I may live my life free from sin. I declare my dependence upon You, and I take my stand against Satan and all his lying ways. I choose to believe the truth, and I refuse to be discouraged. You are the God of all hope, and I am confident that You will meet my needs as I seek to live according to Your Word. I express with confidence that I can live a responsible life through Christ who strengthens me.

I now take my stand against Satan and command him and all his evil spirits to depart from me. I put on the whole armor of God. I submit my body as a living sacrifice and renew my mind by the living Word of God in order that I may prove that the will of God is good, acceptable and perfect. I ask these things in the precious name of my Lord and Savior, Jesus Christ. Amen.

BEDTIME PRAYER

Thank You, Lord, that You have brought me into Your family and have blessed me with every spiritual blessing in the heavenly realms in Christ. Thank You for providing this time of renewal through sleep. I accept it as part of Your perfect plan for Your children, and I trust You to guard my mind and my body during my sleep. As I have meditated on You and Your truth during this day, I choose to let these thoughts continue in my mind while I am asleep. I commit myself to You for Your protection from every attempt of Satan or his emissaries to attack me during sleep. I commit myself to You as my rock, my fortress and my resting place. I pray in the strong name of the Lord Jesus Christ. Amen.

CLEANSING HOME/APARTMENT

After removing all articles of false worship from home/apartment, pray aloud in every room, if necessary:

Heavenly Father, we acknowledge that You are Lord of heaven and earth. In Your sovereign power and love, You have given us all things richly to enjoy. Thank You for this place to live. We claim this home for our family as a place of spiritual safety and protection from all the attacks of the enemy. As children of God seated with Christ in the heavenly realm, we command every evil spirit claiming ground in the structures and furnishings of this place, based on the activities of previous occupants, to leave and never return. We renounce all curses and spells utilized against this place. We ask You, heavenly Father, to post guardian angels around this home (apartment, condo, room, etc.) to guard it from attempts of the enemy to enter and disturb Your purposes for us. We thank You, Lord, for doing this, and pray in the name of the Lord Jesus Christ. Amen.

LIVING IN A NON-CHRISTIAN ENVIRONMENT

After removing all articles of false worship from your room, pray aloud in the space allotted to you:

Thank You, heavenly Father, for my place to live and to be renewed by sleep. I ask You to set aside my room (portion of my room) as a place of spiritual safety for me. I renounce any allegiance given to false gods or spirits by other occupants, and I renounce any claim to this room (space) by Satan based on activities of past occupants or me. On the basis of my position as a child of God and a joint-heir with Christ who has all authority in heaven and on earth, I command all evil spirits to leave this place and never to return. I ask You, heavenly Father, to appoint guardian angels to protect me while I live here. I pray this in the name of the Lord Jesus Christ. Amen.

B

MATERIALS AND TRAINING FOR YOU AND YOUR CHURCH

Christ is the answer and truth will set you free. I (Neil) have never been more convinced of this truth. Jesus is the bondage breaker, and He is the wonderful counselor. The following material will benefit both you and your marriage. It will most likely result in your freedom in Christ and help you to become the person God wants you to be. That would be tremendous, but I think the Lord has something far bigger in mind. Let me explain.

Crystal Evangelical Free Church hosted our "Resolving Personal and Spiritual Conflicts" conference. Immediately afterward, they began their own "Freedom Ministry" by training encouragers. Within three years they had led more than 1,500 hurting and desperate people to freedom in Christ. They have also hosted their own conference to show other churches how to do it. Ninety-five percent of their trained encouragers are laypeople. Because there are not enough professional pastors or counselors in our country to reach more than 5 percent of our population, we must equip the saints to do the work of ministry.

Suppose your church carefully chose 20 people and trained them, as I will outline shortly. If each person agreed to help just one other person every other week, by the end of one year, your church would have helped 520 people. And the ministry won't stop there! These people would become witnesses without even trying. Your church would become known in the community as a place that really cares for its people and has an answer for the problems of life. How can people witness if they are in bondage? But children of God who are established free in Christ will naturally (and supernatural-ly) be witnesses as they glorify God by bearing fruit.

The material for training encouragers includes books, study guides and tape series (both video and audio). The tape series all have corresponding syllabi. The training will best be facilitated if the trainees watch the videos, read the books and complete the study guides. The study guides will greatly increase the learning process and help people to personalize and internalize the message. The cost prohibits some from using the videos. In such cases, the books and study guides can still be effective.

The basic and advanced materials are given as follows in the order they should be taught:

BASIC-LEVEL TRAINING

First Four Weeks

Purpose:	To understand who we are in Christ, how to walk by faith and win the battle for our minds, to understand our emotions and the means by which we relate to one another.
Video/Audio Series:	"Resolving Personal Conflicts."
Reading:	*Victory over the Darkness* and accompanying study guide.
Youth Edition:	*Stomping Out the Darkness* and accompanying study guide.
Supplemental Reading:	*Living Free in Christ*: The purpose of this book is to establish us complete in Christ and to show how He meets the most critical needs of our lives: identity, acceptance, security and significance. This is the first book we have people read after they go through the Steps or pray to receive Christ.

Second Four Weeks

Purpose:	To understand the nature of the spiritual world; to know the position, authority,

	protection and vulnerability of the believer; to know how to set captives free.
Video/Audio Series:	"Resolving Spiritual Conflicts."
Reading:	*The Bondage Breaker* and accompanying study guide.
Youth Edition:	*The Bondage Breaker Youth Edition* and accompanying study guide.
Supplemental Reading:	*Released from Bondage:* This book contains chapter-length personal testimonies of people who have found freedom in Christ from depression, incest, lust, panic attacks, eating disorders, etc., with explanatory comments by Neil Anderson.
Note:	*Breaking Through to Spiritual Maturity* is an adult curriculum for teaching the previous material. *Busting Free* is the youth curriculum for teaching the youth editions.

Third and Fourth Four Weeks

Purpose:	To understand the theology and practical means by which we can help others find freedom in Christ with a discipleship/counseling approach.
Video/Audio Series:	"Spiritual Conflicts and Counseling" and "How to Lead a Person to Freedom in Christ."
Reading:	*Helping Others Find Freedom in Christ* plus the training manual and accompanying study guide. The study guide also details how your church can establish a discipleship/counseling ministry, and it has answers for the most commonly asked questions.
Youth Edition:	*Helping Our Children Find Freedom in Christ* (in process).
Supplemental Reading:	*Daily in Christ:* This is a one-year devotional that we encourage individuals as well as families to read annually.

The following are prerequisites to successfully complete the basic training:

1. Complete the "Steps to Freedom" with an encourager.
2. Complete two or more freedom appointments as a prayer partner.
3. Be recommended by the director of the Freedom ministry and meet the qualifications established by his or her church.

In addition to our basic training, Freedom in Christ Ministries has appropriate materials available for advanced training for specific issues. The topics can be covered by offering additional training, special meetings or regularly scheduled encourager meetings. We strongly suggest that your team of encouragers meet regularly for prayer, instruction and feedback. It has been our experience that cases become more difficult as the group matures. On-the-job training is essential for any ministry. None of us have arrived. About the time we think we have heard it all, along comes a case that shatters all stereotypes and doesn't fit into any mold. This unpredictability keeps us from falling into patterns of complacency and relying on our own cleverness, rather than relying on God. The advanced training material should be studied in the order given:

ADVANCED-LEVEL TRAINING

First Four Weeks

Purpose: To discern counterfeit guidance from divine guidance; to explain fear, anxiety, how to pray by the Spirit and how to walk by the Spirit.
Book: *Walking in the Light.*
Youth Edition: *Know Light, No Fear.*

Second Four Weeks

Purpose: To understand the culture in which our children are being raised; what is going on in their minds; how to be the

	parents they need; and how to lead them to freedom in Christ.
Book and Video Series:	*The Seduction of Our Children.*
Supplemental Reading	
For Youth:	*To My Dear Slimeball* by Rich Miller.

Third Four Weeks

Purpose:	To understand how people get into sexual bondage and how they can be free in Christ.
Book:	*A Way of Escape.*
Youth Edition:	*Purity Under Pressure.*

Fourth Four Weeks (can include one of the following):

Book:	*Freedom from Addiction.*
Subjects Include:	The nature of substance abuse and how the bondage can be broken in Christ.
Book and Video Series:	*Setting Your Church Free*: This book and video series by Neil Anderson and Charles Mylander is for Christian leaders. It teaches a biblical pattern of leadership and shows how churches can resolve their corporate conflicts and establish Christ as the head of their ministries.
Book:	*Spiritual Warfare* by Dr. Timothy Warner.
Video/Audio Series:	"Resolving Spiritual Conflicts and Cross-Cultural Ministry," also by Dr. Timothy Warner.

Schedules for Basic-Level Training

A 16-week format requires meeting one night each week for two to three hours. Viewing two video lessons each night, it will take about 12 weeks to view the first three video series. The last 4 weeks, use the video "How to Lead a Person to Freedom in Christ." It provides four one-hour segments. Showing a one-hour video each evening allows ample time for discussion. This schedule does not include much time for discussing the books and inductive studies or the content of the video series. Another meeting could be scheduled for that purpose, such as Sunday morning. If necessary, the material could be discussed after the video has been shown. A summary of the schedule is as follows:

Weeks 1—4	Week 5—8	Week 9—16
Resolving Personal Conflicts	Resolving Spiritual Conflicts	Spiritual Conflicts and Counseling and How to Lead a Person to Freedom in Christ.
Two video lessons each night	Two video lessons each night; last tape shows the "Steps to Freedom," which can be done as a group in the class or separately with an encourager.	Two video lessons each night for four weeks, then one hour per night for four weeks.

Although these meetings can be open to all who will commit the time, it should be made clear that attending the seminars does not automatically qualify anyone to participate in the ministry. Another possible schedule would be showing one video series on a Friday night/Saturday format each month. This will require only one facilitator giving one weekend each month. It would be possible to cover all the material in four weekends. There is generally less time for discussion of the videos in this schedule, but you can meet Sunday morning or one night a week to discuss the books and the inductive studies.

Weekend #1	Weekend #2	Weekend #3
Resolving Personal Conflicts	Resolving Spiritual Conflicts	Spiritual Conflicts and Counseling
Friday Night—Video Lessons: 1-2	Friday Night—Video Lessons: 1-2	Friday Night—Video Lessons: 1-2
Saturday: Lessons: 3-8	Saturday: Lessons: 3-7 and the "Steps to Freedom"	Saturday: Lessons: 3-8

The fourth weekend could be completed on Saturday only, using the shorter video series *How to Lead a Person to Freedom in Christ*. We realize it is a lot of material to cover, but there are no shortcuts. I cover almost all of this material when I conduct a "Resolving Personal and Spiritual Conflicts" conference in a week. These materials can be purchased from:

Freedom in Christ Ministries
491 E. Lambert Rd.
La Habra, California 90631
(310)691-9128   (310)691-4035 FAX

WHO I AM IN CHRIST

I Am Accepted in Christ

JOHN 1:12	I am God's child
JOHN 15:15	I am Christ's friend
ROMANS 5:1	I have been justified
1 CORINTHIANS 6:17	I am united with the Lord and one with Him in spirit
1 CORINTHIANS 6:20	I have been bought with a price; I belong to God
1 CORINTHIANS 12:27	I am a member of Christ's Body
EPHESIANS 1:1	I am a saint
EPHESIANS 1:5	I have been adopted as God's child
EPHESIANS 2:18	I have direct access to God through the Holy Spirit
COLOSSIANS 1:14	I have been redeemed and forgiven of all my sins
COLOSSIANS 2:10	I am complete in Christ

I Am Secure in Christ

ROMANS 8:1,2	I am free forever from condemnation
ROMANS 8:28	I am assured that all things work together for good
ROMANS 8:33,34	I am free from any condemning charges against me
ROMANS 8:35	I cannot be separated from the love of God
2 CORINTHIANS 1:21	I have been established, anointed and sealed by God
COLOSSIANS 3:3	I am hidden with Christ in God
PHILIPPIANS 1:6	I am confident that the good work God has begun in me will be perfected
PHILIPPIANS 3:20	I am a citizen of heaven
2 TIMOTHY 1:7	I have not been given a spirit of fear, but of power, love and a sound mind
HEBREWS 4:16	I can find grace and mercy in time of need
1 JOHN 5:18	I am born of God and the evil one cannot touch me

I Am Significant in Christ

MATTHEW 5:13,14	I am the salt and light of the earth
JOHN 15:1,5	I am a branch of the true vine, a channel of His life
JOHN 15:16	I have been chosen and appointed to bear fruit
ACTS 1:8	I am a personal witness of Christ's
1 CORINTHIANS 3:16	I am God's temple
2 CORINTHIANS 5:17-20	I am a minister of reconciliation
2 CORINTHIANS 6:1	I am God's coworker
EPHESIANS 2:6	I am seated with Christ in the heavenly realm
EPHESIANS 2:10	I am God's workmanship
EPHESIANS 3:12	I may approach God with freedom and confidence
PHILIPPIANS 4:13	I can do all things through Christ who strengthens me

Taken from *Living Free in Christ*, by Neil Anderson. © 1993, Regal Books.

BEST-SELLERS FROM NEIL ANDERSON!

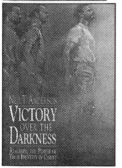
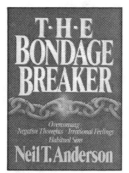
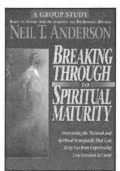

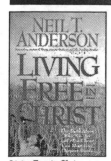

FREEDOM IN CHRIST SPECIAL RESOURCES

VIDEO SEMINARS

Resolving Personal Conflicts PART I
reveals the power of your identity in Christ
in 8 messages covering: The Search for
Identity and Meaning, Faith Renewal,
Walking by Faith, Strongholds, The Battle
for our Minds, Relational Perspectives,
Healing Damaged Emotions, Forgiving
from the Heart.

Workbook 1-884284-02-7

Resolving Spiritual Conflicts PART II
reveals the powerful truth that will break
even the most stubborn habits or private
sins in 8 messages covering: The Position
of the Believer, The Authority of the
Believer, The Protection of the Believer,
The Vulnerability of the Believer,
Temptation, Accusation, Deception, Steps
to Freedom.

Workbook • ISBN 1-884284-07-8

Walking in the Light–
Thomas Nelson Publishing
Neil T. Anderson
Learn to discern God's guidance in an age of
spiritual counterfeits. Dr. Anderson explains
the spiritual dimension of divine guidance and
exposes the nature of counterfeit guidance.

Paperback • ISBN 08407.43866

RESOURCES FOR PEOPLE AT-RISK

A Way of Escape–Harvest House
Neil T. Anderson
We've all faced sexual struggles. For those
who feel caught by unwanted thoughts,
compulsive habits, or a painful past, **A
Way of Escape** provides concrete steps to
overcome the bondage of sexual strongholds battling in your mind.

Paperback • ISBN 15650.71700

Purity Under Pressure–Harvest House
Neil T. Anderson and Dave Park
In this book, you'll find out the difference
between being friends, dating and having
a relationship. You'll see how the physical
stuff fits in. And you'll get answers to the
questions you're asking.

Paperback • ISBN 15650.72928

The Seduction of Our Children –
Harvest House
Neil T. Anderson and Steve Russo
A battle is raging for the minds of our
children. It's a battle parents must win! This
book will prepare parents to counter Satan's
assault by understanding his strategies and
warring against them.

Paperback • ISBN 08908.18886
Video • 1-884284-15-9

SPECIAL READING

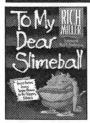

To My Dear Slimeball–Harvest House
Rich Miller
In the spirit of C.S. Lewis, Rich creates the
secret world of Slimeball and Spitwad–two
demons intent on making life miserable for
15-year-old David. As you gain access to
their private plans, you'll see how to detect
their crafty schemes in your own life.

Paperback • ISBN 15650.71875

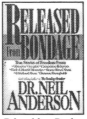

Released from Bondage–
Thomas Nelson Publishing
Neil T. Anderson
Released from Bondage contains gripping true stories of freedom from obsessive thoughts, compulsive behavior,
childhood abuse and many more.

Paperback • ISBN 08407.43882

FOR CHURCHES

Setting Your Church Free
Neil T. Anderson and Charles Mylander
Spiritual battles can effect entire churches
as well as individuals. **Setting Your Church
Free** shows pastors and church leaders how
they can apply the powerful principles from
Victory Over the Darkness to lead their
churches to freedom.

Hardcover • ISBN 08307.16556